STRANGER IN MY SKIN

Stranger in My Skin

~ A Memoir ~

Alysa Phillips

STRANGER IN MY SKIN
Published September 2006

Copyright © 2006 by Alysa Phillips. All rights reserved.

No part of this work may be reproduced in any form, or by any means, without the permission of the publisher. Exceptions are made for brief excerpts to be used in published reviews.

Printed in the United States by
Word Warriors Press, LLC, Minneapolis, Minnesota.
www.wordwarriorspress.com
10 09 08 07 06 1 2 3 4 5

ISBN 978-0-9746940-2-3

Library of Congress Control Number 2006922709
WORD WARRIORS PRESS™

Cover Design by Lance Conger
Typesetting by Zachary Lutterman

The names of people and places have been changed to maintain privacy.

If you receive this book without a cover, you should know that it has probably been stolen, but do not let that stop you from reading it.

To Ray and to Dennis, who never stopped hearing me.

"There is something wrong with this world."

—Irene Hunt, *Up a Road Slowly*

1

I didn't know I was ugly until I met Joel Adams. I may have suspected it now and then, but until I had someone who loved me enough to point out my flaws, I was oblivious.

Joel was almost twenty-five when he received revelation from God commanding him to marry me. I was nineteen. During our first date, which was at a small Salt Lake City Mexican restaurant, he asked me, "Why aren't you wearing make-up?"

"I am." I'd powdered my face and brushed on black mascara.

He said, "You need more."

Joel was one of ten children born to Jeremiah and May Adams. Jeremiah had quit his job as a high school chemistry teacher and now spent all his time researching medical journals and talking to God.

An entire book had come to Jeremiah by direct revelation. One night the heavens had opened in his room and passages of the book poured down. It was all he could do to write the words as they emanated forth. In the space of twelve hours, God explained to Jeremiah how miracles were done and the scientific formulas Jesus used to heal during his earthly ministry. When the final words were written, Jeremiah knew how to cure every disease from baldness to schizophrenia and AIDS, and he became Doctor Adams.

When Joel announced his plans to marry me, his father told him, "Make sure she doesn't have any flaws that might be hereditary. You don't want a woman with skin conditions or bad features. Think

1

about your future children." As an afterthought he added, "And pick a woman who looks good naked."

Joel proposed three weeks after we met. My face was caked in dark make-up. He broke up with his girlfriend the next day. As we sat on the worn couch in his parents' living room late one evening in early December, he said, "I have two questions for you."

I nervously played with the stuffing from the couch, feeling the gritty residue of sawdust on my fingers. "OK."

When we sat down, we were the same height, and he looked directly into my eyes, smiling. "First, will you marry me?"

He reclined on the couch and looked at me studiously, self-assured, waiting for my answer. I swallowed. I was expecting him to ask, but the question still took me by surprise because it wasn't the romantic proposal I'd dreamed of. Still, Joel was a righteous, moral man and he loved me. He lifted a foot and rested it on my knee. As I reminded myself that I hardly knew this man, my hands began to sweat.

"Will you marry me?" he repeated, the same confident smile on his face.

"Yes," I said, and instantly regretted it.

"I thought you'd say that."

"What's the second question?"

"There is no second question." He grinned gleefully. "You answered the first one right."

Something felt wrong. "I have a question for you, then. What about Jaclyn?" Joel had told me about his girlfriend-on-hold during our second date. They were taking time apart to think about their relationship.

"I'll tell her," Joel assured me. Then he leaned over and, taking me in his arms, kissed me delicately on the lips. When he pulled back, he smiled into my eyes and said, "I love you." I felt better.

A car door slammed and the dog ran barking through the

living room. Joel's parents had returned. He abruptly sat up and rearranged the pillows on the couch. A desperate fear rose in my throat. Maybe sharing it would make it permanent. "Let's not tell them yet," I pleaded. "Let's keep it a secret until we get the ring."

Two days later, when I had a shiny cubic zirconia on my finger, I formally met Dr. Adams. Joel introduced me as his fiancée, and he immediately gave me a big hug, saying, "Welcome to the family." But then he gave Joel a long, meaningful look and told his son, "Be careful. Remember what I said about genetics."

After Dr. Adams left the room, Joel confronted me about my nose. "I'm just not sure I want that feature passed on to my children, you know?"

I didn't know. Up to that point, I was unaware that there was a problem with my nose. It's not a straight, Angelina Jolie type nose but until then I thought it suited my face. It's slightly upturned; relatives with similar noses have called it a ski slope.

"There's always the possibility that my genes will be dominant," Joel continued. "I guess I could live with it if you got a nose job."

At first the idea seemed absurd, but as the days went by my nose became my dominant feature. When I looked in the mirror in the morning, all I saw was that glaring flaw in the middle of my face. Every day when I washed at the sink, my nose protruded more. I used a hand mirror to examine it from different angles, always hoping it might look better. I studied my profile for hours, tracing the outline of my nose with my index finger.

It's a terrible, lonely feeling to look in the mirror and see nothing of worth. It's terrifying to know, as you walk down an aisle in the grocery store or along a sidewalk, that you're physically repulsive. But Joel was right. My nose was ugly. Who in their right mind would curse offspring with such a feature?

About a week later, I was hiding my nose with one hand while I told Joel, "I'm thinking about getting a nose job."

"You don't have to do it for me," he insisted, "but I'd feel better being in public with you if you got it fixed."

I grew up like most children do. I had a mom, a dad and five siblings. My parents had the big bedroom at the end of the hall with the big bed and a connecting bathroom. When my mom tucked me into bed at night, I knew that all over the world mothers were tucking their children in at the same time. All the mothers were singing the same bedtime songs. All the fathers were watching *M*A*S*H* in their bedrooms, the eerie tune from the TV supplying the soundtrack to which we fell asleep every night.

That was before I discovered that when I was going to bed in Utah, it was morning in China and little Chinese children were just waking up. That was also before I learned that the theme song for *M*A*S*H* is about suicide.

Perhaps, at the beginning of every generation, everyone's names are put into a hat, then one name is drawn out and that person is considered trash. If one person is trash, everyone else can rest assured that they are not. I never questioned this theory; that's just the way it was. Like a martyr, I succumbed to it, supposing that if everyone belittled me, they'd feel better about themselves. It was a worthy endeavor, I thought. Like the poor victim in Shirley Jackson's short story "The Lottery," somehow my name came up and I was the outcast.

Some people told me I was a misfit. Others told me I couldn't follow directions. Some decided I had a wild spirit that needed to be broken. Others thought I was mentally ill. All I knew was that the world was a lonely place and something was wrong with me.

At my parents' house, I walked cautiously, like I was feeling my way in the dark. One misstep could result in grave punishment. One footfall echoing too loudly in the hallway was sure to awaken the roaring beast inside my father.

Everything in my father's house was white and spotless and silent. My older brother and I played quiet games and conversed in whispers when he was home. We shuffled along the carpet with our feet wrapped in house slippers, careful not to move too much because traversing the same path too many times wore it out. I didn't question the rules because my mom followed them, too.

One time, my mother tripped and crashed to the ground in the backyard, brushing against the tiny branches of a yearling almond tree on her way down. Before she hit the dirt, my father was beside the tree. As he probed it for damage, my disregarded mother clambered to her knees in tears.

When my older brother and I were still in our preschool years, my mom took us on daily walks in the early afternoons. We always walked north down the sidewalk to the green street sign that read "Elysium Drive." There was no intersecting street—the strip of asphalt that I knew as Elysium Drive was a quarter-mile long, and the sidewalk disappeared into dirt at both ends. Orchards of thick fruit trees and wild asparagus acted as bookends to my small street, enclosing my world in a neat tree-rimmed package.

Sometimes, when my mom felt adventurous, she let us explore the borders of the orchard. Some days we picked asparagus and took it home, where my mom boiled it for dinner. Other days we followed a trail at the edge of the orchard that ran along a cliff. Overlooking the mouth of a canyon, the path led to an abandoned shack. Through dirty windows, we could make out the remains of a mattress and an old table.

Usually, though, we stopped walking where the sidewalk stopped. The jagged edge of concrete rose several inches above the dirt and weeds that went beyond. I crouched as close to the edge as I dared and looked down. A rotting apple lay there, its red skin shrinking every day like skin stretches across the bony hands of old people. It reminded me of a tiny red balloon that, day by day, was losing its air.

Every weekday for the entire summer, my brother and I stooped at the edge of the sidewalk and looked down at the apple, watching it die but never stretching a finger out to touch it. Throughout the course of summer, the apple shriveled and rotted. The redness of its once-taut skin faded into brown, and its stem drooped over. The afternoon walks became compulsory; if we didn't check on the apple every day, it might waste away into nothing without us.

After that first summer, the apple wasn't there anymore. I looked for it the following year but it had disappeared with the melting snow. The year after that, a road went through the orchard. People built two- and three-story houses and the sidewalk was extended.

I always counted the number of steps I took between cracks in the sidewalk. During my first journeys, I stepped four times with my left foot and four times with my right. As I grew older, it decreased to three with each foot, and then two. But I always needed an even number of steps between cracks. I'd even pirouette around on one foot, desperately trying to fit step number four or six or eight into the segment. Later on, I began counting steps on staircases, alternating the foot that stepped up first. Moving around in the world became a sort of game in which each player had to have its fair turn.

I thought about that apple many times since the final time I saw it. Eventually, I was glad it left with the snow; I may have been humiliated for it if I'd seen it at its worst.

The culture in Utah is one of strict perfection. Tanning salons, liposuction experts and plastic surgeons fight for advertising space on the billboards that line Interstate 15. If someone doesn't fit the height, weight and coloring requirements, she's ostracized. Designer clothes are a must even when attending church. Women and their daughters, dressed alike in second-skin attire that reveals their flawless figures, sit in pews unofficially reserved for the beautiful people. Their bronzed skin and preened blonde hair mark them as the righteous.

Instead of brand-name clothing, I wore homemade dresses that often hung off my scrawny figure. My hair was usually in disarray, and I wore bangs for years after they became unfashionable. Chronic acne followed me through junior high and high school. If God had a dodgeball team, I would have been chosen last.

It wasn't only physical beauty I couldn't achieve. A friend in college once told me he was looking for an uneducated wife much younger than he was. "What you have to do is marry them really young and then finish raising them right," he confided. "You're a little too old for me, a little too stuck in your ways, if you know what I mean." I was twenty at the time. He was twenty-four. From an early age, Mormon girls are taught that brains aren't as important as a submissive demeanor and a pleasing figure.

So when I discovered I was ugly, my self-worth plummeted like an avalanche. I avoided mirrors at all costs. I also avoided looking people in the eye so they wouldn't see the inherent vileness that I was, that I wasn't worth the space I occupied. I retreated slowly into a shell until I stopped talking. For four months I was silent except in conversations with Joel and his family. They coached me on how to become the person I was destined to be.

I stared at my reflection in the mirror for hours on end every night before going to bed, thinking about my childhood and pulling out photos of myself at all ages. My nose was always ugly, I realized, though I hadn't been aware of it. I became jealous of children, of how they interacted based on age or interests rather than beauty.

After I told Joel I was willing to pay for a nose job, he didn't hesitate in making suggestions for other improvements while I was at it. "Your forehead could use some work," he advised.

My forehead? But as it turns out, anything can be improved with a nip here, a tuck there, if you're willing to pay the price. Plastic surgeons in Utah Valley are eager to please. The first one I saw told me, "If it makes you more beautiful, it's worth it." I'd picked his name out of the yellow pages, stopping at his office on my way home from school.

With his eyes closed, and while he hummed softly, the doctor massaged my forehead. Suddenly his eyes snapped open. "Yes, you do have a deformity in your forehead. It's hard to see in this light, but I can feel it."

My forehead is characterized by a round, protruding bump I can trace with my fingers. When I stand under direct light, shadows make it stand out. Joel had asked me to be careful when choosing where to stand.

The doctor said, "Most likely the deformity in your forehead was caused by a late fusion of the discs in your skull. There are two ways to fix it: I can insert tiny pads of fat on either side of the protrusion or we can pull back the skin and actually sand down the excess bone so it lies flat."

"What about my nose?" I asked.

"You have a very unique nose. Many people without straight noses have them repaired." The air rushed from my lungs as I considered the cost. Leaving the plastic surgeon's office, I wondered when I'd become so broken. My neck and shoulders ached with the burden.

I went home and cut thick bangs.

Sometimes reality shifts. It doesn't shift far—only a half-inch to the left or right of where I'm supposed to be, but far enough to make my world become unbalanced.

The first time it happened I was nine years old and my grandparents were visiting us in Indiana. As a rule, my parents never let us spend fifty cents to purchase a can of soda from a vending machine: "It's a waste of money." As a result, I looked at the shiny, lit machines like I'd watch a ride at an amusement park I wasn't allowed onto. To put money into a soda machine and drink the rich, fizzy liquid was a thought that both excited and frustrated me.

My family was on a tour of the Purdue University campus in Lafayette, with my mother's parents. I'd known for a long time that they had a habit of drinking caffeine. I also knew they'd go to hell for it, but it didn't seem to make them unhappy. I listened to the fresh fizzle as they popped the tops and sipped the liquid, my mouth watering.

Near the stairs in a barren concrete parking garage, my grandmother stopped at a soda vending machine and began to dig in her coin purse. She placed fifty cents into each of our hands. My fingers shook as I slid the coins into the slot. "Push a button now," my grandma prompted.

I read each glowing button carefully, considering my options. A bright yellow button that said "Mellow Yellow" caught my attention, and I pushed it. Gears turned, the machine groaned, and a cold, wet, yellow can descended noisily into the bin. I picked it up and wiped the dew off, never taking my eyes off the can.

Suddenly it was yanked away. I looked up to see my mom reading the label and scowling. "Good going," she said. "You bought something with caffeine in it. Now what are you going to do?"

Although I did it unconsciously, I had simultaneously broken two rules: I'd spent money on something frivolous and I'd purchased a substance that would send me straight to hell. Which was worse—wasting fifty cents or drinking the soda?

The longer I held the can, the stronger was the realization that, either way, I was a sinner. Time stretched on. My concentration circled the can of caffeine. I left my body for a moment and saw myself from above—a scrawny, double-jointed girl with short, unkempt hair, grasping the can that carried her damnation in its thin aluminum shell.

Then, half an inch to my left again, I watched as the can of Mellow Yellow slipped from my fingers and crashed to the concrete, its top splitting and spewing soda at my feet.

❧

People warned me about Joel Adams. They told me something was off with him and that I should avoid him at all costs. As we watched Joel interact across a crowded hallway at church, one girl told me, "He'll date anything in a skirt."

I'd never had a boyfriend. I hungered for a companion I could talk to, a best friend I could also fall in love with. I crossed the hall to stand closer to Joel and waited for him to notice me. It didn't take long; I was a new face and I was wearing a skirt.

Studying me, he said, "I'm Joel Adams. Who are you?"

"Alysa."

Joel grinned, putting his tongue into a big gap between his too-short front teeth. I smiled back. He said, "We should do something sometime. What are you doing after church? Do you want to come home with me and play my piano?"

So after services Joel held his car door open for me, then ran around the back and climbed in behind the wheel. He sped down the road, cutting corners and running stop signs, eventually screeching to a stop in front of a rundown blue house near the high school. I didn't wait for him to open the door for me. I mirrored his movements as he stepped to the ground and made his way up the cracked sidewalk to the front door. The house was dark.

Dirty blue carpet, threadbare and rotting, met my feet as I crossed the threshold. Joel told me to sit on a couch in the living room while he tidied up his bedroom. He didn't turn a light on, so I perched on the edge of the couch in the dark. A dog nuzzled his cold nose into my hand. The only thing disturbing a silence thick as the darkness was the dim sound of a far-off television. Minutes oozed by as my neck grew stiff. Finally, Joel motioned from the stairs for me to join him. I followed him up ten stairs to the top floor of the split-level house.

His bedroom was first on the left. I was surprised at the amount of state-of-the-art technology crammed into the room. Computers, TVs, night-vision goggles, video games, and musical instruments lined the walls. If it weren't for the low twin-sized bed in one corner, I might have forgotten it was a bedroom.

I spent the next hour and a half perched on the footboard, watching as Joel conducted a virtual tour through his electronic world. He played the piano for twenty minutes, improvising a tune and pausing for me to applaud. He skipped through his favorite songs on a sixteen-disc CD player and started a game of Command and Conquer on a big computer screen, narrating his plans of attack and laughing gleefully when large quantities of enemies were destroyed.

Then, with a sudden air of mystery, Joel pulled me closer. I balanced on the edge of his swivel chair in front of the computer. He wrapped an arm around my shoulders to keep me steady. "Have you ever seen porn?"

For some reason I nodded my head. I knew instinctively that any reference that might make me appear more experienced was a good thing. I wasn't in Kansas anymore.

Joel whispered, "This is my brother, Matt." He stretched his right arm out to make sure the bedroom door was locked, and then double-clicked on a desktop folder. Thumbnail-sized pictures popped up, and Joel clicked on the first one.

All I could see filling the screen was Matt's face and bare shoulders. He smiled sensuously at the camera. Joel scrolled down slowly, alternately watching the screen and my face. The man looked a lot like Joel, but with more defined features. Joel kept scrolling down, past the shoulders to a toned, sweating body. Muscles rippled and skin glistened invitingly from the screen. I swallowed. Joel scrolled further, down to a hard abdomen. Sculpted pelvic bones jumped from the screen. Matt's hands, placed on his hips, summoned the eyes downward. Joel scrolled more slowly, studying my face. When the first dark bristles of pubic hair appeared on the bottom of the screen, I turned my head, dizzy and nauseated.

Joel grinned. "Now, that's physical perfection!" He banged a hand appreciatively on top of the computer.

A knock came suddenly at the door. Joel jumped and turned sheepishly toward the sound. In a single practiced movement, he shut off the computer and eased the door open a crack. A face appeared in the gap. "Hi," it announced.

"Oh Alysa, this is my brother, Matt," Joel said, winking at me.

About a week after we got engaged, Joel and I were at Matt's apartment on a Friday night, sharing an overstuffed couch. Matt and his pregnant wife Laura perched on a second couch. It was only the second time I'd seen Matt.

Shy and afraid of my own voice, I sat listening to the men talk. Laura piped in occasionally with a comment. I tried to appear attentive, smiling every time someone made eye contact. After a lull in conversation, Matt addressed me. "So, you're going to get married. Are you a virgin?"

All eyes were on me. I cleared my throat.

"Come with me," Matt said. He took my hand and led me into the hallway.

Joel followed us to Matt's bedroom. Once we were inside, Matt patted the space beside him on the king-sized bed, so I perched on the edge. Joel stood in the corner, but he watched me with hawk eyes.

Without preamble Matt blurted out, "Have you had an orgasm?"

I gasped, "What?"

"Your responsibility is to please your man, and I told Joel I'd look out for him. I was married once before," he explained. "My first wife wouldn't give me sex. When we were first married, she gave it to me every night, but then she slacked off. I had to beg her for it. Then I had to bribe her for it. Eventually she made me take it from her. One night she said she was sick. I told her I needed sex and she threw a plate at me. I had to divorce the bitch."

I didn't respond.

"I'm not being crude. I'm just trying to prepare you."

But I wasn't prepared for what came next. Joel adhered stalwartly to his conviction to remain a virgin until marriage, but he had also told me repeatedly that he couldn't marry me unless he knew we were sexually compatible.

"Turn around slowly," Joel said as he and Matt watched. I stood up and spun.

"Her chest is really small," Matt noted. "Can you deal with that?"

"We can do hypnosis and work on it," Joel answered.

I kept turning because it was the only way I was participating in the conversation. I felt my mind drifting toward the left and stumbled on something invisible in the carpet.

"Well, I wouldn't marry her," Matt decided. "Not with that nose."

2

Swirls of exhaustion danced in front of my eyes as I lay motionless, my face pressed into the carpet, the threads tracing psychedelic patterns into the softness of my cheek. I was too tired to move, too tired even to close my mouth against the rotten smell of mold. Ragged clumps of yellow shag drifted in and out of focus as my gaze alternated between them and the cheap plywood wall beyond.

Joel punched the thin basement wall, making thousands of termites fall from their perching places inside, skittering downward and ricocheting off each other. The sound reminded me of an African rain stick someone brought for show-and-tell in grade school.

He said softly, "I can't live without you," but his voice got lost before it reached the low ceiling. We were lying side by side in the semi-darkness of a tiny sub-basement at Joel's parents' house. The only light came from an industrial-sized flashlight Joel had propped up in the middle of the bare room. "If you leave me, I might as well just commit suicide."

I wasn't about to leave—not right then, anyway. It was two a.m. and I'd told my parents I was having a sleepover with my best friend. I had nowhere else to go. Besides, Joel's body blocked the door. He hit the wall and the rain stick began again. Joel's threat wasn't new, but goose bumps formed on my neck and shoulders anyway and I shivered.

I finally said, "I'm not leaving. I love you."

"I love you, too," he whispered, pulling me toward him. As

Joel wrapped his arms around me, my stomach turned and I held my breath.

That was another lost chance, I thought. Why hadn't I just said it? Why didn't I just stand up and tell Joel that I didn't love him, that I never had and I never would? What was wrong with me? Instead, I let him kiss my forehead, my nose and my lips.

I shifted and sat up. "It's cold down here," I said flatly. "Why don't we go upstairs?"

Joel was happy. "OK. I'll get blankets."

I followed him down a dark hallway and up a flight of six stairs to the regular basement. We settled directly underneath the guest bedroom, where a hobo named David—pronounced with a soft *a*—was staying with his wife, Elidah. The Adamses were famous for their hospitality, and these two street dwellers had been dorming with them for nearly a month.

Joel scurried around, building a nest of bedding. Then he disappeared for a moment and came back wearing flannel pajamas. "Ready for bed?"

"Sure." In the Adams house, it was strictly a sin to spend the night with a member of the opposite sex, but that didn't seem to bother Joel. He even hummed a silly made-up song as he slid in and beckoned for me to join him under the covers.

After I was situated, he asked, "Do you have a special place you go to? I mean, like when you're stressed or something, a peaceful place in your mind?"

"I guess so."

"Tell me about it."

"Well, there's a stream and some trees and the moon is out. It's just . . . peaceful."

"Am I there?"

I hesitated.

"Am I there?" he asked again.

"Yes," I said, but the word felt dirty coming out of my mouth.

Content, Joel turned away from me and drifted to sleep. Alone, I replayed the events of the evening until I was worn out.

I had checked my email at a kiosk between classes at Brigham Young University. My mother's message started, "I have a confession to make. I've been reading your journal and I know what's going on. I know you are kissing that boy, that you are physically involved." A lump rose in my throat. "Alysa, you're sinning. You're following the devil. If you insist on marrying Joel, I will not be at your wedding."

This was the only way my mom communicated with me ever since I met Joel. She refused to talk to me directly anymore. Instead, she emailed me or copied inspirational thoughts and scripture onto pink cards, decorated them with stickers and left them in my shoes, under my pillow, or in my backpack. Her small notes added pounds to my backpack after I found them, but I never had the courage to throw them away.

Unable to control my tears, I had logged out and hurried to the nearest courtesy phone to call Joel. "My mom's right, you know," I told him. "We're following the devil. We need to fix things or she'll never accept you." A long line of students waited impatiently behind me, shuffling their feet and clearing their throats. I ignored them, talking lowly into the phone as I cried.

"Calm down," Joel said. "Come to my house tonight and we'll work things out."

I must have finally drifted off to sleep in the basement because I woke to a loud banging in the room directly over my head. "What?" I mumbled from half-sleep.

"Hear that?" Joel whispered close to me. "They're having sex."

The bed in the guest room was slamming against the wall in steady rhythm, vibrating the ceiling above us. The light fixture swung back and forth, throwing eerie shadows across the room from the streetlight shining through the basement window. Thin animal-like yelps echoed in the dark. It was the first time I heard the act of sex. It frightened me. I lay still, fascinated and terrified at the same time. I put my hands over my face as if blocking out the darkness of the basement room would hush the ugly, hungry sounds.

Gradually, I became aware that Joel was breathing heavily beside me. I turned toward the sound, opened my mouth to say something, and he pulled himself on top of me. His teeth dug into my neck and he sucked violently. At the same time, I became aware that he was thrusting himself against my body. I felt the hardness of his crotch, which he rubbed up and down my torso.

Terrified, I let out a scream. Joel silenced it with his hand, seething, "Do you want to wake up my parents?"

As much as I wanted to be free of him, the thought of his parents coming to my rescue was less than pleasant. I bit my tongue and bucked against Joel. He released me for a second and I rolled over. An arm wrapped around my neck, forcing my face roughly into the carpet. The grip was uncomfortable but not tight. Twisting his arm gently to cut off my air supply, Joel said, "I could break your neck this easily."

I could feel the residue of his saliva on my neck and face. I didn't struggle anymore. Instead, I waited, breathless, for him to make a move. I almost wished he would just break my neck.

Finally, Joel said, "I would never actually do it. I just want you to know I could." He released his grip, and I pulled myself into a sitting position. I don't know how long I sat there in the dark, rocking back and forth. I don't even remember thinking.

The next thing I knew, Joel was crouched next to me on the floor, sobbing into his hands. "I didn't mean to do it, Alysa." His voice was thick with moisture and emotion. "I heard them upstairs and I couldn't help myself. I couldn't stop."

I never learned how to say "no" to a man. I was taught, at least at a subconscious level, that I was inferior. Women answer to men. Women look up to men. Women stand in men's shadows. As a woman, my role was to marry and raise a family. I was supposed to stay home to cook, clean, and have children while my husband acted as bread winner. As a single woman, even at nineteen, my foremost goal was to marry such a man.

I was enamored with Joel's better sides. His confidence and stature alluded to an inner elegance. A student of martial arts, he moved with an ease and grace that defied my outlook on men. When I watched him moving arms and legs together into beautiful Kung Fu stances, I imagined a kind of poetry.

The dance that defined our romance started with a cleft foot at the end of my ankle. From the beginning, Joel was superior—physically, emotionally, spiritually and intellectually—and it was that superiority that had me infatuated. I constantly had to prove my worth to Joel because he threatened to lose interest in whatever blonde thing was passing by. I had to fight for his attention, and once I got it, I needed daily assurance that he still wanted me.

Though I never noticed other men, Joel was fond of saying, usually while gazing out the car window at some scantily-clad beauty, "You can look at the menu. You just can't order."

A week after we got engaged, Joel planned a road trip to visit his ailing grandmother. Joel's brother James and his wife Kristi drove us in their new Chevrolet truck. Joel was the eighth of the ten children, seven of whom were sons. James was the sixth child, and Matt was situated in between him and Joel. I rarely saw Joel's eldest siblings.

Joel made tuna and cheese sandwiches on cracked wheat, and we munched them in the covered truck bed, where we lay side by side on a pile of blankets. Kristi kept yelling at us through the connecting window, "Don't be having sex in the back of my truck!"

She sat close to James in the spacious cab and kept leaning over to tease him. He'd grab her thigh or hips, constantly veering to one side of the icy road or the other in the process. I was glad I couldn't see the dangers standing on either side of the road, waiting for James to lose control or hit a patch of black ice.

My ears were fuzzy with travel when we got to Grandma's house and I stood awkwardly in front of her for inspection. She asked Joel while scrutinizing me, "Is this one a keeper?"

"Yes, Grandma," Joel said. "We're engaged."

"She's awfully thin," Grandma sighed. I felt like a slab of raw beef. I couldn't tell if she was disappointed or just tired. She looked to be about ninety years old.

The drive home was long because James and Kristi were ornery with each other. "Let me drive," Kristi whined. "I'm getting car sick."

James shot back, "I'm not letting you drive my new truck in the snow."

Joel and I sat in the back of the truck, perched on either side of the window that looked into the cab, afraid to interrupt the argument. Occasionally, Joel touched me on the knee and winked like we shared some inside joke. I smiled back.

Kristi made a leap for the wheel, but James pushed her into the passenger side door, holding her there with his arm extended. The door rattled, and Kristi glared at James, saying, "You're lucky that's locked."

"I'm lucky . . ." James started. He interrupted himself when he caught sight of something out the window. "What the . . ."

He slammed on the brakes, threw the driver's side door open and ran toward the back of the truck. Joel and I followed his movements, crawling around the interior of our carpeted cage. For a second, I thought James was going to open the back door for us, but he rushed right past. Kristi hopped out and followed him. From the tiny steamed-up windows, Joel and I watched as James waded through knee-deep snow toward a barbed-wire fence.

I gasped when I saw what he was running toward: a large animal standing upright in the snow. I thought it was an enormous deer, but it didn't have antlers. James approached the animal, motioning for Kristi to stay behind. He edged up to the animal's thick hind legs and swatted one with his fingertips, turning at the same time to run. But the animal didn't move.

"It's dead!" James's voice struck the side of the truck and bounced back. He ran toward the road; the deep snow no longer held him back. "It's dead, it's dead," he kept screaming.

Kristi cried hysterically, "What?"

"It's frozen, and it's dead." James was regaining his composure. I looked at the animal again and saw it was a horse—a big, sturdy horse that had died and frozen into place. Or maybe it had died because it froze.

James leaped back into the truck, the argument between him and Kristi forgotten. Kristi pulled herself in and leaned up against James as the truck roared to life.

A picture of the big dead horse, frozen in place where it had been grazing or scratching itself against the fence, fixed itself in my mind, and I could think of little else. I saw suddenly the fragility of life, and the image of death was imprinted on the inside of my eyelids. I think it was the sturdiness of the horse that bothered me, that something so powerful and robust could succumb to something as simple as weather. Witnessing the defeat of the horse made my survival less likely.

The death affected Joel, too. He used the occasion to teach me about lymphnogenesis. "Did you know that you have a system of lymphatic vessels that parallel the blood vessels all throughout your body?"

I had no idea what he was talking about. "Um, no."

"The lymphatic vessels keep the body healthy," he said.

"Without them, we'd all be dead within five minutes. I'm going to tell you the health discovery of the century. People are killing for this knowledge."

He rapped on the window and asked Kristi for a pen and piece of paper. She handed back a page torn from an atlas. Joel took it and began scribbling. "Lymphatic vessels pull the poisons out of our blood stream. This is what a healthy cell looks like." A big hollow circle looked back at me from the atlas page. "See all the oxygen in that cell?" I imagined oxygen into the circle.

"Now, if you have a diseased cell, it's collapsed because there's not enough oxygen in it," Joel said, drawing a flattened circle.

Then he wrote out the formula for life: Pressure + Massage + Stroke = Healthy Cells. "The only way to get oxygen back into your diseased cells is to turn on a sodium-potassium pump, and the only way to do that is to put pressure, massage and stroke on the damaged area.

"Your cells get diseased when you eat salt, sugar, meat, or anything that isn't pure. The government puts that crap into our food so we stay sick. The only way to survive is through this science." I thought I was going to laugh. Then I thought I might be sick. Joel didn't notice. His face had taken on cherubic features. "It's actually more like a religion than a science."

I remembered watching religious fanatics on the public service channel. They stood behind lecterns and beat their fists into the wood for emphasis. They called to their congregations like shepherds to sheep, impelling them to follow. In turn, the people shouted, "Amen!" The evangelists' rantings echoed poetic phrases, which usually had to do with sinners experiencing eternal damnation and burning in the soul fires of hell.

As Joel launched into a well-practiced speech about the secrets of human life, I could imagine him on one of those shows, pounding repentance into the lost. I could almost hear his fists flying toward the trembling wood of a lectern; the rhythm of his chanted science lent itself to the scene.

Joel forced me out of my reverie with a sudden silence. After a moment, he said, "God told me not to marry someone unless she accepted lymphnogenesis. I need a woman who'll support me in my life's calling."

Somewhere in the awkward silence, I decided there were worse things than joining a religion. "I accept it."

"If you truly accept it, it will be the most important thing in your life. More important than your family, your friends or your education."

That part I'd heard before. It came straight from Dr. Adams. Late one afternoon he'd told me, "You're learning the wisdom of Man at that university." His tall and heavy body was crammed into one of six dark blue recliners in the den. The chairs all pointed toward a big-screen TV. Outside the sliding glass doors that led to the backyard, dirty snow lay on the ground and fence. The mud-covered purity made me sad.

Dr. Adams's voice was dignified and commanding as he said, "Come with us and learn from God." When Dr. Adams spoke, people obeyed, and I was accustomed to doing whatever a man told me to anyway. I hung my head.

His eyes roamed over my body and I felt naked and vulnerable. But although large, Dr. Adams didn't seem threatening because he had a gimpy foot. Decades earlier, he'd been hit by a garbage truck and his foot was smashed beneath a wheel. Doctors wanted to amputate but he prayed for healing. Though he kept his foot, Dr. Adams was permanently maimed. The experience had prodded his later medical research.

But I couldn't stop going to school. I still lived with my parents and they wouldn't allow it. I didn't know which was worse— breaking off an engagement or quitting school.

I spent as much time as possible at Joel's house with his parents and David and Elidah, who were fond of rousing religious discourse.

David was a gentle, soft-spoken man. In his eyes was a clearness that echoed his claim of being spiritually cleansed. I couldn't have known that in five years the entire nation would see his face on television screens and newspapers in connection with a horrific crime. He wore his brown hair long and knotted, but it was clean. He parted it in the middle of his head and the ends fell softly on his shoulders, tangling at times with his beard. While not monotone, his voice had a calming stillness about it and he projected his words at a volume just above a whisper. His voice had a quality that made me stop and listen. Perhaps it was the pitch—low enough that I was forced to concentrate in order to hear. Perhaps it was the words he said. He rarely spoke directly to me, so when he did, I made a point to listen.

I came upon him one evening in the kitchen. Dr. Adams was in his recliner in front of the TV and Joel was in the living room with Elidah, who was pounding on one of two upright pianos. She'd been a concert pianist before she married David, so she often sat on a stool in front of the piano, her fingers gliding expertly over the keys, hitting chords with absolute precision. If the piece had words, Elidah sang along in a clear, beautiful voice. I could listen to her for hours, and I wondered why she only sang for us.

Elidah never wore make-up or jewelry. She tucked her long hair underneath a blue handkerchief that was bound around her head. She wrapped a light blue, floor-length robe around her body and secured it with a belt around her waist. On her feet she wore leather sandals or boots.

David donned the same kind of homemade robe, except his was always white. Both wore long sleeves that nearly covered their hands. The main difference between the two was the expression etched into their faces. David's was serene and almost blank, while Elidah's was stiff and hard. David rolled up his sleeves when he cooked. During intervals between stirring boiling liquids on the stove, he was making bread out of spelt.

"Spelt is the only pure kind of flour," he told me. "It's spoken of in the Bible."

Even though an entire room in the sub-basement was full of cans from government programs, David refused to use any of it. He claimed it was contaminated. "The government is the last thing I'm going to trust with my food."

When Joel dismissed his ex-girlfriend Jaclyn and proposed to me, she didn't exit his life. Instead, she befriended Kristi and frequented the Adams house, where she continued with her lymphnogenesis training. Early one Friday evening in January, Jaclyn appeared on the doorstep in Spandex. Her hair was pulled into pigtails and tied with colorful scraps of cloth. She invited Kristi and me to go to a private health club.

Kristi immediately went to get her workout clothes, but James blocked her way. "Where do you think you're going?"

"To work out," she said. "With Jaclyn and Alysa."

"I don't want you going out with that whore."

Kristi's face started to go red. "I don't care what you want." She maneuvered around James and started down the basement stairs.

As he followed her, James repeated, "You're not going."

For the next fifteen minutes, Joel and I could hear them shouting at each other from where we sat in the living room. Their bedroom was directly underneath us. Jaclyn stood at the door, awkwardly waiting for the argument to be over. Then Kristi emerged again, triumphant, with a bag of exercise clothes in one hand and a pair of athletic shoes, tied together by the laces, hanging over her shoulder.

Kristi followed Jaclyn out the door, calling to me from the front porch. "Come on, Alysa."

I pulled my hand from Joel's and stood up to follow them. "You're not going, Alysa," he said.

I looked at him in surprise and then said, "Yeah. See ya."

I tried to pull the door shut behind me but Joel caught it and threw it open. His voice rose to a shrill. "I said I don't want you going with them."

I looked at Kristi and Jaclyn. Neither of them seemed frightened. Jaclyn even rolled her eyes, but neither stood up to my defense. Joel grabbed my hand and pulled me toward the house.

Kristi said, "Don't let him tell you what to do or you'll end up wiping his butt for him after you're married."

I looked down, mumbling, "I'm going with them."

"What was that?" Joel demanded.

I said more loudly, "I'm going with them." As I pulled my arm free from his grasp, I looked him in the eye. I turned and climbed into the backseat of Jaclyn's car, but the hair rose on my neck and I pictured Joel running across the snowy front yard in pursuit, hands raised to come down at me.

I shut the car door without incident. Only then did I venture a look back toward Joel. The front door was shut—probably slammed—and the house looked relatively serene. I breathed a sigh of relief and then became aware of a loud buzzing noise in my ears. I looked around. Jaclyn was backing the car out of the driveway.

Kristi was talking and laughing, gesturing largely with her hands. "Did you see the look on his face when you walked away?" she asked me.

The volume of the buzz decreased and I realized it was my heart beating in my chest. I gasped in a couple of deep breaths and then allowed myself to laugh with the other girls.

"If he thought I was going to just obey him . . ." I started. I couldn't finish. I'd glanced back at the house as Jaclyn drove slowly toward the stop sign. The front door had flown open and Joel was running toward his car.

I yelled to no one in particular, "He's coming!"

In sync, Kristi and Jaclyn swiveled around to see Joel's car start up in a cloud of exhaust and peel away from the curb. The same look of horror and disbelief crossed both their faces, and Jaclyn hit the automatic door lock button. At the same time, she brought her right foot down on the accelerator, speeding through the intersection.

At Center Street, Jaclyn pulled into the turn lane and slid through a red light. Cars twisted in their lanes, narrowly missing us. Horns blared through the drums beating in my head. I held on to the seat belt cutting across my chest. Out the back window, I watched Joel's car follow the same crazy track and close in on us.

Time went into slow motion as both cars slipped across the icy lanes, headed toward the center of town. Kristi screamed. Jaclyn cursed at Joel under her breath. His car was on our right side, swerving into us. The front end of his car clipped the side of Jaclyn's. The sound of metal scraping on metal seemed to snap Joel out of his mission. He stepped on the brake. Jaclyn followed suit and turned her car slowly around to follow Joel back to his house.

For about five minutes, all was calm as Jaclyn and Joel examined their cars. The two agreed not to call the police or insurance people on the minimal damage. Instead, standing awkwardly in the cold with two steaming cars, they became apologetic and even a little bit sheepish. It looked safe to creep from the back of Jaclyn's car and make my way to the front door.

Only then did I realize another argument had begun.

Joel demanded, "No, you are not going to work out! Don't you see you almost got killed? Give it a break, already!"

"You're the one who almost got us killed," Jaclyn pointed out.

"We're going. We planned on going all day, and you're not going to stop us."

I nodded my head at her as I backed into the house, so she'd know I was on her side. Joel came through the door just after me. Before I knew what was happening, Jaclyn—a large woman, nearly twice my size—charged at Joel. As she bolted through the front door, he slammed it on her to keep her out.

I heard glass shattering and then an awful wailing coming from Jaclyn's wide-open, red-rimmed mouth. I had to peek around Joel, who was still standing with his hand on the closed door, to see what had happened. Jaclyn stood outside, but the stained glass in the middle of the door had ruptured under the force of her arm. The reds and blues of the glass, dulled in hue by time and sunlight, had collapsed on either side of Jaclyn's thick arm, which was gyrating weirdly. Blood dripped down her arm in large gooey trails from dozens of tiny cuts and pooled on the ground. It had splattered on Joel's clothes and shoes. He stood frozen as Jaclyn's arm, looking strangely dismembered, stuck in through the glass, pulsating in what could only be the dance of shock.

Slowly, Jaclyn eased her arm back through the window, wincing as the glass cut her again and again, sending fresh rivulets of blood trickling toward her hand. When it was free, Joel opened the door. She collapsed onto the carpet, moaning with pain and trying to hold her arm without pushing any of the shards of glass further into her flesh.

Joel stared down at his former lover with fear and disgust. James, who stood in the kitchen, grabbed a handful of towels and threw them in Jaclyn's general direction. For several moments, no one moved. The only sound was Jaclyn sniffling into her wounds.

Then I moved. "We need to take her to the hospital."

Joel backed me up. "Alysa knows First Aid. We have to do what she says."

The cult that didn't believe in conventional medicine meekly followed my directions. "Put a towel under her arm for support. Jaclyn, we need to make a sling until we get to the hospital. James, get some gauze out of the First Aid kit for the bleeding. Joel, get Jaclyn into your car."

We all piled into cars and reconvened at the Emergency Room. Jaclyn was taken immediately. The glass was removed and her bloody arm stitched up.

Hours later, as we returned home, Joel smiled at me. "I told you that you weren't going to work out today."

3

The first red flag should have been Dr. Adams's title. He wasn't a doctor of anything but called himself one anyway. A doctor of natural healing, of osteopathy he said, borrowing terminology and "revelations" from real medical journals.

At first the science seemed innocent enough, even with some merit. Dr. Adams encouraged people to not take too many prescription medications or get unnecessary surgeries. His life and death formula worked through a simple method of applying pressure to the diseased body part, massaging it to break up the poisons, then stroking the area to get the poisons to leave the body through the lymphatic vessels. People with diseases simply had too many poisons in their systems, and Dr. Adams could move those back out. "It's the health revelation of the century," he told me.

Dr. Adams selected the ideal location to propagate his science. Utah was filled with genuine seekers. Borrowing biblical lexicon, he passed lymphnogenesis off as religious doctrine. Like sheep, people yearning for a higher purpose pulled checkbooks from their pockets and purses and went home with the precious oracles.

He'd tell his audiences of half-believers, "This is the key to Christianity. Everyone who denies it is bound for hell." I studied his face as he preached and could see he sincerely believed what he was saying. In front of my eyes, half-believers became true believers and pledged away their money and souls to help Dr. Adams's ministry.

When disbelief flickered in the eyes of skeptics, Dr. Adams pushed more forcefully. "Of course, some people won't accept this science because they're not ready. They're to be pitied because they'll experience hell on earth from their diseases and ignorance."

I imagined myself going to hell.

Dr. Adams had a financial benefactor. Randy Miller was a middle-aged man who had just married for the fourth time. He preached more than pressure, massage and stroke. He taught the importance of not wearing elasticized waistbands and not carrying a backpack or even a wallet in the back pocket. Randy would say, "Even the smallest thing will set off an imbalance, and that's where illness and violence come from."

When he read Dr. Adams's manuscript, Randy agreed to pay the publishing costs since Dr. Adams already had two mortgages on his house. "This is the work of God," Randy declared. "It must be made available in all languages to all the people on the earth."

I went to Randy's home one evening. He was preaching to his wife about a man named Nimrod who was not a believer in God. Nimrod was stricken with diseases of all sorts, and in his last days he lost all his limbs to become little more than a helpless torso. The way he said the word *torso* gave me goose bumps.

When Joel and I got back to his house, I asked him to find the Nimrod reference in the Bible, since I'd never heard of him. He couldn't, so he called Randy and asked for the chapter and verse. "Can't you leave a man alone?" Randy demanded so loudly that I could hear him from across the room. "I'm having sex with my wife, and you call with an air-headed question like that? The story's in the book of Nimrod, from the Bible's lost pages." He hung up.

Joel turned to me. "Randy has prophets' writings that aren't included in the King James version of the Bible. He's a spiritual giant and has knowledge we can't even imagine."

I started to cry and I didn't know why.

About a week later, Randy came to the office to bring a transcription of his latest revelation. God had told him that we were supposed to stop wearing watches. "Wearing those things on your wrist takes years off your life. They create negative thoughts and reduce the amount of love you can feel."

Right then, Joel forbade me to wear a watch. I'd worn one for ten years. My life revolved around catching public buses and making sure I arrived in time for my classes. But wearing a watch was diminishing my capacity to be in love with him, Joel said. He also told me I had to give up all sugars and salt. I could eat only natural foods, preferably those spoken of in the Bible.

I'd only been engaged for three weeks and I was already drowning. Rules kept pouring in and I had to watch my every action. I had to dress in a certain way, eat only approved foods, and watch what I said. I wanted to rewind the last month and start over. When Joel asked me, "Do you know that you have a set of lymphatic vessels that parallel the blood vessels all throughout your body?" I'd laugh. Maybe I'd slap him. Hopefully, I'd at least have the courage to walk away.

Suddenly I was a scared and inexperienced nineteen-year-old, and I wanted my mom. So the next day after school, as I slipped off my shoes, I called out from the front door, "Mom?" I heard a sniffle in response. Padding down the hallway to her bedroom, I found her lying on her bed sobbing.

Alarmed, I asked, "What's wrong?"

She took a few moments to compose herself. Her face was screwed into a wet red ball and her voice was moist, piercing my heart. "Don't you see that you're ruining your life?" She dissolved into tears again.

She refused to talk to me until I broke up with Joel, but didn't seem to realize that I needed support to do that. I backed out of the room, my heart breaking, and called Joel from the basement phone.

"Can you come and get me?"

I half-hoped he'd say no and our relationship would be over, but he had a habit of being sweet when I was hurting. In a single breath, he said, "What's wrong? Are you crying? I'll be right there."

I hung up and felt some of the pain leave my body. I could talk it out with Joel and everything would be all right. But a couple of hours later, I returned home still brokenhearted. I wanted nothing more than to be free of Joel's mind games, to be a teenager again. I couldn't tolerate my own thoughts and, without my parents as a support, I turned again and again to Joel.

Although my mom would have nothing to do with me until I broke off my relationship, she and my dad were getting ready to go out with Joel's parents. Dr. Adams had called and invited them to dinner. The object, from the surface, seemed to be the celebration of families getting to know each other before the marriage of their children. The real motive of course was for Dr. Adams to convert my parents. As they drove away in Dr. Adams's banged-up blue Astro van, I had the vague feeling I might never see my parents again.

Joel and I stayed at my house, making awkward conversation with the acute awareness that our parents were talking about us. My four younger siblings were home, and Joel and I idly played games with them. Then Joel suggested we play Truth or Dare with my twelve-year-old sister, Sarah.

Sarah went first. "Truth or dare?" she boldly asked Joel.

"Truth," he said.

"Have you ever kissed someone?"

Joel looked at me and snickered at her naiveté. "Nope. Now it's your turn. Truth or dare?"

"Truth," she said.

"What would you do if I kissed you?"

"If you kissed me, then you'd have to marry me," Sarah declared.

I remembered thinking the same thing when I was her age. Kissing was not recreation in my family. My parents married without having ever kissed each other or anyone else.

Without warning, Joel leaped on Sarah, pinning her to the carpet. As he put his tongue into her mouth, her eyes grew wide with shock. I pulled Joel off her. He sat back on his heels and grinned. "How did you like that?"

Sarah looked like she was going to cry or throw up. Maybe both. Her fingers clenched together tightly and her fingernails dug into her palms, but she faced Joel directly. "That was gross."

I couldn't stand to look at her face, so I turned to Joel instead. "Do you want to go spy on our parents?"

My parents and Joel's sat at a table in the middle of the restaurant. We took a table in the corner so they wouldn't notice us. At first I thought it would be difficult to overhear their conversation, but with Dr. Adams pounding on the table for emphasis as he drilled his science into my parents, not a person in the restaurant was immune. Next to her husband, May was little more than a whisper perched on her chair. I watched my parents struggle to eat under the scrutiny of the surrounding people. They left most of their food on their plates. I wasn't hungry either.

Dr. Adams's food grew cold as he bellowed out his formula, his face flushed red with excited animation. "Every healing art on earth involves getting oxygen to cells. Repeat after me! Every healing art on earth involves getting oxygen to cells!" Hesitantly, my parents mouthed the words with him.

"The pumps generate the electricity that gives the eyes the power to see and the brain the power to work," he said. My parents repeated it. It all sounded like a silly nursery rhyme and I hid my face in my hands. My dad's face was pink from embarrassment but he repeated the formulas anyway.

Dr. Adams calmed down for a moment and stared at my parents

as if he were just meeting them. "Do either of you have pain or disease? I can demonstrate right now how to heal you."

My mom adamantly shook her head. My dad said, "We don't have any health complaints."

Dr. Adams stared at them a moment longer and seemed to lose interest. "I know the cause of pain, cancer, heart disease, diabetes and every other degenerative disease on Earth. I know how it's possible to relieve pain and suffering at home faster and easier than you've ever dreamed possible. I know how to keep your body free from disease as long as you live.

"A baby was born blind and brain damaged," Dr. Adams continued. "Doctors said he'd never recover but I healed him in five days. A man with five bypass surgeries was given up to die but I healed him in two months. I broke my fingers but I set them myself and they healed within eight hours. I had a brand new hand! These are things you won't learn anywhere else on the face of this earth and I am giving them to you!"

For two and a half hours my parents sat at the table, picking at their food and avoiding eye contact with anyone in the room. I wanted to laugh and cry at once, seeing how ridiculous the party looked and still wanting more than anything for my parents to believe.

Dr. Adams's force reverberated through the room, creating an unnatural hush among the diners. At moments of intense excitement, he struggled to his feet, towering above my dad. In amazement, I watched my dad wither under Dr. Adams's dominance. For a moment he looked like a child picking at his food, hanging his head in the presence of obvious authority.

"Let's go," I whispered to Joel. "I want to go home." I couldn't stand seeing my dad wiggling feebly in the palm of Dr. Adams's hand.

Pressure, massage, and stroke. Dr. Adams was given that formula in one night, but he was marketing it to the world for $350 a pop. Some people were buying it. His sons worked eight-hour shifts in a rented office space, calling from a list of numbers, launching into their marketing speech as soon as the phone was picked up on the other end. I watched several Saturdays in amazement as they called home after home.

Of course, they were usually rejected. Matt was fond of saying after an unproductive afternoon, "The destruction of the world is nigh at hand. The people shall lead themselves to the grave by their own choices."

In contrast, when someone agreed to send $350 for the book, the videocassettes and the tapes, the brothers, after gently setting the phone down in its cradle, blessed their father with a morbid righteousness for providing them the knowledge and the means to save the world.

Pressure, massage, and stroke. It all worked fine in theory. It was Dr. Adams's practice that I had a problem with. One night I rubbed my neck and Joel pounced on the movement. "Do you have a headache?"

"My neck is just stiff."

"You're probably not eating right. And I'll bet anything your joints are out of place."

Before I could respond, Joel called his dad, who was shoveling food into his mouth in front of the TV. Dr. Adams hobbled into the room, favoring his good leg. "Where are you hurting?" he asked.

"My neck is just a little bit stiff."

"Stand up straight and turn your back to me."

I obeyed.

He put his hands on my shoulders and breathed in deep. As he exhaled, he put pressure on my muscles. Then, with the balls of his hands, he massaged my shoulders. With quick movements, he began stroking at my neck and traversing the length of my arms to my fingertips. After he finished my shoulders, he moved on to my back. Then, breathing deeply and gyrating sensuously, he massaged and stroked my hips and thighs. I cringed when he put his large hands on my butt and probed the muscles. Heat erupted between my legs and he pulled my hips backward until they rubbed against him. The way he was breathing in short jagged gasps reminded me of the love-making session I'd overheard the week before.

When he was done, Dr. Adams asked, "How do you feel?"

I said, too quickly, "Fine. It feels much better." I moved to hover near the piano, crossing my arms over my chest.

With a satisfied smile, Dr. Adams sat in a faded arm chair and looked at me. "By stroking and transferring my positive energy into your body, the lymphatic vessels will activate and heal you. You won't have pain, loss of energy, or disease when your cells are in this condition.

"Imagine you've burned yourself. What happens? The cells are damaged and the skin blisters. If you compress the tissue, the wound can't expand. By applying pressure, you've just healed the burn. Now put positive energy in it, add massage and stroke, and in five minutes you've got a brand new hand!"

I flashed back to when I was seventeen. Red-hot searing pain shot up my arm. A second and then two seeped by as intense agony surged through my body, numbing my mind. Then nothing. The smell of burning flesh permeated the air, but the pain was gone. Muscles throbbed from exertion. My eyes clenched tight. I opened them and turned my hand palm-up in front of my face.

A blister the diameter of a nickel stared back at me, the same size and shape as the mound of cooling glue on the counter. The edges of the wound curled up slightly and pus was already inflating the middle. Gently fingering the hardening bubble in my palm, I wondered at the lack of pain. Time stopped. My life up until then ceased to make sense.

Emotion caught in my throat, threatening to choke me. I swallowed. I wanted to cry but tears wouldn't come. I'd been using a hot glue gun to put the finishing touches on a Christmas ornament that would be delivered the next day when my family made the annual trip to visit relatives in Southern Utah.

Despite my age, I still wanted my mother to take care of me. I called to the adjoining room, where she was folding laundry, "Mom, I burned myself." Going to her, I held out my hand, palm up, for her to inspect. She continued stacking the towels. "It doesn't look bad. Run it under cool water and I'll get some first aid cream."

As she walked toward her bedroom, I sat down on the cool tiles of the laundry room. Something about the wound calmed me. I felt like I could sit on that hard floor forever. I still couldn't feel the burn.

The wound began to heal but it pulled my skin toward the center, making my hand look disfigured, like an animal's claw. A big green pool of putty-like infection brewed in a perfect circle in my palm. I started prodding the pus and discovered that if I pushed it around, it pulled the skin with it and caused pain. The pus dried and cracked and I picked at it until it came off in leaves. Finally, I saw beneath it a gaping hole that led to the inside of my hand. There was no skin in that nickel-sized hole. I started screaming.

Two days later, I sat with my mom in the doctor's waiting room. She worked on a cross-stitch ornament as I flipped nervously through a dull magazine. I habitually tore pages from these magazines and hoarded them in a box I kept under my bed. My parents didn't subscribe to magazines and doctors' offices were the only place I got to read them. They were full of beauty advice—how to get shinier hair, how to lose thirty pounds in thirty days, how to clear up acne-prone skin, how to select clothes that flatter the shape of your face.

Seven or eight other patients waited in the same room, some reading, some staring straight ahead. No two people sat next to each other. The room was silent. I wondered about that space people always reserve around themselves, and how strangers always seem to know where that space starts and ends.

Pictures lined the walls, labeled "Before" and "After." I studied them. Women in the "Before" column hadn't fixed their hair, put on make-up, or remembered to smile. In the "After" column, women smiled seductively at the camera, hair falling in curls around the flawless skin of their faces. They showed off bare shoulders and deep necklines. They seemed to invite people to come into their frames and be beautiful, too.

When I looked more closely, I noticed more subtle differences between the two columns. I saw higher cheekbones in some, fuller lips in others, a stronger chin or a straighter nose. I ducked my head and stared at my hands while waiting for someone to call my name.

A nurse stepped out, the rubber soles of her white shoes soundless on the hard wood floor. "Alysa," she read from a clipboard. I stood up. My mom tucked her sewing into her purse and followed. The nurse told me to sit on a table and then asked my age and what part of my body we were going to look at. I couldn't help wondering what she thought needed the doctor's knife.

The doctor was a tired man who didn't even introduce himself before asking me to extend my left hand. My fingers curled toward the palm and the skin pulled taut when I tried to extend them. Hardened dead skin lined the wound and the light green bubble of infection persisted from inside the hole. Less than ten minutes later, we were scheduling an appointment for plastic surgery. The procedure was simple, the doctor said. "All I'm going to do is shave some of the skin from the side of your hand and use it to fill the hole in the center."

"Can I watch?"

"Sure. We'll give you a local anesthetic and you'll be awake for the whole thing."

What the doctor didn't say was that he'd give me so many

sedatives before the surgery that during the hour he cut, patched and stitched my skin, I'd babble away, telling him and his assistants that I burned myself on purpose. If the doctor passed along my confession to my parents, they never said anything.

Afterward, my hand had a damaged, decaying sort of smell to it. An elastic bandage covered a thick wad of gauze in my palm, and it was constantly sweaty and warm. Every time the panic began rising from the pit of my stomach, I put my nose next to the bandage and breathed in, comforted. As long as I had the polluted bandage on, my hurt was strictly on the outside. I dreaded the day my hand healed and I'd be forced to expose it to the world.

I sat in Joel's living room one Monday morning finishing my statistics homework. I'd been awarded permission to continue my education if I agreed to use it to benefit the cult. Dr. Adams told me I could be an asset to him if I got a degree: "We can always use someone who's played the government's game and knows the inside secrets."

Because my parents wouldn't let me drive their cars, I relied on public transportation to get to and from school, and the trip took nearly an hour each way. When Joel wasn't calling all over the world trying to sell lymphnogenesis, he drove me.

In the kitchen, May was trying to console Karen, the wife of Joel's eldest brother. Karen was twenty when she married Isaac, who was fifteen years older. She had never learned to read and Isaac forbade her from learning. She wore floor-length skirts and balanced a grimy toddler on each hip. Even though her eldest was nearly three, she wasn't crawling yet. She hadn't been weaned off breast milk either.

May cooed to Karen, "Every Eve is different."

Karen sniffled. "But I'm displeasing to God."

"It's true that women are here to please their men and bring children into the world, but you have to let it happen naturally."

Karen's voice got higher. "I want to bring as many children into the world as I can, but I'm failing."

"I had ten children and you will, too," May assured her. "God will give children to his chosen followers."

All the Adams children were born at home. May taught her children that electronic tracking devices are placed into infants' feet during the moments between birth and when the baby is put into its mother's arms. "That way the government can watch you for your entire life," she said.

I found it difficult to concentrate on my homework, so I called into the next room at Joel, "My class is starting."

He strode forward to embrace me. Then he spun me around, positioning his hands in front of my stomach, massaging an imaginary fetus and saying, "I can't wait until you're pregnant."

I decided to stop talking.

I spent my time watching people, wondering what went on in their heads. Mostly, though, I wondered how I could act like they did. I wondered if their hearts ached all the time, too. I couldn't figure out how to nonchalantly push a cart around a store or wait in the line at a library without confiding to everyone that my heart hurt. I isolated myself as often as possible. When it was necessary to mingle in common situations, I avoided making eye contact, choosing instead to focus above people's eyes at an invisible spot on their foreheads. I wandered around in a sort of half-life, my feelings so big I felt I would burst.

Pain isn't a socially acceptable emotion. People are expected to act a certain way in public, and some sort of unspoken code mandates that emotions be kept inside. But my pain was too big; it leaked to the outside. I started cutting my left wrist, little cuts in the shower

40

after I shaved my legs. Before going to school in the morning, I used my mom's blunt bread knives to chafe the skin. During the day, I scratched at my wrist with pieces of sharp plastic, unbent paper clips or pop tops from aluminum cans. I only cut in one place and I wore a wide watch to cover it up.

I started playing a mental game with myself. I'd give myself a deadline to stop hurting so I wouldn't have to cut. "After Valentine's Day, you won't hurt anymore," I'd tell myself. I'd allow the pain to rage inside until that day, when it would miraculously disappear.

Then I started bribing myself: "I'll buy a new book if you can go a week without the pain."

Every morning, my goal for the day was to survive. When that got to be too much, I started whispering under my breath, "Just one minute. Just get through this one minute. Then move on to the next."

4

"I'm going to kill myself," I blurted out when I was nine. My mom grabbed me by the back of my neck and yanked me up the twelve stairs to my room. She hissed through her teeth, "Don't you ever say that again. I want you to sit in your room and make a list of all your blessings."

It was nine p.m. All I had to look forward to was another day of elementary school, where the other students would taunt me, destroy my homework, tear off my homemade clothes and kick open the bathroom stall door when I was inside. I was always in the principal's office, though I never knew why. One time a girl I'd never seen before told the principal that I bit her. Teary-eyed and nursing a red spot on her arm, she pointed a finger at me as I walked into the office. "That girl bit me! She bit me right here." She pushed on her bruise and grimaced to add emphasis.

The principal asked me, "Did you bite this girl?"

He was too tall for me to look in the eyes, so I stared at his striped tie. "No."

But even as the syllable escaped my lips, I knew it was pointless. I took my punishment with as much dignity as I knew how, sitting on a long black leather couch and writing "I will not bite other students" fifty times on a piece of bluish copy paper.

People don't take the pain of children seriously.

A boy I knew killed himself later that year. He used a knotted sheet to hang himself from the top bunk in his bedroom. He didn't leave a note. Students and teachers began talking in whispers. The principal cut pieces from his black mourning tie and handed them out to students in need of consolation. He said generically to the boy's grieving classmates, "We'll always remember Daniel. His positive outlook and good sportsmanship will never be forgotten."

But students kept talking in hushed voices in the hall before lunch and on the bus rides home. We asked questions but no matter how much we talked, we were never satisfied with our answers. "Did you hear his little brother found him?" someone whispered.

Another student answered, "I heard he tried it before and everyone knew it was coming."

I stored these conversations away in my imagination to think about Daniel when I was alone. I half expected him to come back to school and tell us it had all been a joke. But of course he didn't come back. I pictured his face growing red from lack of oxygen and blood. Then bluish gray as his heart stopped beating. I tried to imagine paramedics forcing air into his lungs while his mother prayed. But nothing in my mind could save him.

The school year continued on, and with it the quiet urge to bleed. I followed the craving like a fish pursues a hook. I gave in to the compulsion to cut my arms and legs, even though it delivered pain and mutilation along with protection. Most people won't understand the protection part, but that's because when my blood trickled from the thin cuts, I existed in a warm, safe place.

Girls my age spent time in their rooms surrounded by groups of beaming, laughing pre-adolescent peers. They experimented with their mothers' make-up and tried on brand-name clothes with assorted styles of shoes. I sat in my brown-carpeted, white-washed bedroom trying to find my lost time. While waiting for a call from a friend I didn't have, I'd take a broken razor and run the blade gently across my arms and legs, letting blood seep from the wounds and then dry. I wore the dry blood as a badge, as a way to account for the time I felt was slipping away.

I lost time whenever reality shifted. I was never prepared for it, and the resulting anxiety added to the confusion. It snuck up, pitching a cape of dread over me. Sometimes it lasted only a moment. Other times I walked along as a shadow-self for days before re-entering reality.

When I turned twelve, I was required to attend a weekly religious gathering to learn skills for my future family. The congregation I attended—known as a ward—was two square blocks and about four hundred members strong. All the girls in that area walked to the church on Wednesday evenings for instruction on cooking, cleaning, and sewing.

One night we were making Christmas crafts in one of the building's multi-purpose rooms. Foam brushes and paint lay scattered on long tables covered with newspaper. We were each given a piece of wood shaped like Santa Claus's body. Two smaller pieces of wood had holes drilled through the sides, designed to have a length of yarn strung through them and tied to Santa's body so his legs could bend and he could sit down.

I figured Santa might grow bored with his red suit year after year. As I watched the mob of girls all reaching for the same paint, I couldn't color mine red anyway. It went against my nature. Green paint drizzled from its plastic tube like liquid energy, and I dabbed the end of a clean brush through a puddle on a paper plate. Then I caressed the block of wood, enjoying the clash of textures when liquid met solid. My brush moved quickly as I blotted a green suit on the old man, thrilling at the shiny paint. Bent in concentration over my work, I painted faster, washing my brush in a plastic cup of water to give Santa white and green striped socks and red boots.

A church leader suddenly yelled in my ear, "What are you doing?"

All around the table, girls stopped painting to stare at me. The leader continued, "You're ruining your Santa! What's wrong with you? Why can't you follow directions?" My face grew red and I ducked it down, hiding behind a curtain of my hair.

For a little while objects became too big and everything was too loud. I floated two feet above the table, staring down at the tops of the girls' heads. Their stiff bangs jutted out from the fronts of their heads like balls of dirty cotton candy. Gradually the world slowed down and I drifted back to my seat. My Santa Claus was almost dry and I could have repainted it red. Instead, I pitched it into the economy-sized trash can on my way out of the room.

I knew even when I was twelve that I didn't fit the right molds. I was smart and creative but I didn't look or act right. Adults ignored me and peers ostracized me.

My physical inferiority was especially obvious when I once stood next to a classmate in front of a bathroom mirror. I reached for the soap to wash my hands while the girl curled her upper lip. Bubbles slid from my wet hands into the white basin while she examined her face. "My mascara's smeared," she said, digging through her purse.

I waited until she'd touched up her makeup and left. Then I took her place in front of the mirror and mimicked the way her lips opened to emit their graceful, silent song as she applied mascara. My mom made the same expression when she put on makeup, but her face was older and I could see the blue veins criss-crossing under her skin. My peers had soft firm skin and cheesecake complexions. I had no idea how to achieve that.

When Joel proposed seven years later, my skin was still marred by subtle imperfections. But I'd caught his attention and I was desperate to keep it. On the shiny top of a bureau in his bedroom, he kept a line of small picture frames. From each frame smiled one of his gorgeous ex-girlfriends. I cried happily when Joel finally asked for my picture, framed it, and put it at the end of the line. He said, "The other girls were mostly shallow, and you have a pretty smile. You're the last girl I'm going to date."

Joel was fond of driving in the Utah mountains. He'd often, after picking me up from school, steer his car onto one of the highways that led up the nearby mountain. He followed the route into cool air where Aspen trees gave way to pines, and where the road forked frequently to take its passengers to secluded groves of trees or peaceful streams.

Cascade Springs was Joel's favorite destination. It closes at dusk and an ornery old man living in a mobile home enforces the rule with a rifle. He carries it around with both hands, stalking in darkness, keeping his eyes open for trouble-making teenagers. Joel rationalized entering the park in the dark. "We're not vandalizing or anything. We're just making out." I hated making out and I hated the pine trees. They reminded me of summer camp, which I attended five years in a row.

Camp was the female equivalent to Boy Scouts, a church program designed for young women between twelve and eighteen. Split into groups by congregation, we traveled a hundred and fifty miles from home in hoards of fifty or a hundred. Buses dropped us off in a clearing full of cabins next to a lake. The drivers dumped our luggage into the dust and sped away, leaving us to struggle up the hill towing packs bigger than we were.

We lived there for a week at a time, learning about nature, survival, spiritual reawakening, and ultimately which of us would bear the group's pain of growing up. The world of adolescent girls is poison. Camp meant waking up to find a bra hung on a flagpole and groups of girls chanting about their victory, even to the tune of embarrassed sobbing. Those were the days of fierce competition that ended in fist fights or nasty nighttime pranks.

Two cabins were assigned per group, one of them filled to the brim with those who passed the tests. Places to roll out a sleeping bag on the wooden floor of the popular cabin were in high demand. The other cabin was for outcasts and camp leaders.

The youngest campers were called yearlings, and they were forced through a series of sorority-type tests to prove their worth. One of the first tests was to play "Cheeky, cheeky." After the popular girls staked out places in their cabin, they immediately started looking for their first victim. One girl would stick her head out the cabin door to lure a yearling over. "Hey!" she'd call out. "Come over. We want you to play a game."

The invitation dripped in honey sweetness and the invitee never turned her back. She'd eagerly climb the four roughly-hewn wooden stairs into the cabin. A girl would move over and offer a seat on the edge of her sleeping bag, and then the game would begin.

Like all good jokes, "Cheeky, cheeky," grew with excitement and anticipation with each passing moment. A tube of dark lipstick was passed around the circle as the game went on, and girls leaned toward the middle as things got more intense. Then, without warning, the game would be over, all fingers pointing to the yearling while laughter echoed from the cabin. In confusion, the yearling would take the mirror that someone readily handed her to discover that she was the only one in the group with lipstick smeared all over her face. She'd been so engrossed in the game that she failed to realize there was no game. The object was to make her cry. I don't know what the rules of "Cheeky, cheeky" are; I was never invited in. But I saw the faces of yearlings and even leaders as they slumped back to our cabin, faces mixed with lipstick and tears.

Camp was going to be especially bad the year I turned fourteen. As part of the camp requirements for third-year girls, we had to go on a three-day adventure hike two weeks prior to camp. I carefully packed in preparation for the wilderness area where we'd pitch tents and survive by our own means for seventy-two hours.

The only way I could fall asleep before going on trips was to take a sleeping pill. I woke groggy the day of the hike and, with a feverish energy, packed and repacked my backpack. I couldn't dismiss the feeling that I was leaving out something important. I didn't discover what I'd forgotten until dusk the first night. The girls dug a latrine about fifty yards up the hill from where the tents were pitched and I didn't have a flashlight.

The day's hike had left me exhausted. I was a small thirteen-year-old—at least twenty pounds lighter than the other hikers—and I had to struggle to keep up. When we reached our camp site, the girls split into groups of two or three and pitched their tents.

There were four tents and ten campers counting the chaperone. I wandered from spot to spot asking for a corner to sleep in, but there was no room at the tents. Even the chaperone, who'd packed a six-man tent, insisted I'd have to find someplace else. Eventually two girls had pity on me and invited me in. But they'd pitched their tent on top of a fallen tree and my space was on the log. Three days later, lack of sleep and depression slowed me down and I finished the hike last. When I finally joined everyone in the parking lot, the chaperone was saying, "You all did well. Now we can look forward to camp."

The pressure to get emotionally ready for another disaster gave me a migraine the day before camp. I lay in bed all day as jagged pain shot through my head at every noise, light, or turn of my head. The headaches never lasted less than eight hours, and they usually spilled over into the next day, leaving me disoriented and woozy. As I moaned, my mom kept reminding me to get over it or I wouldn't be able to go to camp.

"But I don't want to go to camp," I protested. She pretended not to hear me.

The pain finally subsided at nightfall. With my camping supplies lining the walls, I downed a sleeping pill and fell into a fitful sleep. Five a.m. came too early; my alarm blasted through the darkness with a deep sense of despair. Ten minutes later my dad came downstairs to make sure I was awake.

Hundreds of teenage girls swarmed the church parking lot when my dad pulled in. Bleary-eyed and anxious, I dragged my gear to one of the charter buses. The migraine had left me disoriented and my coordination was sloppy. I just wanted to go home.

An hour later, the bus was piled high with shrieking girls as it headed up the canyon, and my reality shifted. When the bus stopped at camp, everyone began gathering their gear without a thought. But I had to concentrate on my hand as it moved into my line of vision and then attached itself to my sleeping bag. The hand was not mine. The image made my heart race and a sense of despair draped over me. Five days was a long time.

When I went to bed that night, I hoped I'd wake with reality shifted back to normal. I had no such luck. Each night that entire summer—long after camp ended—I wished the same thing, sometimes staying awake for hours to avoid the inevitable reentry into a world that had ceased to make sense. Colors were not the same in the muted world. Lines couldn't make shapes. Angles didn't add up. Mathematical equations defied linear planes. I existed not because I wanted to, but because I had no choice.

Pine trees began to represent isolation to me. Year after year as I traveled to camp, I dreaded seeing that first stand of the spiny trees more than I dreaded five days of filled latrines and practical jokes. So every time Joel started the hour journey toward Cascade Springs, I groaned quietly. I wouldn't say anything, forfeiting my desires to satisfy his, but once I protested. "I don't want to go make out. I want to stay in town and talk or go walk around the mall or something."

Keeping his eyes on the road, Joel asked, "Do you love me?"

"Yes."

"I need you to show me that you love me."

"What do you mean?"

Joel said, "You tell me you love me all the time, but when I want to go somewhere to make out, you get all touchy. If you really love me, then show me you mean it."

Mormon girls are expected to start dating at sixteen, and most marry by the time they're twenty. Like my peers, I prepared most of my life for the day I'd say "I do" and live happily ever after. I had a hope chest in the corner of my bedroom filled with things I'd use after I got married—towels and potholders and homemade wall hangings. Someday I'd be the perfect housewife. I even crocheted booties for my children and hoarded pacifiers and baby bottles. My hope chest filled up so quickly that I had to buy a plastic tub to catch the overflow. I was so prepared that I sometimes forgot I wasn't married. When Joel showed up, he fit into my life like the one missing link; it was all too easy to overlook his flaws.

Still, that link to happily-ever-after began to tarnish after Joel asked my grandfather for money. My grandfather was a turf farmer and wasn't hurting for money, though he didn't live high. He gave much of his money to charity, often writing out checks for thousands of dollars to help young people go to school or serve a mission for the church. Then Joel approached him.

"Hey Grandpa," he said jovially, assuming a birthright. "How about some cash for my dad's science?"

Dr. Adams's sons had all recently signed a legal statement, promising the United States government they'd live in poverty, emulating Christ in his mission to heal. Their vows ensured that the International Academy of Lymphnogenesis had a tax-exempt status. "It's really easier this way," Joel told me. "The government knows I'm on a mission from God and will be more likely to help support me. Besides, I never have to worry about taxes."

I had a brief image of the two of us growing old, never owning anything except cans of government chicken. For some reason, the image showed us living out our lives in his parents' basement.

When Joel asked my grandfather for ten thousand dollars, I blurted out, "How are you going to explain that to the IRS?"

Joel turned toward me. "It's a charitable donation, money given to God, not us." He turned back to my grandpa. "What do you say, Gramps?"

"I say that you're not welcome in my house. And take your science with you." My grandfather turned and walked off.

~⁓

One Friday night, Joel and I went to the dollar movie theater to see *Men in Black*. We were at the end of a long line when Joel turned to ask an attractive girl standing next to him, "Did you know you have a system of lymphatic vessels that parallels your blood vessels all throughout your body?" I sighed.

The girl was in her early twenties and looked bored. "No."

"Well you do, and in the next ten minutes I can tell you how to live without pain or disease for the rest of your life."

"Are you some sort of doctor?" the girl asked.

"I'm training to be one," Joel said.

The girl looked impressed. "Do you live around here?"

"I'm going to school. By the way, do you know you have pretty eyes? We're going out for dinner after this. Do you want to come?"

I looked at Joel in confusion. Was he asking her out? Apparently she had the same thought. "You mean like on a date?"

"Yeah, like a date," Joel said.

She motioned toward two other girls in line with her. "I'm here with my friends."

"So that's a no?"

The confused girl looked at me for an answer. I shrugged. Then she quickly grasped at one friend's arm and the three left without looking back.

51

I asked, "What was that?"

Joel turned toward me. "My dad told me to prepare for the future. God will again command men to practice polygamy. She was a pretty girl and she would have given me good children."

⚓︎

In a final effort to accept me and Joel, my mom invited him over for dinner on a Sunday night. She served baked chicken, rice, steamed broccoli, and strawberry Jell-O. Joel rang the doorbell at the appointed hour and my dad let him in. Joel stood straight and tall, with one arm draped across his body in a formal sort of way. He tilted his head back and smiled at everyone.

"Have a seat," my dad offered. Joel sat down at the table and folded his hands in his lap. I sat next to him and my siblings took their chairs.

"I'll pray," Joel offered. I looked up. My mom was frowning. I closed my eyes again. We bowed our heads as Joel began. "Thank you, Lord, for this opportunity to partake of thy bounteous food as a family."

When we began to fill our plates, Joel looked uncomfortable and began bombarding my mother with questions. "Do any of these dishes have MSG in them?"

"I don't know."

"I can't eat it if it does," he said. "I'll have some broccoli. That should be safe."

He heaped his plate with the green vegetable and I passed him the Jell-O. He said, "Jell-O is a poison that goes directly into your lymphatic vessels, causing cancer. You shouldn't eat it, either."

Wordlessly, I passed the Jell-O to my dad without taking any. When I reached for the rice, Joel said, "If that has any salt or niacin, it'll kill you." He took a quick look at the chicken being passed.

"And if you eat meat, you'll take on the characteristics of the person who butchered the animal."

I put down the rice spoon and helped myself to a small portion of broccoli. My family was silent but Joel didn't seem to notice. He scooped some broccoli into his mouth, though no one else was eating. "Well I can't live on just broccoli," he announced. Then he addressed my mom. "My dad can teach you how to prepare food in a way that will benefit your family. The way you're cooking now, you're going to kill everyone in a matter of weeks."

After dinner, Joel and I migrated to the living room. Sarah followed. Joel situated himself on the couch and took my hand. Directing himself to both of us, he said, "I'm going to tell you something important. You'll have to accept lymphnogenesis in order to be saved. I have to admit I was surprised to see the way you eat around here. You're good people but you're living ignorantly and that will only send you to hell."

Sarah looked at me but I was speechless. Joel continued, "I want you to bear testimony to the truthfulness of lymphnogenesis. I know you believe in God but I want to hear the same conviction about lymphnogenesis. It's the word of God, too."

I didn't realize my mom was listening from the hallway until she stormed in, her mouth set in a hard line and her eyes flashing. "You get out of my house," she seethed. "I never want to hear the word lymphnogenesis in my home again. If you ever say it, you will not be welcome within these walls."

As Joel calmly stood and walked toward the front door, he told my mom, "You're following the devil. You'll realize your fault and bow to my father." He spoke without any malice and I found myself believing him. Joel let himself out and I followed, not so much because I wanted to be with him, but because I feared my mother's wrath would be directed at me in his absence.

When we got back to Joel's house, Dr. Adams was in his usual spot in the recliner in front of the TV, a plate balanced on his large stomach. He was devouring a large steak. Using a fork and a dull knife, he tore off pieces and shoveled them in. Blood drooled down his chin from the corners of his mouth and soaked into his shirt.

I looked at Joel with a question. He understood. "My dad can eat whatever he wants. His cells are in a perfect healthy condition; they pull the poisons from the meat as soon as he eats it. It won't affect him."

I decided to stop eating.

5

My throat tightened as if hands gripped my neck. Blackness seeped into my sleep, threatening to smother me if I didn't wake up.

I'd had this dream before. It was abstract, like watching dark creatures from a Salvador Dali painting melt into an even darker tank of oil. Even as I slept, I tried to make sense of it. Then the darkness erupted suddenly, violently, into a faceless figure that crawled toward me, panting, sucking, evil.

I stopped breathing and woke up gulping at the dank air of my bedroom. I kicked out wildly at my imaginary enemy, thrashing around in bed as if rising to the surface of deep, suffocating water. My sweat-soaked sheets tangled in knots around my ankles and stomach.

I breathed deliberately, forcing myself to relax.

"It's just a panic attack," I said out loud. "Just breathe."

Out of habit, I pressed the ring and middle fingers of my right hand to my left wrist and felt for a pulse. My heart beat so quickly it was almost whirring. I counted while staring at the red numbers on my clock radio: 142 beats per minute—the fastest it had ever been.

My breathing slowed gradually and my heart rate followed after. Calmer, I disentangled the sheets and sat up, trying to get oriented. In my sleep, I'd twisted around in bed. The basement window wasn't where I remembered it. Pale orange rays from the streetlight cast weird shadows, making the furniture look bigger than it should be.

My panic attacks lasted anywhere from ten minutes to several hours, and they happened almost every night. In a strange way,

I was comfortable with them because they were so familiar. The attacks were like a constant irritating background noise; if suddenly removed, the silence would become unbearable. I needed my nightly panic attacks to reassure myself that I was still alive.

The panic I felt whenever I disobeyed Joel was also familiar to me; joining his cult was an easy transition from my home life. The rules, though somewhat different, were dictated in the same manner as my father's laws.

My father ran his home like a kingdom, and he sat on the throne. There were rules for everything—what to wear, what to eat, how much to eat, when to eat, what to say, act, and feel. Between-meal snacking was prohibited and food was counted in my parents' house. If one of my five siblings or I got too hungry and ventured into the pantry for a slice of bread or a cookie, punishment was inevitable.

My dad would organize "truth tables" to find the culprit. We'd sit around the dining room table while our dad asked us, one at a time, if we had taken the slice of bread from the box on top of the dishwasher, or the cookie from the pantry, or the apple from the refrigerator. We even had truth tables over who had used the last of the roll of toilet paper, signifying our use of more than the two allotted squares per sitting.

"Michael, was it you?" my dad asked, making eye contact with his oldest son.

"No," he'd say, squirming anyway.

"Alysa, was it you?"

"No."

"Nathan, was it you?"

And on and on, until the culprit buckled under growing guilt and confessed. It took us more than a decade to realize that if we all confessed to the crime in question, none of us would have to bear the entire punishment.

My dad also kept track of mileage on the van. He took a

passenger car to work every day, leaving the eight-person van home, with specific instructions that my mom drive it only in an emergency. If she had to go grocery shopping, she called my dad at work to ask his permission. If she had to take one of us to the doctor's office, she called my dad to tell him where we were going. Sometimes, if we begged long enough, she gave in and drove one of us to a friend's house or to the mall, and occasionally even to Ginger's Dairy for an ice cream cone. But we all learned quickly that taking the van without permission wasn't worth the penalty.

Upon returning home every evening, my dad analyzed the position of the van's tires in the garage. If he determined that they were an inch forward or backward from the position they were in when he left, he confronted my mother: "Did the van go out today?" Whenever he asked that question, we tried not to exist.

My mom would say quietly, "I went to the store." This conversation usually took place while she was preparing dinner, but she'd stop her chopping or sorting or cleaning.

My dad's voice would rise in anger. "Out gallivanting around, running back and forth! I work all day, and you and these lazy kids sit around and take, take, take. You're all a bunch of moochers."

It only took a few minutes for my mom to start crying. I think she cried partly because her children were watching her public flogging and partly because my dad left the room when she cried.

Everything in my dad's house belonged to my dad. I learned never to say I was going to "my room." My dad would always correct me: "It's my room. I'm letting you use it."

Borrowing a bedroom from my dad came with certain responsibilities. One such responsibility was to never shut the door. He needed to be able to see what I was doing in that room at all times. One time I challenged that rule so I could write in private. But then my dad wanted to know what I was writing in my journal. I felt my very person was being intruded upon.

57

"Stuff," I told him, shutting the book before he could see any of the words.

He made a grab for my journal, but I put it behind me and yelled for my mom. As he tried to reach around me for it, my dad muttered, "Ungrateful, immature brat!"

"Get out of my room!" I yelled at my dad, pushing him toward the door.

"Your room?" he spat. "I'll show you how much this is your room." He went to the furnace room for a tool box. When he came back, he removed the hinges on my bedroom door. "Let's see if you appreciate your privacy now."

My heart often ached from stifled feelings. In my father's house, emotions were unacceptable at best and sinful at worst. I wasn't allowed to express anger, sadness, or disappointment, and I wasn't even allowed to be too happy. Happiness was light-mindedness, my dad always said. So I learned to display only half an octave of emotions, nothing too high or too low. Any breach of the norm was penalized.

My dad's leverage for punishment came from his ability to remove us from his house whenever he wanted to. If we ever talked back, he'd ask, "Do you want to go sleep outside?"

We'd hang our heads. "No."

"Then you'd better find your attitude adjuster."

I never knew where my attitude adjuster was, or how to adjust the silly thing, but I knew exactly what my dad needed. He needed to be right about everything, no questions asked. The sooner I bowed my head and squelched whatever emotion I was feeling, the better.

Dr. Adams's cult also worked like a kingdom. I glided easily from the tyranny of my father to the confines of the cult, readily forfeiting my will to Joel and Dr. Adams. I didn't realize the two kingdoms were at war until I was on the battlefield. The panic attacks every night reminded me that I was only fighting myself.

I broke off the engagement in January after wearing the ring for a month. I hoped my pain would subside if I gave the metal band back. To Joel, with his $400 ring around my finger, I belonged to him. When I told him I wanted to slow things down, he demanded I give it back.

"I just need some time to think about things," I told Joel as I handed the ring to him. We were hovering near the dying Christmas tree in the first sub-basement of his parents' house.

He asked with a sneer in his voice, "Are you saying you don't love me?"

I sat down on the ragged carpet and he seemed larger than life standing above me. The overhead light cast a halo around his head. "No, I'm not saying that," I started. "I'm just . . . confused."

"You're not going to find anyone better than me."

When I didn't answer Joel, he sat down beside me and reached out for my hand. I moved away. "I'm just not sure," I started again. "We hardly know each other and we got engaged so fast. I think we should just date for a while and see if we really want to do this. I mean, there are things about you and your life . . . I just don't know if I'm ready to live with that forever."

I was feeling brave so I continued. "Like your debt . . ." I trailed off. Joel was buried under more than $30,000 in credit card debt with nothing to show for it. Dr. Adams's debt was more than triple that.

Joel demanded, "And what else?"

"Well, I kind of always thought I'd marry someone with an education. I think if you went to school you'd find lots of other options and you wouldn't have to rely on your parents."

"You said you supported lymphnogenesis." Joel's tone was accusing.

I appeased him quickly. "I do support it. I just want to make sure that we can be financially secure."

As I spoke, I imagined that the pain plaguing me every waking hour would disappear as soon as Joel registered for classes at the local community college. He'd glimpse a whole world awaiting him and he'd leave the cult, taking me with him.

But Joel's tone hardened. "I wasn't sure either. I never wanted to marry a brunette or a woman with physical flaws."

I sat upright against the wall. "What is that supposed to mean?"

"I don't like your nose," Joel started. "And I don't like the moles on your arms and face. And I really don't like your hands. They're too big for a girl."

I slid my hands underneath my thighs. "What else?"

"Your weight."

"What about my weight?" I was 5-feet-10-inches and 130 pounds.

"Well," Joel said. "Look at Kristi. She's at least twenty pounds lighter than you." That was true. Kristi ate even less than I did, sometimes existing only on lettuce leaves.

"I'm losing weight," I countered. That was true, too. Since the beginning of the year my appetite was non-existent. I'd been losing a couple of pounds a week. My ribs poked out from under my skin, and my cheeks were pale and taut.

"And your breasts . . . Well, there's not really enough to grab onto, if you know what I mean."

I crossed my arms around my chest and began to cry. Suddenly exhausted, I leaned over and rested my head on the floor.

Joel's voice shifted. "When I look at you and really see you, I think, forget this. Beautiful women line up to go out with me. Why would I choose you?"

I didn't have an answer.

Joel continued, his voice gone gentle. "But I love you in spite of your flaws. It's like, when you let yourself be mine, I can see past your physical imperfections. I think I can see your spirit."

"You can?" I looked at Joel through teary eyes, but I could

barely make eye contact. I didn't want him to see my face or notice the mole on my left cheek again. I could no longer imagine anyone loving a hideous monster like myself.

Joel said, "Just put the ring back on and we'll forget this whole thing." The size six, dull gold ring was comforting as I slipped it back onto my finger.

Later that night I faced myself in the mirror. The dark brown mole, about the circumference of a pencil eraser, protruded gently from my left cheek. As I scrutinized my reflection, I found a similar smaller mark on my right cheek, wondering why I'd never noticed it before. A third little mole nestled against my hairline above my ear, and yet a fourth one glared at me from my left eyelid. I stretched out my arms and saw hundreds of the colored marks there. Despair settled over me like a snowdrift.

Joel was right. I was lucky to have him, lucky he was willing to look past my disfigurements and love what was underneath. But as I stared at my mole-covered reflection, I suddenly couldn't remember if there was anything underneath.

I picked up a pair of toenail clippers and positioned them over the mole on my left cheek. The jaws of the clippers encased the mole like they were designed for it. I pushed gently on the levers and a current of pain darted across my cheek. I pushed harder and a crease appeared around the mole. I pushed the levers completely together, and with a soft crunch the mole came off between the blades. A gaping hole quickly filled up with thick blood that seeped down my cheek, branding me in blood-red ink. I triumphed at the sight of my mole-free cheek even as blood continued to ooze from the wound. But then I remembered the hundreds of other moles on my arms.

January was the start of a new semester. I took a job in the kitchen of the university cafeteria. From seven to ten a.m. every day, preparing for the kitchen to open, I chopped bell peppers, steamed rice, and put the ingredients into sweet and sour and egg drop soup.

During the first week of my job, I arrived at six thirty to dress in the white button-down shirt with "Food Services" embroidered on the pocket in blue thread, the white apron—one size fits all—that I wrapped around my body and tied in the front, and the blue and white mesh hat that kept my hair from falling into the food. By seven I'd punched my social security number into the time clock and gone into the walk-in freezer to pull out a five-gallon tub of frozen chicken to thaw.

By the second week of the semester, I was lucky to arrive on campus by seven. I had to hurry to get to the kitchen before my boss noticed my tardiness. At the start of the third week, my boss called me into his office. "Alysa, you started out well but you're getting sloppy. I want us to put together an action plan and stick to it." He pulled out a legal pad and a pen. "What can I do to help you?"

I wanted to blurt out that I was in a relationship I couldn't control and I was drowning. Instead, I swallowed the lump in my throat and said, "I like my job. I just wasn't sleeping well but things are better now." I willed myself to believe the words coming out of my mouth. My boss must have felt sorry for me because he let me keep my job until the end of the semester.

I wasn't doing any better in my classes. By the middle of February, I had failing grades in every class. My Music 101 teacher called me into his office. "What can I do?" he asked kindly.

"Nothing," I said. "I've been stressed out lately and I need to put more time into studying."

He looked at me closely as I left. My eyes filled with tears as I withdrew from what felt like safety in his office to face the world alone again. I was surrounded by people eager to help, but it wasn't the help

I needed. If someone could help me get away from Joel, I was sure my grades would improve.

February also brought Valentine's Day, a day Joel was looking forward to. He wanted to set a wedding date that night. Kristi and I planned a meal for our sweethearts. The two men arrived on the doorstep of my parents' house at seven p.m. Kristi and I had prepared mashed potatoes, breaded chicken, corn and green salad—no salt, sugar, niacin or MSG added.

With her face hardened in disapproval, my mom put a bowl of conversation hearts on the table before retreating to get ready for a date with my dad. "I didn't want Joel in my house," she explained to me later, "but I'd rather have had him there than worry about you being with him somewhere else."

Joel handed me a long-stemmed pink rose before we sat down around the dinner table. I inhaled its aroma and put it into a tall vase. But I didn't like real flowers because I couldn't stand watching them wilt.

I went through the motions of being in love with Joel that night. I held his hand while James and Kristi spoke of their marital bliss. I stroked his permed hair, pulling gently on the stiff curls as he read messages from conversation hearts to me. I put my tongue down his throat when he told me he loved me enough to be with me forever.

It was all a lie.

After dinner, Kristi and I piled the dishes into the sink. We linked arms with our beaus as they escorted us to the car. Our destination was the movie theater but halfway there, James and Kristi got into a fight about circumcision. The week before, Kristi had found out the baby growing in her womb was a boy. James had already named it Amos.

"I don't care what you say, the baby is getting circumcised," Kristi said. "My dad and my brothers are all circumcised."

James looked at Kristi like she was ripping off his manhood.

"You're willing to put our son under the knife just for convention?" he accused.

"James, there are medical reasons, too," Kristi started. She sighed. "We've already been through all this."

"I'm not sitting in this car with you," James told Kristi. "I'm not talking about our son and his weenie right now. I'm taking you home."

Kristi pleaded, "But it's Valentine's Day."

"Yeah, and I'm married to a cow," he said. "A fat pregnant cow."

We didn't make it to the movies that night. James pulled into the Adamses' driveway with a screech and let himself out, slamming the door behind him. As he stormed toward the house, Kristi ran after him, begging him to stop. "James, let's just forget it. Let's talk about it later."

James didn't turn around, so Joel and I followed Kristi into the house. Dr. Adams and David were kneeling in the living room with thick candles in the center.

"Oh God," David droned. He swayed back and forth, his white robe billowing around him. "Oh God, it is I, thy chosen one. I kneel before thee and bare mine arm, for gross darkness covers the earth and gross darkness envelopes the minds of the people. For Satan reigns and his dominions are great. The peoples of the earth stumble and grope in darkness at noonday. Make thy paths and directions known to me, oh God."

As he talked, tears streamed down David's cheeks and got lost in his beard. Dr. Adams wiped tears and perspiration off his own face, which was screwed into a grimace of concentration. Elidah perched on the piano bench and wrote rapidly with a ball-point pen into a spiral notebook.

Then revelation dumped from the heavens onto Dr. Adams and David's heads. David reeled backward with a weird light in his eyes, and deciphered the vision in his head while Elidah scribbled. "And

I, even Jesus Christ, do call thee to be my servant and a light and a covenant to the world in these last days. I have called you and given you a name to be had in remembrance before me, even the name Immanuel David Isaiah, which name being interpreted means God with us, beloved God, the Lord is salvation."

Dr. Adams looked up and motioned for us to sit down. Joel took my hand and led me toward the couch. The revelation continued. "My servant Immanuel has the fullness of the gospel," David chanted. "One who is mighty and strong have I ordained, for there has never been from the beginning of man upon the earth such great wickedness among its inhabitants as there now is. And I, the Lord God, hold in reserve a swift judgment against every soul who does not humble himself before me and before my servant, Immanuel David Isaiah."

Dr. Adams bowed himself to the floor, placing his head between his hands on the carpet. Joel slid from the couch onto his knees. I knelt next to him. During the following hour, David received revelation instructing him to begin a new church called Testaments of Jesus Christ, a study and fellowship society. "The prophet of my church has been led astray, therefore I have chosen Immanuel to lead my people," God told him.

Before the revelation ended, God also told David to renounce his citizenship in the United States and to destroy all his government documents. Social Security numbers were the government's way of branding its citizens, God said, and the government was Christ's most formidable enemy. Carrying a driver's license was agreeing to let the government control our lives.

After saying "Amen," Dr. Adams hobbled up the ten stairs to his room and returned with a box of social security cards and mortgage information. One by one, he fed the documents to the tiny candle flame and let them burn. Only when the fire threatened to consume his fingers did he drop the charred corners onto the carpet, where the papers fizzled for a second longer, melting the plastic fibers. James and Joel followed suit with their Social Security cards. David and Elidah had ignited all their own papers months before, at the same time they'd embraced their new names.

I thought about how I put my trust in the Bible and the words of the prophets. God had called prophets before. Why not now? The room glowed before my moist eyes. David was the chosen one.

As Joel drove me home after David's revelations, the digital speedometer on the dashboard read 74. The speed limit was 35.

Joel always drove at least twenty miles over the speed limit. He was immune to death, he always told me, because he was a messenger from God. Initially, I'd ask him to slow down. Then, when he flattened the accelerator, I pled with him to consider his own life and mine. Later on, I simply closed my eyes when he drove; I'd read somewhere that victims of car accidents sustain less injury if they keep their bodies relaxed. I figured if I didn't see the accident coming, I'd have a better chance at surviving it. Then finally, I decided I didn't care. A fatal car accident didn't sound all that bad. After four months, I even started praying that Joel would lose control and I'd be killed instantly.

The journey from Joel's house to my parents' house was about two miles, but we traveled the first mile in less than a minute. I had closed my eyes but they jerked back open when Joel suddenly slammed the brake. Thinking death was near, I looked for a vehicle or a tree in the car's path, but the road was clear. Then I saw the red and blue flashing lights in the rearview mirror.

Joel pulled to the side of the road and slammed his hands against the steering wheel. He reached across me to rummage in the glove compartment. An officer knocked on the window. Flustered, Joel pushed the automatic window button. Nothing happened. With an embarrassed giggle, he turned on the ignition and tried again.

The officer was not amused. "License and registration," he demanded.

Joel handed over his driver's license and insurance papers, which he luckily hadn't burned. The officer pawed through them and returned to his vehicle. Several minutes went by as Joel and I sat in silence. Then a second police car pulled up behind the first, lights flashing. Two officers approached Joel's car.

The first one said, "Step out of the car, sir."

With a defiant demeanor, Joel pushed the car door open and stood up.

"We have a warrant for your arrest," the officer said, yanking Joel's arms behind him and securing them with a pair of handcuffs. Then he began to pat Joel down. "Spread your legs," he ordered. Joel complied.

The second officer stood at my door shining a flashlight at my eyes. "Step out of the car, please, ma'am." My legs shook violently as I faced him. He asked, "Do you have identification?"

I shook my head. "Just my checkbook."

He took my checkbook and went back to his car, then returned with a thumbs-up. "No record on you. You're free to go."

I looked at Joel, who was staring at the ground humiliated. "What's the warrant for?" I heard him ask.

"Failure to appear in court," the officer said gruffly as he frisked Joel's legs. "I'm also arresting you now for criminal speeding."

The officer turned toward me. "Bail is set at $180. We'll hold him at the station for two hours, but then we'll have to move him to the county jail." The officer escorted Joel to his car and slammed the door.

The other one asked, "Are you a licensed driver?"

"Yes."

"Go ahead and drive the car then."

I slid into the driver's seat with my legs shaking so badly that I even had trouble pushing on the gas. Joel's cell phone was lying between the seats so I picked it up to make a call. I blurted into the phone, "James, Joel got arrested."

James's voice was heavy with sleep. "He what? OK, come to the house."

When I got to the Adamses' house again, James met me at the front door. It was after midnight. "How much is bail?" he asked, yawning.

"A hundred and eighty dollars."

"How much do you have?"

"Twenty maybe." I searched my pockets.

James bounded up the stairs and banged on his parents' door. "Dad, Joel's in jail. We need a hundred dollars to get him out."

The dim hall light shone through Dr. Adams's thin blue pajamas, and I turned my face away. "What's he in jail for?" he asked James.

"I don't know. Speeding, I guess."

Counting out bills from his wallet, Dr. Adams said to no one, "How many times do I have to tell you to stay away from the law?"

Leaving Kristi sleeping in the basement, James jumped behind the wheel of Joel's car as I took the passenger side. The speedometer edged over the speed limit as James pumped the gas, cursing Joel under his breath. When we arrived at the police station, we found Joel on a bench, hands still shackled behind him. He was crying.

James counted out the bills into an officer's hand. The officer then unlocked Joel's cuffs and presented him with papers ordering him to appear in court. Joel was the first one out the door but James followed at his heels. I dragged my feet, glancing back at the officer before following because I had an impulse to tell him that I wasn't really one of them, that I was different.

The house was lit up when we got back. Dr. Adams and May sat in two of the recliners. Kristi paced the floor, but she jumped at me when I walked in. "What were you doing with my husband?" she demanded.

Taken aback, I muttered, "Nothing. We were just getting Joel out of jail. You were asleep."

Accusation dripping from her voice, Kristi said, "Uh-huh." She glared at me through red, sleep-deprived eyes. "I'm watching you. Just remember that."

Joel suddenly started punching holes in the walls. May pleaded quietly, "Joel, please stop." But her tranquility only fueled Joel's outburst. He punched the wall over and over until sheet rock hung from his scraped knuckles and tears spewed from his eyes.

When he finally stopped, Dr. Adams confronted him. "What was the warrant for, son?"

"Failure to appear in court. But you told me not to go. You said the government couldn't track me or make me pay." Joel looked at his father with confusion.

Dr. Adams said, "We're exempt from paying the government anything, but that means you have to keep a low profile. The devil influenced you to speed because he knew the government already had the warrant. He had you in a vulnerable position and he was ready to take advantage of you."

"I know Dad, I know," Joel spit through his tears. "It's just hard to live in this world of unbelievers. It's hard to be on God's side when everyone else is against me."

"We are God's chosen people. He will prepare the way, and all who rebel against our cause shall be smitten."

Later, Joel and I sat in his car. The key was in the ignition but Joel didn't turn it on. My eyes stung from exhaustion. He said, "So I'm thinking May fifteenth should be the day."

"May fifteenth?" I repeated blankly. Then I got it. Three months.

"We have plenty of time to prepare." Joel started the car and pulled away from the curb. His left hand was on the steering wheel and he put his other on my thigh. I didn't move. Setting a date seemed solid. The world rejected me and my new religion, but Joel would always be at my side.

My parents' house was dark when I got home, the orange glow of the front porch light the only welcoming sight. I knew my mom was still awake, lying in bed and worrying about me, so I slid off my shoes and padded down the hall. The boards creaked obviously, and I wondered why I even bothered to sneak.

"Mom," I whispered into the darkness of my parents' bedroom. I felt funny standing there listening to my parents' breathing, like I was eavesdropping on a private conversation. There was no answer. "Mom," I called again, louder this time.

When she still didn't answer, I shrugged and went downstairs to bed. I lay there hugging my arms around my body until morning.

Everything was different in the morning. My mom was up early making Malt-O-Meal for breakfast. Music blared through the intercom system. Bedroom and bathroom doors creaked open and slammed shut as everyone got ready for the day. But I stayed in bed wide awake, thinking about how pointless everything was. The world was about to be destroyed and my family was following the wrong prophet. Or was it the wrong prophet? I suddenly couldn't remember. I finally put my pillow over my head and went back to sleep.

6

Dr. Adams's injured leg was getting worse; he couldn't climb the ten stairs to his bedroom anymore. I walked into the living room in March to find him facing the wall and urinating into an empty mayonnaise bottle. "Uh," he said when he saw me. A row of bottles lined up against the far wall, each filled to the brim with cloudy yellow liquid.

I jumped at the sound of Joel's voice. I hadn't realized he was behind me until he spoke: "How's the old leg doing, Dad?"

"It's in bad shape."

Joel brushed past me to help his dad sit in the recliner. Then he stood a couple of yards away, breathing in deeply. As he exhaled, Joel circled his arms like a giant windmill, and then brought his hands together in front of his stomach. Shoulders thrust backward in a hyper-military stance, Joel churned his hands in front of his naval, fingertips nearly touching. Chanting under his breath, his hands moved faster and faster. In a sudden movement, he threw the invisible ball of energy he'd gathered toward his father. Then he knelt beside his father's leg and began chanting as he stroked the damaged foot.

When Dr. Adams yelped in pain, Joel stepped back to form another energy ball. He softly explained to me, "When the patient is in too much pain to touch, we have to create energy to heal them. I'm pulling energy from my center—the belly button, the key to life—and transferring it into my dad's leg."

Dr. Adams was breathing more easily, looking as if he were in some sort of trance. His eyes glazed as he watched his son conjure the forces of the heavens into balls of energy to thrust at his damaged leg.

Due to his illness, Dr. Adams stepped down from his throne and forfeited leadership to David. I still answered to Dr. Adams, but he in turn answered to David. David, of course, spoke directly with God. Rules in the cult were based on Dr. Adams's revelations about health and on David's continued communication with the Creator. As the revelations grew in intensity over time, the gap between us and the rest of society widened.

"It's us and it's them," David often said. "It doesn't have to be that way, but God will punish those who don't accept us." He welcomed ridicule whenever he preached to groups of people waiting at a bus stop or stood in line at the grocery store. Resistance to God's way only reinforced his conviction of its truth.

David handed jurisdiction of healing sessions over to Dr. Adams. During those times, he'd sit quietly in a corner or pour over a book of scripture, occasionally raising his head to affirm the small gathering of followers. Dr. Adams instructed quasi-classes of five or six adults at a time in his living room. Some people came with only minor aches and pains but others came with debilitating diseases like cancer. Usually at least one curious person played devil's advocate. But all stood in weird positions, arms stretched across their bodies to insert energy into their pain. Many closed their eyes and swayed gently. "Thank you, Lord, for perfect health," they chanted in unison.

During one session, Dr. Adams told his patients he was going to restore perfect eyesight to them all. Hands positioned over their navels, people then cupped their other hands over one eye at a time. "Thank you, Lord, for perfect sight," they chanted.

"Keep at it until your sight is perfect," Dr. Adams instructed. "Even if it takes months."

Meanwhile, David spent all his time absorbed in the scriptures, the Constitution of the United States, and talking with God. He began to receive new revelations about the wickedness of the U.S. government. On the rare occasions he still preached, he only allowed an audience of cult members.

His eyes glistened with the spirit of God as he spoke, and we were spellbound. "Enemies are seeking our lives. The government makes food delicious and desirable, regulating all of it. But disease is caused by the very foods we put into our mouths. How could the devil better control the people of God than to tear us down with disease and misery? Hearken, oh my people, and beware thy government. It would have us all addicted to the food of the flesh, the food that will destroy us."

David commanded us to partake only of fruits, green vegetables, and the grains of the earth. "It will be difficult to break free of this parasite that we call the government," he said, "but we will do it."

I struggled to ignore the hunger that plagued my thoughts every day. "You will hunger for the poisons of the flesh until you are free of the devil's influence," David told me. "When you reach the point of perfect health, no one can stop the spirit of God from residing in your body, as it does in mine."

I moved out of my parents' house at the end of the semester, getting a second-floor apartment south of campus. I shared it with a twenty-one-year-old nursing student who split her time between studying and making out with her boyfriend on the couch.

Since passing my classes with a D average, I'd decided to take the summer off from school and figure out what I was doing with my life. I got a job as a janitor but was fired after the first week for sleeping in. Then I got a part-time custodial job that didn't require me to be at work until five p.m. I got fired after the first week for sleeping in. So I decided to take the summer off from work as well as classes. I paid rent and bought groceries with a credit card, spending all my time sleeping or hanging out with Joel, and I never went to my parents' house.

After the first month, I stopped answering the phone. I'd sleep until noon every day and then wander around the apartment in boxers and a T-shirt, waiting for Joel to get done selling lymphnogenesis. He'd pick me up as soon as he was done and I didn't get dressed until he arrived. We used credit cards to go out to eat every day and then went back to his house to make out or study God's word.

"Your unemployment is a blessing," Dr. Adams told me one evening. "It has been well received. If you don't bring in an income, you're not a slave to the IRS. If we're faithful, God will provide everything for us." I knew better than to question any revelations pouring in through the roof of the Adams house, and I was happy I'd done something to please Dr. Adams.

David told us we needed to gather in more followers and the easiest converts were those who already had strong faith. So in June he sent Joel and me to Temple Square. Temple Square is a sacred site for members of the Church of Jesus Christ of Latter-day Saints (LDS), a place both historical and religious, where people learn about the Mormon pioneers who traveled to Utah from New York and Illinois, looking for a peaceful place to practice their religion. But Joel challenged everything about it. He climbed up onto a cement pillar and began shouting. "The modern church has gone astray. I have been chosen by God to call you to repentance."

Most of the visitors ignored him; Joel wasn't the first to threaten damnation on Temple Square. Others snickered as they passed. Eventually, a man in a gray summer suit and tie asked Joel to leave. When Joel responded, "Did you know that you have lymphatic vessels that parallel your blood vessels all throughout your body?", the man said something into a Walkie-Talkie and gripped Joel's bicep, pulling him toward the gate. "This science will change the course of history," Joel hollered as he was dragged from the square. "You will accept this."

I followed Joel through the gate, giving what I hoped was an apologetic look to the security guard. Joel straightened his shirt, put a hand over his naval, and began stroking negative energy from his body. A beggar sidled up to me and asked if I had any spare change. I dug into my pocket to produce a dollar bill. But before I could even extend my arm, Joel grabbed it back. "What are you doing? That's good money and he's not of the chosen people."

Joel took my hand and we began to circle the block, stopping at every potential audience so he could preach his monologue again. It was midnight when we started home. I'd slept until noon so I wasn't tired, but Joel's brain quit functioning at about ten every night. Halfway home, he began to veer recklessly from one side of the road to the other, cutting across lanes of traffic. Horns blared and Joel sat up straight, mumbling, "Can't stay awake."

"Pull over and I'll drive. You stopped paying your insurance anyway."

When we got to the Adams house, it was lit up like a bonfire. I entered cautiously. Kristi was screaming at James in the first sub-basement. James had apparently used his dad's science to heal a woman stricken with polio, and Kristi was furious. "James, I'm your wife," she shrieked. "How am I supposed to feel when you're out fondling everything that moves?"

James defended himself. "The woman was ill. It's my calling to heal the earth and rid its inhabitants of disease."

"James, listen to yourself," Kristi pleaded. "What's happening to you?"

"Nothing is happening to me. God is working through me. Can't you see that? Or are you blind and stupid?"

75

In answer, Kristi's long plastic nails lashed out to scrape James's cheek. A pencil-thin line of blood appeared. He grabbed her arm before it even had a chance to return to her side, twisted it behind her back and forced her to her knees.

Kristi screamed, "James, stop it, let me go! Stop it!"

James ignored her pleas. In a mask of anger, he shoved her face into the carpet, his hand lost in the tangles of her red hair. He banged his wife's head against the floor two or three times and then shoved her away from him. Kristi tumbled into a ball face-down on the carpet, cursing him.

James finally looked up and noticed Joel and me at the top of the stairs. Grinning sheepishly, but offering no explanation, he leapt up the eight stairs to the main floor and went into the kitchen for a drink of purified water. Joel and I followed. Books and pamphlets were strewn all over the kitchen table. David and Dr. Adams sat at opposite ends, engaged in deep discussion. "We have means of recreating the miracles of Christ right here at our fingertips," David said. "It is a sin to keep this to ourselves. It is our solemn duty and moral obligation to share this message with every people."

Dr. Adams agreed, but he wanted the religion to progress more slowly. "I have research to complete," he argued. "God has warned us not to run faster than we have the strength."

"Let God decide how much strength you have," David urged. "This is life or death for some people. It is peace or war. Every inhumane act on the face of this earth can be stopped if people only accept the truth." I thought suddenly of Kristi crumpled into a broken ball beneath us. David continued. "And how will they accept the truth if we keep it from them? By staying silent, we are paving our own roads to hell."

James pulled out a chair from the table, swiveled it around and straddled the seat. He turned toward his father. "We've been preparing for this step all our lives. You left us at home for more than a decade while you researched this science. It's time to spread it to the world. I'm right here with you."

Joel took a seat on his dad's other side. "It's time," he said simply.

With wet eyes, Dr. Adams nodded and raised his voice in prayer. "Oh God, we are truly thankful for thy word and for thy instructions. We ask thee to consecrate our travel as we take thy word to all thy children. Amen."

David decided the best way to attract converts was to pull members from other churches. Religious people already had the door open for further revelation, he said. So one Sunday Joel and I accompanied Dr. Adams and May to church. It was the first Sunday of the month, when the worship portion of the service was open to any man who felt moved by the spirit.

David and Elidah entered from the back and made their way slowly toward a pew near the front, walking with their heads bowed and hands at their sides. Worshippers tripped over themselves to get out of their way, heaping themselves on top of each other to clear the aisle for the strange robed beings. The scene reminded me of Moses parting the Red Sea.

David was the first one to reach the pulpit, and the room quickly grew silent. "I am a humble messenger from the Lord," he began. "I am called to preach repentance unto the wicked, and every one of you has sins. You sin when you partake of God's beloved animals for food. You sin when you give of your substance to our corrupt government. You are on the swift road to destruction. Follow me and be saved. I can lead you to your salvation. I am Immanuel."

Saints didn't amass around David when he finished speaking. The chandeliers didn't fall to destroy the wicked. Instead, a void filled the room as members of the congregation searched each other's faces for explanation. David returned to his seat next to Elidah and the meeting continued. After the final "Amen," the bishop introduced himself to David and asked him not to preach again from his pulpit. David brushed off his feet symbolically before leaving the building, never to return.

"What a waste of God's children," he mourned.

Another of David's ideas was to convert children. God smiled on people who took care of his children.

Once a week, Dr. Adams and May went swimming at the public pool, where lots of children gathered. Joel and I often went along, taking turns flipping from the boards into the deep end, or diving for pennies in the shallow end. May hovered near her husband, performing peculiar gestures from a water aerobics class that she had half-forgotten.

At one of our weekly swimming ventures, I stayed near Dr. Adams to learn about healing mental illnesses. I was interested to hear how pressure, massage and stroke would work with something as abstract as schizophrenia. Dr. Adams had a small audience of youth gathered around him as he preached. His lymphnogenesis body language even held the interest of some very young children.

I stepped back to view the scene as an outsider might. An elderly, half-naked marshmallow of a man was surrounded by eight kids who watched with awe and disgust as he bounced in place, one hand covering his hairy belly button and the other massaging wrinkles on his forehead. His voice carried over the water as he uttered his prayer: "Thank you, Lord, for mental health."

Dr. Adams didn't even know he was making a fool of himself. I played with the idea of telling him but instead turned to go in search of Joel.

When I returned to Dr. Adams's corner, one solitary girl was all that remained of his audience. He'd taken her inflatable toy and she was trying to get it back. He held it just out of her reach, forcing her to lunge toward him. Then he'd move the toy at the last moment and poke her in the chest or rear end. This continued for several cycles until the girl was near tears. With unusual courage, I grabbed the toy from Dr. Adams's grasp and handed it to her. As she took it, I whispered, "Get away from him."

<hr />

I kept contact with one friend outside the cult. Marina hated Joel because he monopolized my time. Joel hated Marina because she'd try to set me up with men she met in Internet chat rooms. I liked Marina because she'd send men to my apartment, and whenever Joel perceived competition, he was nice to me. It was my only weapon.

Russ was twenty-seven and lonely. Marina didn't know anything else about him when she invited him to drive from his home in Magna and spend the day with me. She told him that I was a lonely and troubled young woman who could stand some cheering up. Russ showed up at my door at nine a.m. I was no longer working or going to class so I didn't even know what day it was.

"Hello, gorgeous," Russ said by way of introduction. "You can call me Pooh—as in Winnie the Pooh—because he's my hero."

He had bright blue eyes but a shadow seemed to cover his face. I ignored it. It was welcome to be gorgeous. Russ was nice for about fifteen minutes—until after my roommate left for class. Half a second after the door closed behind her, Russ tackled me. Holding my arms down with one of his, he bathed my face in saliva. I twisted my head around, trying to keep his lips off mine.

"Come on, be a good sport," he coaxed, shifting his weight and sprawling across my body, securing my legs to the floor with his. A coffee-and-cigarette flavored tongue probed the inside of my mouth. I gagged.

Russ released his grip and allowed me to sit up. Feeling dizzy and disheveled, I got to my feet, a saliva trail still on my cheek. Russ grabbed my left hand, noticing right off the scar in the center. He peered at me more closely. "Why did you do this?"

I stared past him at the blank wall and pretended to be studying something significant. "Because."

"Because why?" he asked. "What's so wrong in your life that you're doing this?"

For a brief moment I imagined he actually cared. But suddenly I was very tired. "Stuff."

Russ stooped and picked me up from the floor, then carried me like a baby down to his car, where a friend sat waiting in the driver's seat with the engine running. Russ deposited me in the backseat and climbed in after me. I didn't resist any of this, thinking only, *This will really make Joel jealous.*

Russ pulled me against him. He was several inches taller and about a hundred pounds heavier than I was. Dressed in black sweat pants and a T-shirt, he was soft and almost comfortable to lean against, or he might have been if I'd known him longer than twenty minutes. At the moment I didn't care. It was simply nice to be away from Joel. I was wearing cut-off jean shorts and a big T-shirt. My hair tumbled down my back, nearly brushing my belt-loops, but I hadn't combed it in days. I must have looked pitiful.

Russ cooed into my ear, "You just need someone to hold you, baby girl."

The journey back to Magna was short. I watched out the window as houses and stores gave way to farmland and ranches and then yielded to cities again. After forty-five minutes, the driver dropped us off at a tiny apartment near the freeway. I followed Russ through a courtyard to his front door and then allowed him to lead me inside. With the door shut, the rumble of cars and trucks whizzing by on the freeway muted to a dull hum. Using a key, Russ locked a deadbolt on the door from the inside.

"I have to make a quick phone call," he said. "Make yourself at home."

He disappeared up a flight of fourteen spiral stairs and I sat down on a lumpy couch. The blinds were drawn and the living room looked like the aftermath of a natural disaster. Stains dotted the thin gray carpet, and couch cushions and pillows littered the room, along with CDs, beer cans, and magazine pages.

"Whatever you do, don't come up here," Russ's voice filtered through the low ceiling. "Do not come up here. I'm naked."

"I'm not coming up," I hollered back while fidgeting with the front door. The deadbolt held. There was no way for me to unlock it without the key. I went back to my perch on the couch, trying to look nonchalant, like I was used to being locked into a strange house with a strange man.

Russ descended the fourteen stairs still wearing the sweat pants, but he'd shed the T-shirt. I wondered if he'd really been naked upstairs. He sat on the floor next to the couch and ran two or three fingers up and down my leg. I wished I'd worn long pants. My white thighs looked exposed and vulnerable, and I tried to pull my T-shirt down to cover them. Still sitting on the floor, Russ dragged me from the couch and sandwiched my body between his legs.

"Don't," I said, kicking against him. But he pulled me closer even though I stiffened every muscle against him. His chest was warm and balmy against my face though.

"Settle down, kid. There's nowhere to go."

His words rang true. The apartment was my prison. I let myself go limp in his grasp, lying under his body. Every time I exhaled, gravity caused his body to melt into mine. I began to worry that I'd lose myself in him.

After a few moments, Russ rolled over. I writhed in his grasp, but he held my legs between his and my arms at my sides. He brushed the tangled hair from my face. "You're beautiful," he told me. I believed him and stopped struggling. Perhaps beauty wasn't as costly as I'd thought.

In the early afternoon, after another make-out session, Russ put on a shirt and ran across the street to Burger King. While he was gone I investigated the kitchen. The top shelf of the fridge was occupied by the remains of a birthday cake—the kind grocery stores sell, covered with gooey white frosting and dozens of huge, sugary roses. The cupboards were empty except for a couple cans of Campbell's soup and a stale loaf of bread.

As Russ set a greasy bag of Whoppers on the table, he said again, "I have to make a phone call." He bounded up the stairs. The smell of fast food made my stomach rumble, and I tried to remember the last time I'd eaten. Russ shed his shirt again before rejoining me on the couch. I devoured the thin, mayonnaise-soaked hamburger meat.

"Hungry?"

"I guess so. Can we go outside?" The dark living room was beginning to depress me.

"I can't." Russ set down his half-eaten hamburger.

"You can't?" I repeated.

He swiveled on the couch to face me, lifting one leg and resting it on my knee. The rolls of skin on his naked stomach folded over each other like dough. Russ pulled the leg of his sweat pants up and pointed to a black box clamped around his ankle. "See that? That's a monitor. I can't leave the house without permission, and then I have to call in as soon as I return."

Feeling naive and stupid, I asked, "Permission from who?"

"The cops," Russ said, dropping his foot to the floor. "I'm on house arrest."

I'd never heard of house arrest, but I assumed it had something to do with staying in the house. "For what?"

He said casually, "My ex-girlfriend said I assaulted her. Her and our son."

The fear that had been absent for most of the day returned all at once. I felt like I was going to pass out so I laughed instead. "I know," Russ said. "It's ridiculous to think that I could do something like that. I'd never hurt a flea."

I edged away from Russ, asking, "How did you get to Salt Lake City this morning?"

"I told them I had to get something from my mom's house." He paused as if to let the information sink in.

"I want to go home," I said.

Without looking up, Russ told me, "Not an option. I can't leave the house and there's no way I'm sending you out there alone."

I tried to determine whether I was being held against my will. The door was locked but I hadn't specifically asked Russ to open it. Then he jumped on me again, pushing me into the couch. I wriggled out of his grasp and slid to the floor but he followed. The more I bucked against him, the tighter his grip became. He seemed to get off just by holding me down. "Can't breathe," I gasped.

"It's not comfortable down here anyway," Russ said. He grabbed both of my hands and yanked me to my feet, then began dragging me upstairs. When I resisted, he picked me up and slung me over his shoulder. I beat his back with my fists as he charged up fourteen stairs. I didn't hit him too hard; I was afraid of the consequence.

Russ hurled me onto his bed and then launched himself for a heavy landing next to me. "This is better," he said, pulling himself back on top of me. I couldn't tell if he was kissing or just slobbering all over me. I twisted my head violently from side to side.

"Knock it off," he ordered, anger creeping into his voice. "I'm not going to rape you."

"Well, that's a relief," I said sarcastically. "Get off me."

Russ ignored me. Spread-eagle on top of me, he effectively held both my hands and my feet down and his body weight kept my torso paralyzed. The only thing I could move was my neck so I kept wagging it back and forth, trying to avoid his tongue.

Eventually I had to breathe and I was tired of fighting. "OK," I said. "I give up."

He loosened his grip and I breathed in, tasting his spit and sweat on my lips. "Let's just lie here like this," he said. I let his sweaty arms encircle me and his legs wrap around mine. I felt vaguely like I was in a cocoon. A Russ cocoon. I wondered briefly if a butterfly could emerge.

Russ fell asleep but maintained his grip on me. A cuckoo clock kept track of lost time with a silly bird popping out from a window on the miniature house every hour to deliver its mocking message. "You're still here," the bird taunted as each hour passed.

At five a.m., Russ woke with a start. He checked his watch and then leapt from the bed, pulling on a clean T-shirt in the process. "I have to go to work, girlie-girl," he announced. "If you want to stay here, you can. I'll be back by ten."

He sailed down the fourteen stairs with me behind. When he unlocked the door, I darted under his arm and into the bright sunlight of the courtyard. He tugged a Burger King hat over his greasy hair and jaywalked across the busy street. Pausing on the median to wait for traffic, he blew me a kiss and then was gone. I started walking.

It's almost impossible to get lost in Magna because all the streets are numbered. I needed to be in the center of the city to catch a bus back to Salt Lake, and I knew Russ's apartment was on the west end, so I walked eastward. Several times I came across construction worker crews. Men without shirts spread concrete or held on to rattling jackhammers. I crossed the street every time. I didn't think I could stand facing a man.

After walking for three miles, I used a credit card to withdraw money from an ATM, and then found a bus stop on the southbound side of the street. I sat down to wait, draping my arms around my legs and resting my head on my knees, trying to disappear.

"Miss, are you all right?" someone asked. I ignored it but the person was persistent. "Miss? Miss?" I finally looked up. A bus had stopped in front of me and all the passengers were on board. The driver had his head bent over me with a concerned look on his face. "Are you all right?" he repeated.

"Yes," I said. "I'm sorry."

The driver looked like he didn't believe me. "Are you getting on this bus?"

"Yes."

I handed the bus driver two dollars and found a seat near the back. The ride took almost two hours with all the stops. A man sat in the seat directly in front of me, and I spent most of the ride staring fixedly at the back of his head.

The bus dropped me off a few blocks from my apartment. Once inside my bedroom, I locked the door. Then I dragged my bed across the room and positioned it in front of the door. No one would get through without me knowing it.

I ignored the world for two days.

7

One morning in June, May didn't get out of bed. Dr. Adams had spent the night in his recliner in front of the TV, but when his wife didn't appear in the morning to serve him breakfast, he decided to hobble up to the master bedroom to investigate. I'd arrived at the Adams house half an hour earlier, hoping to persuade Joel to give me a ride to my new part-time job. Joel and I followed his father up the ten stairs.

May's limp body sagged into the mushy cavity of a deteriorating king-sized bed. A sprout of red-gray hair peeked out from beneath the comforter, and her hands lay impassive at her sides. The only indication that she was still alive was the faint up-and-down movement of the blanket as May breathed. I concentrated on its steady rhythm but it seemed to diminish in front of me.

Joel stood rooted in the doorway, unwilling to take the first step in. "Mom?" he called from where he stood beside me.

Dr. Adams busied himself with doctor-like duties, taking his wife's pulse and propping her eyelids up to peer into her yellow, watery eyes. May didn't even blink.

I crossed the threshold into the room, noticing a difference in texture as my foot met newer, thicker carpet. Their bed dominated the room and aside from a rocking chair that looked near collapse and two mismatched bedside tables—one with a lamp perched precariously on it—the room was unfurnished. Dirty clothes and underwear, as well as clothes freshly laundered and folded, lay in heaps on the floor.

My intent was to take May's hand or utter some word of consolation. Maybe I just wanted to break the heavy, deathlike silence. But as I neared the bed, Dr. Adams stopped me with his eyes, which were suddenly bloodshot and frightening. So I feigned interest in a jumble of books that lined the walls in short, unkempt stacks. They were of all sizes and included textbooks, dictionaries of homeopathic and herbal remedies, and religious doctrine, including several copies of the Bible.

Dr. Adams began to apply pressure to various parts of May's body, chanting, "Thank you, Lord, for health and life. Thank you, Lord, for thy healing power. I command you, May, to rise and be whole." The praying and chanting continued for about fifteen minutes but Joel and I didn't move. Dr. Adams's strokes became violent in urgency, and May's body bounced under his weight. She moaned softly but didn't open her eyes.

Finally Dr. Adams took a step back from the bed. He eyed his limp wife like a schoolboy trying to comprehend a bad grade on an assignment. "We'll have to get her to a doctor," he said, exhaling long and heavy with a deflating sound that gave voice to May's appearance. Joel looked at his father in surprise and started to say something but changed his mind. A minute ticked by in silence. Still staring at his wife, Dr. Adams finally ordered, "Joel, get the car ready."

Dr. Adams sighed again, pulled a suitcase from under the bed and began to throw some of May's things into it. I followed Joel downstairs, half expecting him to say something, but he grabbed his father's keys from a hook in the kitchen and went silently into the garage without a glance back. With his gimpy leg, Dr. Adams tried to lift May's dead weight. From where I stood on the sixth stair, I heard him grunt and her cry out with pain. At least she was conscious.

"Joel!" Dr. Adams bellowed from the bedroom. "Come help me lift your mother."

Joel bolted past me, bounding up the stairs three at a time. He lifted his mother like a rag doll and carried her down. I opened the door, and he whisked her out and into the back seat of the van. Dr. Adams made his way down the stairs slowly, his breath coming in painful gasps whenever he stepped on his bad foot.

I hesitated too long on the front porch, and they sped away with their comatose bundle nestled behind them, so I got a ride with James.

We'd been in the hospital waiting room for two hours. Dr. Adams was arguing with the receptionist, who'd asked for insurance information. "We live in the U-nited States," he enunciated, lips curled away from his uneven teeth. "Send the bill to the U-nited States."

I traced my finger along the grooves of a sterile plastic chair. James and Kristi sat silently beside me, contempt for the medical system readable on their stony expressions. James's moodiness was left over from our ten-minute ride to the hospital, during which he cursed his mother for submitting to illness and his father for caring more about diseased and ignorant strangers than for his own family. His silence was eerie, but I watched the emotions dance across his face as clearly as if they were characters on a television screen.

Finally, a doctor emerged from behind two swinging doors that closed silently behind him. He held a clipboard in his hand and looked up from it as he entered the room. "Adams?" As we gathered around him, the doctor explained in a monotone, "May has lymphoma and it's in a progressed stage." He continued to explain that lymphoma is cancer of the lymphatic system and recommended immediate surgery.

Dr. Adams looked stunned, then muttered, "Impossible. I can't believe I didn't see it." He brushed the doctor's shoulder roughly in his haste to hobble toward the door, calling back quickly, "Thank you, Doctor. We'll take her home now." The door was locked but Dr. Adams didn't seem to notice. In an excited frenzy, he jimmied it violently, causing the hinges to squeal.

"Sir," the doctor said. "Did you hear me? Your wife needs medical attention. Now. She needs chemotherapy. If we operate now, we can buy her some time . . ." The doctor's voice trailed off and then he repeated, "Sir, are you listening?"

"Yes, I hear you," Dr. Adams said. "My wife will receive the attention she needs, but not here." The doctor looked curiously at Dr. Adams and then shrugged and motioned for the receptionist to buzz the door open.

After a week of rest and Dr. Adams's treatments, when May was functioning again, though still weak, she got a library card. Because she'd dropped out of high school and married at sixteen, she was sixty before she ever stepped into a public library. But now, once a week, May drove the long white Chevrolet across town and returned, face flushed in excitement, with a stack of books about the power of nutrition.

Besides the lymphoma, ten pregnancies had left May's body sagging and worn. The red and gray hairs springing from her head reminded me of the threadbare carpet of the first sub-basement, where Joel had masturbated while sitting astride my body like a knight on his horse. In my mind, that carpet and May's head were inextricably connected. One Monday afternoon, she bustled into the house with her carpeted head and an armful of books, only to trip and send the whole stack flying. Leaving Joel in the kitchen with David, I went to help her. Embarrassed, she crawled around the room scooping up books, smoothing bent pages and mumbling to herself. Since she'd started reading, May's speech had become less coherent, like she used all her energy to study and didn't have enough left over to form complete sentences.

In spite of his belief that women should remain unlearned, Dr. Adams encouraged May's research. Soon she even became his scribe, jotting down new revelations that were strangely uniform with May's studies. Niacin and red dye number five were put into our food to control us. May also declared salt a poison: "Any food that makes you thirsty is destroying your cells and causing cancer." She began eating only simple water-based foods, a diet to replenish her cells.

As meat at the Adams house became increasingly rare, Joel and I nibbled on steamed potatoes and carrots. However, May continued to deliver plates of steamy, blood-raw steaks to Dr. Adams, who masticated like a tiger tearing through a live animal, blood soaking into the towel he tied around his neck.

Despite her diet, May's body continued to deteriorate. She decided everyone should participate in a two-week lemonade cleanse, grating lemon peels and mixing them with twice-purified water. As the lemonade aged, it became cloudy—from impurities in the lemon peels, May said. To me, the lemonade looked more every day like the bottles of Dr. Adams's urine that lined the living room walls, so after four days I replaced the lemonade with plain water. As Joel and his brothers drained glass after glass of the bitter yellow liquid, I imagined their insides taking on the same characteristics.

After starting the cleanse, even David's odd concoctions caused my tongue to salivate and my stomach to ache with hunger. Since David and Elidah weren't participating in the diet, I'd find them hovering over the stove each evening. David would add a pinch of something or other to a strange-smelling mixture bubbling in a pan. Elidah would stir it around and around until it dissolved into the whole. I imagined one of those particles was me and, as I whirled around and around, I kept losing pieces of myself until

I disappeared. After a week on the water diet, though, I stopped craving food, even Dr. Adams's steaks. In fact, the smell of meat made me sick; I dry heaved when I thought about chewing through a piece of dead animal. Even the prospect of buttering a slice of bread could send me into a panic. I'd finally baptized the inside of my body and I couldn't bear to taint it with even the smallest morsel of government-poisoned food.

A month after she was diagnosed with lymphoma, May declared that she felt healthier than she ever had. Dr. Adams began spending three or four nights a week in bed with his wife, and prayers became something of a violent celebration. "Oh God," Dr. Adams moaned, swaying side to side, face bathed in tears and arms stretched to the heavens. "I, your humble servant, do thank thee for healing us, even thy chosen children, in the face of our greatest enemy, even the government of the United States."

I celebrated my twentieth birthday at my grandparents' house in Southern Utah. The five-hour drive through desert heat left us off-balance and irritable. We staggered into my grandparents' manufactured home and melted into the various couches and armchairs that cluttered the living room. The house sat on a hill outside the Pintura city limits. It overlooked a golf course, with the backdrop of a broken-down, sun-faded town that my mother knew intimately, as only a child growing up on its streets could.

As family conversation turned to health—how Uncle Rodney who had cancer was doing, who was dying and who was already dead—I wandered into the back bedroom for a cool place to lie down. I stretched out on the old bed, careful of the footboard that had bruised my legs during previous naps. My hand drifted to the side and brushed against a stack of envelopes, so I propped myself up and dragged a bundle to the bed. Most were addressed to my grandmother in my mother's handwriting. I expected small talk and news, but the letters extensively detailed my relationship with Joel.

"I don't know what to do with her," my mother wrote. "She's ruining her life and taking us all with her."

I put the letter back and picked up the next. "If I could just get her to go on one date with someone else . . ." The black cursive letters blurred before my eyes. I read another. They went on and on. My mom had anxiously listened in on my phone calls, asked church leaders for advice on how to split us up, policed the front porch windows when Joel brought me home. Once she'd even sent my older brother to follow us when we went out, to make sure we didn't get too close.

"I feel like giving up," the last letter read. "I've tried everything and she's just too stubborn. Sometimes I think she does it just to hurt me . . ."

I thought back to my own months of sleepless nights, of crying into my pillow, of praying for the strength to tell Joel it was over, of begging God out loud to make it all stop. I knew I was ruining my life, hurting myself and others, but I was too small to fight it on my own.

Much later that evening, I was taking a shower when Sarah knocked on the door and called my name.

"What?" I shouted back, though I had a general policy of not answering when someone spoke to me from behind a door.

"Joel's here."

"What?" I gasped this time. I grabbed a towel, wound it around my hair, threw on my jeans—sticking to my wet legs—and T-shirt back on and ran upstairs.

Joel stood casually in the tiny dining room of my grandmother's house, looking harsh and powerful against her background of delicate knickknacks and collectibles. My head spun at two distinctly different worlds colliding. My grandma's house represented a safety I didn't have anywhere else, and her tiny town gave me an anonymity I craved. She stood with her back to the open front door. Insects rushed from the darkness into the house, congregating at the ceiling light and buzzing contentedly. She let her hand fall from the doorknob to her side, but she made no movement to close the door.

"Hi," Joel said.

"What are you doing here?" I demanded.

Joel didn't seem to notice that neither I nor anyone else seemed happy at his appearance. "Happy birthday!" he said. "I left home in a hurry and didn't have a suitcase, so I packed in a box." As if to prove his point, he thrust a medium-sized cardboard box at my face. A green plaid pajama sleeve flopped over the side.

My mom said, "Put your box down, Joel. I'll get some blankets; we can make up the hide-a-bed for you."

The only thing I wanted was for Joel to leave and I didn't know what to say. After an uncomfortable silence, I turned on my heels and crept back down the twelve spiral stairs to the basement. Fully dressed, I crawled under a blanket on the big fold-out couch, hid my head under a pillow and willed myself to sleep. But even through the fog of cotton and goose feathers, I heard doors open and shut upstairs and the toilet flush. Sheets snapped out, and then I knew they were being stretched tight and positioned over the living room couch. Joel's cackling laugh was louder than anything else.

"It's so good to meet you, Grandpa," I heard him say, cringing as I imagined him shaking my grandpa's hand.

I forced my head deeper into the couch but heard someone coming down the wooden stairs, then my mom's voice. The couch sagged under her weight as she sat and put a hand on my shoulder. I sat up to face her. The fluorescent light from the ceiling slashed at my eyes. "You have a guest, and you're being rude," she started.

"Why don't you just send him home?"

"He drove 250 miles to see you. How could we send him home?" An hour earlier, she had hated him. Now she was so accommodating that I wanted to throw up.

In the morning, I woke to the sound of my grandpa moving around upstairs. He wasn't a graceful man and he bumped into things when he walked. When he was fifteen, a dump truck bed had fallen on his head and crushed his vertebrae. He spent every day since in excruciating pain. My grandpa could tell me what every doctor's office in the country looked like, and what the doctors' bedside manners were. He knew that medicine wasn't advanced enough to offer him relief but he kept searching anyway. Every conversation I ever had with my maternal grandparents started with a detailed account of his pain and how no one could help him. Every letter my grandma ever wrote to me mentioned that Grandpa was still surviving the pain, though he didn't sleep well and could hardly walk. Sometimes the pain was so great that it blurred his vision.

All these thoughts went through my head as I listened to him move toward the living room, where Joel was no doubt still sprawled on the hide-a-bed. I bolted from the couch and sprinted up the twelve stairs, trying to get to Joel before he got to my grandpa. I was too late.

"You don't have to live in this pain, Grandpa," Joel was saying when I got to the main floor. "I can relieve it. It will take some time and you'll have to commit to some lifestyle and diet changes, but I can heal you."

Ashamed, I ducked back into the stairwell. I willed my grandpa to dismiss Joel before he could get started. It was silent, so I peered around the wall. Joel was perched on the edge of the bed, one hand placed over his belly button, the other stroking his own shoulders roughly.

"I'm moving the poisons from my body," Joel explained. "I put one hand on the center of my energy to keep myself balanced, and I use that energy to cast out everything evil from my blood through the lymphatic vessels." He stood up and approached my grandpa.

No! Don't touch him! My thoughts were so loud I was sure Joel could hear them. But if he did, he ignored me. He instructed, "Now you do the same. Where does it hurt, Grandpa?"

With an expression on his face I didn't recognize, my grandpa put his hands on his shoulders. "Here," he said. "And here, and here, and here. I have some crushed vertebrae, and pretty much everything hurts."

"It's nothing," Joel said. "You'll be amazed at how quickly you'll feel better. I can't imagine carrying around so much negative energy for so long. First I need you to let go of any hate. Any bad feelings for anyone, I want you to just let go of them. Now, get into a comfortable position."

"I don't have one," Grandpa replied. He didn't move.

"Just sit on the edge of the bed then." Joel pulled the covers up to make a smooth area. My grandpa lowered himself carefully, grunting in pain. "Now put one hand over your belly, your center of energy. I'm going to put pressure on your spine."

"Don't touch . . ." my grandpa started to say, but it was too late.

Joel suddenly heaved his weight into my grandpa's back. Grandpa sucked air in so sharply that it whistled. "Stop," he winced through his teeth. A vein stood out on his forehead and another one pulsed in his neck.

"What happened?" Joel asked.

Grandpa breathed in a dozen times before he could answer. He gasped, "Don't . . . touch . . . back."

Something in my heart broke when I saw my grandpa's pain written across his face like that. The little pain in my heart grew and grew until I could feel it trying to strangle me. My breath caught in my throat and tears sprang to my eyes as I swallowed to force it down. Then I felt a valve in my heart turn off. Something died in me and, instead of pain, I felt hollowness.

That afternoon my mom's brother, sister, nieces and nephews bombarded me with congratulations for leaving my teen years behind. I ignored Joel. I hadn't forgiven him for the incident with my grandpa, and I could tell my grandpa hadn't, either. But my dad told me to be polite. "Sit right here, next to Joel," he instructed. Joel grinned at me from the couch.

My grandma served up cake and ice cream and my mom piled my lap with presents. But I wasn't hungry and I didn't want presents. "Open your presents, Alysa," my dad prompted. When I sat still, he repeated his command, a tinge of anger in his voice. "Don't be ungrateful."

Suddenly the room tilted on its side. My cousins' animated faces whirled like horses on a psychedelic merry-go-round. Reality slipped and I left my body. After I'd opened the presents from my family and stacked them neatly on the floor, Joel handed me a boxed collection of Beatles cassettes and one ripe red apple. "Happy birthday, babe." He leaned over for a kiss and I obliged. After all, the girl sitting on the couch with birthday wrapping strewn around her and ice cream melting in her bowl was not me.

After the party, it was time to start for home. I packed my things and clambered up into my parents' minivan with my siblings. Joel watched from his car, one hand resting on the open door. Then he shot a searching glance at my dad. My dad said, "Joel drove down here for you. You ride with him." Something in his tone ended the argument before it started. I hung my head, grabbed my suitcase, dumped it into the backseat of Joel's car, and slid into the passenger side.

As we left town—ten minutes ahead of my family—I unwrapped the Beatles tapes and pushed one into the cassette player. "Help!" the band screamed from tiny car speakers. *Help,* I thought. *Help.* After driving for about an hour, Joel spotted a hitchhiker crouched in the sparse shade beneath a mesquite tree. He stood when he saw

Joel's car and waved wildly at us. "And the meek shall inherit the earth," Joel said as he pulled over.

The interior of the car was suddenly permeated with the mixture of body odor and cigarette smoke. I coughed once and then held my breath as the man crawled into the back seat with two loaded backpacks. "Thanks," he breathed into the front seat. "Can I smoke in here?"

Wrong question. I stared out the window at sage brush and dry red dirt as Joel began, mouthing the first familiar words along with him: "Did you know that you have a set of lymphatic vessels that parallels your blood vessels all throughout your body?" Half an hour after we picked him up, the terrified hitchhiker asked Joel to pull over and let him out. Only desert sand and sage brush stretched for miles in every direction, with waves of heat spiraling up from the earth, making the air hazy. We left the man coughing and staggering outside and Joel punched the gas pedal before I even had the door shut. "Moron," he said under his breath.

Later, as Joel rounded a turn to merge onto a freeway, it began to rain. I cracked my window an inch to enjoy the fresh air. My head cleared and everything became solid again. Joel reached out for my hand and I let him take it. He looked at my face and I let my features soften, even squeezing his hand.

"I love you," he said quietly.

"I love you, too," I said. I even thought I meant it.

"Gimme a kiss." Joel leaned toward me and I met him halfway, our lips filling a void that had spanned the long distance between us since he'd arrived at my grandparents' house. But suddenly the car also moved. Joel jolted upright and grabbed the steering wheel with both hands, but the car continued to move toward the shoulder.

"Shit," Joel said. "Hydroplane."

Red, sandy mud pirouetted away from the tires and the car bounced over clumps of sagebrush. It finally slid to a stop next to a barbed-wire fence fifty yards from the road. I looked back to see long twisted skid marks in the soft mud. Joel put the car into reverse and slammed his foot on the gas. The tires spun and mud spewed onto our windows. Joel tried again with the car in drive. It moved forward a few inches but then stuck again. Back and forth, Joel coaxed the car until it was six inches deeper in the muck. Then he got out and tramped to the highway.

The first car to approach was my parents' van. I climbed out and followed in Joel's footprints to the road, then climbed into the van to escape the rain. My dad and older brother hiked down to the car with Joel. With a few well-placed rocks, my dad got enough traction under the tires for Joel to back out his car. He quickly inspected the vehicle and proclaimed there didn't seem to be any damage.

Joel thanked him and shook his hand. As my dad came back, Joel got into his car and honked the horn. "Let's go, Alysa," he called.

I looked at my dad. "I'll ride with you."

"He's your fiancé," my dad said. "Get in his car."

Joel honked the horn again. I looked at my mom but she didn't say anything, so I trudged the distance and plopped in as Joel started the ignition. I looked at him and saw his lips wagging as he talked, but the only sound I heard was a thin whine, like an insect buzzing in my ear or static on the radio. Reality slid and proportions changed again. It had been happening more and more lately. What I once relied on as solid, I now doubted. I existed in a world separate from what was real, where the laws of physics didn't hold true. Cars and people moved in slow motion, and then moved faster to make up for lost time. Street signs and trees changed their positions when I wasn't looking.

I'd somehow stumbled onto a world in which I didn't belong. If I slept, maybe time would sort itself out and the world would make sense again. I shut my eyes against Joel, against the road and the rain, and against the absence of noise that cluttered my mind.

After three hours of driving in near silence, Joel dropped me off at my apartment. As I gathered my things, I saw the birthday apple on the floor of the car, bruised and split, but I carried it into the house anyway.

During the following month, I watched the apple where it sat on the kitchen counter. Like my childhood apple on Elysium Drive, it rotted, transforming from a hard, crisp piece of fruit into a deflated, twisted monkey head.

It took several months of pleading before my mom relented and took me to a head doctor. My dad was of the firm opinion that MDs meddled in areas in which they had no right to be, and his opinion of head doctors was even lower. "Quacks," is all he'd say whenever someone mentioned a therapist or psychiatrist.

But I knew something was wrong with me. In the family doctor's office, I complained about being detached from my physical self. The doctor said "hmmm" a lot and then referred me to a specialist. The specialist asked if I had friends or long-term plans for my life. I couldn't figure out what that had to do with being separated from my body. He wanted me to talk to someone who had more experience with cases like mine.

So when I finally sat down in front of a psychiatrist, the words poured from my mouth. He couldn't get up and leave; my mom was paying him to listen. I talked about losing myself, how my hands weren't my own, how my voice spoke in a foreign language. I told him about the summer I turned twelve when I spent all my time trying to accumulate enough saliva in my mouth to swallow. I also told him how I loved Joel, but that it hurt to be with him as much as it hurt to be away.

The doctor leaned back in his chair, crossed one leg over the other, and tapped his foot against the desk. A diamond stud shone from his left ear lobe, and a neatly trimmed beard and mustache framed his soft face. He read lists to me and asked me to repeat them. He read a series of numbers, then told me to reverse them in my head and spit them back out.

I mentally drifted away from the room and the doctor didn't notice or follow me. So I stuck out my damaged hand and mumbled something about inner pain bleeding to the outside. He just looked at it in a disinterested sort of way and pulled out a book of ink blots. I'd watched enough TV to know that I was supposed to say "sex" every time he turned the page, but I couldn't say the word out loud. Not to a man anyway. Instead I saw butterflies, angels, and castles. Even as I spoke in the gargoyle voice that wasn't mine, I could tell how normal I sounded. "But I'm not normal," I wanted to blurt out. "I'm sick."

I wanted to tell him how scared I was that I'd disappear—that my hands and voice had already gone and it was just a matter of time until the rest of me followed. But he was too busy writing out prescriptions for Paxil and Lithium, a combination I later learned was effective for manic-depressive or bipolar disorder. I wished I was dying of cancer so at least my illness could be acceptable, understood.

When I told Joel I'd seen a psychiatrist, he was furious. He screamed, "You're putting poisons into your body!" We were sitting side by side, crunched into one of the recliners in his living room. "You're setting yourself up to be controlled by the government. What were you thinking?"

I hung my head, trying to hide my nose.

"What do you think we're doing here?" Joel continued, shifting away from me and standing up. The recliner was suddenly huge and cold without him. "We're preaching the gospel, the true religion, and you're putting that crap into your body on purpose?"

But the medications stabilized my emotions and I stopped slipping from reality. By August, I felt more like myself.

The soundtrack of my life with the Adamses that summer had the constant bang of hammers in the background. David and Elidah were spending all their time on the back porch pounding away at a wooden structure designed to be a handcart, though hearty enough to double as shelter from the winter cold. David's eyes were bright. He was excited about preparing for his new calling to go into the mountains. By the time the handcart was completed, his excitement had turned into a feverish fury. Climbing to the top of a mountain was the best way to communicate directly with God, he said. Being away from the small-minded, faithless people who littered the earth would be cleansing to him. After his long commune with the Maker, David planned to rejoin society and go about God's work with renewed commitment.

David and Elidah began to bow in prayer for more than an hour at a time, and David walked around the house with a sort of weightlessness, like he'd discovered the secret for walking on water. The long spirited sessions of revelation continued, but Dr. Adams rarely took part in them anymore. "They've gone too far," he told Joel and me one day. "David is running faster than he has the strength. He will be weary and he will faint."

The chasm between the religious leaders widened, but David didn't give up on Dr. Adams. Late one night, Joel and I slipped in the front door after a midnight movie to find them pouring over the Bible on the kitchen table. Yellow legal pads were strewn about the table top, covered with tiny, sinuous characters. Elidah crouched in a dark corner of the living room, her robes tangled around her body and shading her face from view.

David looked toward the door where Joel and I had stopped, but he didn't see us. I had the vague, uneasy feeling that he was looking right through me. It was obvious we were interrupting something extremely important. David's face was animated in a weird electric way. Dr. Adams also seemed hypnotized in the moment, gazing in awe at David's effulgent features. David's eyes brightened until they glowed with an ethereal power, and he spoke in a deep, sepulchral voice I didn't recognize. "I, the Lord of all the earth, the Creator of all things, speak unto you. I have called one to be a light and covenant to the world in these last days."

The room was silent for a few moments. Elidah approached the table and began writing David's words furiously onto one of the legal pads. Then the voice that was not David's continued. "I the Lord make bare my holy arm in the eyes of all nations, for gross darkness covers the earth and envelops the minds of the people. I the Lord God will not be mocked. My people have rejected me, so one who is mighty and strong have I ordained. I will lift him up and clothe him in mine own power and glory, that of the Father. Amen."

The revelations continued all night. When the heavens were finally silent, there were seven revelations—diamonds, as David called them. David and Elidah were to shed their mortal ways, to set aside all vain and foolish things and begin a new religion. They should rule the society equally, in full fellowship and brotherly love, God said. They should also live with much mourning, weeping, fasting, praying, rejoicing, testifying and praises. In short, David said, they were to "live after the manner of happiness."

The seventh diamond was directed to Elidah. "Wherefore, Hephzibah Elidah Isaiah—meaning My Delight is in Thee, God Adorneth, the Lord is Salvation—thou wilt take into thy heart and home seven sisters. Thou wilt recognize them through the spirit as thy dearest and choicest friends from all eternity. They shall bring thee great joy, even a multiplicity and an eternal weight of blessings and glory. And lo, thine own womb shall be opened and thou shalt bring forth a son to sit upon the throne of his father David. And thou shalt take into thy heart and home seven times seven sisters, to love and care for, forty-nine precious jewels in thy crown. And thou wilt be the jubilee of them all, first and last, for all are given unto thee for thy glory and honor and exaltation, even as thou art given unto them, for thou art a queen."

In one hour, God unsaid everything he'd told the early leaders of the LDS church. In one paragraph of small cursive script, he'd reinstated the eternal law of polygamy and commanded Elidah to accept forty-nine sister-wives. But oddly enough, it wasn't the seventh diamond that caused the final break between David and Dr. Adams. It was the eighth revelation that came a few nights later, when God told David to expect hardships beyond belief. "My son and humble servant, Immanuel David Isaiah, you will be marred beyond human likeness and numbered with the criminals."

Dr. Adams countered with, "God is a God of mercy. He will not suffer his children to experience pain or grief or death. You've gone too far, David. I cannot in good faith submit my family to this."

David and Elidah didn't say good-bye. One morning they were just gone. When I got to the house in the early morning, Joel was on the back porch standing where the handcart had been, scratching his head at the sudden space. "They didn't say good-bye. And they took most of our food."

I followed Joel to the pantry in the second sub-basement. Where cans of vegetables and fruit and cans of rice and flour had once been, dusty shelves stared back at us. Perfect dark circles stood out starkly on the dust-covered shelves. All that remained were a dozen large cans with faded labels that read, "Whole bottled chicken."

Without David and Elidah, Dr. Adams's revelations increased and Joel even began to speak intimately with God. "I know that you are to be my wife," he told me. "He has made it very clear to me that you are the chosen one. You will be my queen and I shall rule thee with my right hand. When the time is right, I will take another wife. But you will always be my first and my favorite."

While I was repulsed at the thought of sharing a man with other women, I felt a comforting peace at knowing I'd be favored above all the others.

I was in school again and Joel worked part-time at the Lymphno-genesis Academy. At my insistence, he started to hunt for a second job and he found one that suited him fine: Amway. Joel explained breathlessly to me, "All I have to do is sign people up under me and I earn money."

He'd purchased several large boxes of merchandise and spent the afternoon sorting it into piles—nutrition supplements, personal hygiene items, household cleaners. The items littered the living room floor and spilled into the kitchen and dining room, transforming the house into a convenience store. I knew that people bought into pyramid marketing schemes every day, but I was still dumbfounded. "You bought all this stuff to make money?"

"Look," Joel said. "People will see this stuff. They'll want to buy it. They'll want to sell it. Pretty soon, I'll just be sitting around collecting checks from all my employees."

Tired, I sat on the dirty carpet in a small triangular space between a stack of coffee filters and an array of laundry detergents. "Is this really what you want to do?"

Joel pouted. "I feel really good about this. If it doesn't work out, I'll register for college."

My parents were the first victims of Joel's new job. It was the first job he'd ever held outside the Academy, but the verbiage of a lifelong salesman was intact. I waited in the car as I imagined him asking my mother, "Did you know that eighty percent of regular shampoos are poisoning your hair? Companies force us to think losing hair is normal, but when it falls out, it's dying. Just by using your regular shampoo, you're signing your life away to the government and to companies that work for the government."

My mom walked Joel to the front door and locked it behind him.

When Joel didn't sell anything over the next few weeks, he picked up a course catalog from the local community college. But because he'd barely passed his high school classes eight years earlier, he had to take a year's worth of prerequisite classes before even qualifying as a freshman. That was the first blow, and Joel dropped out after his first semester.

But college proved to be a good place to meet young inexperienced blonde girls, girls who were only at college to meet career-driven men looking for wives. Joel decided he'd fallen in love with a girl named Julie. "She's everything I always wanted," he told me over the phone. "She's beautiful, she's blonde . . ."

"OK. So are you dating her?"

"I think you and I should take a break from things so I can see where this goes."

In a matter of days, Joel was asking me to take him back. "She was beautiful and would have given me perfect children, but she just wasn't you . . . and she didn't accept lymphnogenesis. Can I take you to dinner tonight?"

Our second break-up during this period was due to pornography. I was lying next to Joel on the big trampoline in his parents' backyard, a big "lymphasizer." He was wearing a short-sleeved polo shirt with a minuscule geometric pattern on it—the kind professional golfers wear during tournaments on TV—and matching slacks. They were clothes left over from the wardrobe he'd bought to sell Amway. A wardrobe that stunk of failure and hundreds of dollars of debt.

He was painfully confiding in me. "I was in a gas station and I saw the magazine. I couldn't control myself. I had to look at it and then I had to buy it. I don't know what came over me. The women are so perfect, hair in the right places and shaved in the right places, too." I wasn't exactly sure what he was talking about and I was too tired to ask. "I feel so guilty," he said. "But it was like something took hold of me and made me look. Then I had to buy it. It wasn't me."

This was my chance. I swallowed hard. "Joel, this isn't working," I mumbled. "I can't do this."

"What are you saying? I said I was sorry."

I raised my head from the trampoline and gazed at the house, where soft beams of light peeked through spaces in the blinds. "I don't think we should be together."

To my surprise, Joel began lightly crying. "You're right. I'm not good for anything. I should just kill myself, just jump off a cliff. Then you'd be happy."

Dr. Adams suddenly poked his head out the door, punishing us with the bright glare of the porch light. "Joel, it's ten thirty, time for your girl to go home. Now. It's late. I don't want any funny business going on." He pulled his head back inside the house like a turtle going back into its shell.

I bounced to my knees and crawled to the edge of the trampoline. Joel followed and we picked our way stocking-footed across dry prickly grass to the porch door.

"Alysa," Joel said, "Don't leave me. I'll never look at pornography again. I love you."

I crouched on the porch carpet to tie my shoelaces. I made a bunny ear, circled it, and tucked the other end into a knot. Joel hovered larger than life above me, his shoes forgotten on the cold cement. I slowly moved on to the other shoe. My breath caught in my throat and my heart pounded. If I let Joel touch me, my courage would be gone. My stomach knotted in pain.

I finally stood and, when Joel held out his arms, I melted into his embrace.

"I love you," he said into my hair.

"I love you, too," I whispered.

Joel had told me that I wasn't strong enough to live without him and he was right. I needed him like I needed air, like Dr. Adams needed to lymphasize. The pain of being with Joel was less than being without. Besides, I was nothing without the cult. My identity hung intertwined with it. Life was easier after I made this discovery. I forfeited my will to the greater good. When I talked, my voice left my throat but the cartoon sounds escaping from my lips weren't my own. My fingers went through solid brick and wood, and air was heavy and hard to breathe, but my life was no longer my concern. I was only a puppet head that needed to remember to bob in agreement.

Instinct was harder to stifle but I developed an ingenious method for coping. When the little automatic voices threatened to revolt, I forced them back into submission by hammering the inside of my right wrist against hard surfaces. Banging had two benefits. First, it reassured the logical part of my brain that wanted to know if things were still solid. Secondly, it served as punishment for a rebellious will.

Blue-black bruises formed but I continued banging. They spread, yellowing at the edges and spanning my entire arm. They reminded me of my own reality with a constant dull ache. I banged on desks, doors, bricks on the sides of buildings—anything immovable, sometimes banging so rapidly that I could strike an object two or three times a second. By banging faster, I numbed my arm to the bruising of an already damaged area. Blood vessels burst. Hard purple blisters formed under my skin. Still I banged. I banged until my heart stopped arguing with my brain and I could lie underneath Joel on the shaggy red carpet and feel nothing.

8

I survived in grayness, too frightened and tired to commit to either black or white. But in my shadow world the blacks, whites, and grays were more varied than a box of Crayola crayons. That is until December, when the contrasting hues began to separate into two groups. White symbolized the years before I met Joel, and I assigned black to every memory after I met him. That was when I realized I was going to kill myself if I stayed with Joel, that there was no gray area in the matter. Leaving Joel was empty but it was empty and white. White's future was less clear, but at least I knew it was there.

The clarity of that oracle both liberated and scared me. I knew immediately what my decision had to be but I didn't know how to do it. The first step was getting out of my parents' house, which I had returned to when money got too tight. I got a new job and an apartment, instructing my new roommates, "Whatever happens, don't let me go out with Joel." Five pairs of unfamiliar eyes studied my face, probed the sincerity and urgency of my request, and finally agreed. "No matter what I say, no matter how much I cry, do not let me see him," I repeated.

Uncannily, the phone rang. I felt my face redden with guilt. Guilt at hurting Joel, and guilt at picking up the phone only seconds after promising I wouldn't talk to him. I covered my mouth with my hand, as if my roommates sprawled across the adjoining room were unaware of what I was doing.

"Whatever I did, I'm sorry," Joel choked. He was crying so hard I couldn't understand what he said next. Then he asked if he could come over. I hesitated. The seconds crawled by, and Joel sniffled, waiting. "Just tell me where you are and I'll be right there."

"Six hundred North. . ." I started, but then the phone went dead. Panicky, I jiggled the cord. Poised to dial Joel's number, I clicked urgently for a dial tone but the phone remained mum. Then Christine handed the other end of the cord to me. She'd pulled it from the wall. I finally noticed that all five of my new roommates—I wasn't even sure of all their names yet—were in the kitchen with me.

"Don't," one of them said.

"Hang up the phone," another prodded.

I balanced the receiver on the cradle and followed the herd back into the living room, disintegrating onto the carpet. One girl said, "Suppose you tell us who Joel is."

"Joel is my fiancé." I burst into tears, stroking a pillow from the striped couch and then cradling it in my arms like an infant. Nurturing the pillow, I was able to let the words drip from my mouth. "It felt right at first," I blubbered. "Then things changed and it wasn't good, but I couldn't stop it. . . . If I could just be a better person . . ." I had to stop talking so I could breathe. "I think I'm still in love with him," I finished, suddenly feeling stupid and conscious of my profile—the hideous uplifted nose and protruding forehead. I buried my face into the pillow and sobbed, trying to minimize my body mass.

Still strangers, an awkward distance separated me from the other girls. Christine silently traversed the room and plugged the cord back into the wall. She jumped when the phone immediately began ringing. "Hullo?" she said. "Just a moment." She shot a meaningful glance my way as she handed over the phone.

Joel was done crying. His accusing voice berated my ear. "You hung up on me! You can't leave me. Just tell me where you are."

I put the phone back on the receiver. It rang again.

Joel's voice was brimming with anger. "You call this a mature way of handling the situation?" he demanded.

I hung up again. The phone rang again. My roommates and I counted the rings. One, two, three, four, and then the answering machine clicked on. Joel's voice filled the room: "I know you're there!" I backed into a far corner of the room. Another girl pulled the blinds down to cover the front window. "You're probably all sitting there listening to me, so I'm telling all of you that I will find you."

Seconds after Joel slammed down his phone he called again. This time he snarled into the answering machine, "You're keeping my wife from me. I'm on my way and I'm going to break down your door!" One roommate slipped the dead bolt and another one propped a kitchen chair under the doorknob. Still another roommate pulled the telephone cord from the wall. I flipped off the lights and huddled, quivering, in the corner with my five new friends.

Knowing what Joel was didn't lessen the pain. Every morning started with a panic attack. Although the attacks had also occurred while I was dating Joel, the intensity multiplied after I dumped him. I saw his face on the inside of my eyelids when I blinked. I saw his features in the outline of the curtains and in the patterns of the carpet. I heard his voice in the silent seconds before I fell asleep and again right before I woke up. I saw him in crowds, on buses, always in sight but never within reach. His face hovered at the edges of my sight.

Darkness invaded my life, waking and sleeping. Like strong fingers encircling my neck and choking the air from my lungs, shadow pressed in from all sides. Weeks after I stopped talking to him, I still heard him commanding my actions: Don't eat that; Hold your shoulders straight; Look people in the eye; Don't let them know you're insecure. I watched everyone around me devour poisons and ignore the simple steps I knew would bring them health and happiness. I imagined they were all going to hell. I woke frightened several times every night, expecting to find Joel on top of me or to hear David and Elidah whispering revelation and judgment from their upstairs bedroom.

My goal, I decided, would be to simply get through school so I could leave the state for employment. The key to my literal survival was to finish school, so I began to pour every effort into it. Progress was slow. I dedicated two or three hours every morning to overcoming the panic attacks. I'd wasted a year, skimming by with C's and D's. My class schedule for the first semester after I broke up with Joel looked strangely familiar, and I bought all the same textbooks over again. It was a giant-sized déjà vu event. But after one semester of near-perfect grades, I pulled my GPA up to a 3.0—the bare minimum for entrance into the journalism program.

It was an assignment for a history class that changed my perspective about Joel, and my mourning of him. The teacher, a seventy-something, silver-haired man who tottered across the front of the room on unsteady feet, asked the class to produce pictures, journal entries, or letters from progenitors, preferably from more than a century before. If I've ever met a pack rat, it's my mother's mother. I'd even found candy wrappers in her basement that I presented to her in my preschool years, with "I love you" scribbled on the backs. They were brittle and yellowed but still filed away. If I was going to discover the history of my family, it would be in her basement.

I called my grandma and began probing her for pieces of my past. Instead of pulling out a few pictures or letters, as I expected, she sent me a suitcase full of unsorted, ancient paraphernalia. Digging through the dusty artifacts late one night, I came across a

111

picture of Christian Lingo Christianson, some odd relative from the 1800s. Something about the way he stared out from the tarnished photograph unnerved me. I imagined I heard him speak. "Who is this?" he asked, pointing at Joel. "Is this who you chose to marry?"

I was ashamed thinking about introducing Joel to any of my ancestors. If life did continue after death, and if families lasted beyond the grave, there was no way I was going to bind my family to Joel's.

Religion was different without Joel. I continued to go to church but I doubted everything, especially whatever came out of men's mouths. I stopped listening to their words, warily watching their eyes instead. Work was different without Joel, too. During my year with him, I was hired by twelve different companies, most jobs lasting a week or two. It was time for that to change.

I got a job in the cafeteria of the mission training center. The 1970s-style orange-brick building housed long lines of busy dishwashers. The supervisor instructed on my first day, "You'll stand here—always wear your ear plugs so you don't damage your hearing—and make sure all food is scraped from the dishes before they go to the loader."

He allowed a five-minute tour of the kitchen before leaving me to a silent world. All the usual sounds of a kitchen were masked by the orange foam disks I jammed into my ears. Other students, dressed in the same rubber boots and white plastic aprons, daydreamed to the same dimmed clinks and crashes. Sometimes plastic crates full of glasses sprayed down on us from atop a precarious tower. Other times a conveyor belt broke and dishes piled dangerously, leaking the reds and oranges of what had once been beautiful food. As employees, we bonded through our shared catastrophes with facial expressions.

Something about the act of getting dressed for work, boarding a city bus, and entering my social security number at the beginning of each shift was almost too much for me to handle. The individual tasks required more energy than I had. I envied other workers for the ease with which they came and went, as well as the students of gospel principles and foreign languages who ate together. Life went on as it always had for them. Mine halted and coughed like the dying transmission of a car struggling to make it up one last hill. I knew I was going to crash and burn but I tried not to think about it.

I pressed on and as the days warmed up, things gradually got easier. They got easy enough that I decided I could start a friendship with Joel. Without consulting my roommates, I called him. "Hi. It's me."

Joel's tone was softer than I'd ever heard it. "Hey, babe. I miss you."

"I miss you, too. Can you meet me somewhere? Will you pick me up?"

Half an hour later, Joel roared down the street in his Pontiac. My stomach fluttered when I glimpsed him. He screeched to a stop, the front tire of his car coming within a couple inches of my feet. He leaned across to open the passenger door for me and I slid in, feeling the familiar leather grind against my skin. Joel pounded the gas pedal and the car lurched away.

As he drove down familiar, ice-encrusted streets, his hand edged toward mine. I let the meatiness of his fist envelope mine and, for the first time in five weeks, I felt safe. Electricity pulsed from Joel's hand to mine and he smiled at me. "I still love you."

I said, "I love you, too," but a familiar turmoil began stewing in my stomach.

He pulled into the lot of a park we frequented when we were dating. Ducks padded along the banks of the river. Walking hand-in-hand with Joel down a paved path tracing the river, I felt like the last weeks hadn't happened.

"Have you been practicing lymphnogenesis?" he asked suddenly.

"Yes," I lied.

"I can tell. You're thin." He squeezed my hand. "I knew you had it in you. This whole thing has been a test. Satan is trying to tear us apart, but you were meant to be with me. Can you feel it as strongly as I do?"

I watched the freedom I'd gained dissolve as I dissolved into Joel. He held me as we sat on a bench by the water, the drip, drip of melting ice trickling from icicle-laden trees and pooling on the ground. I felt like I was gaining back something important, something I had blinded myself to when I decided to leave Joel. I leaned closely into him, sharing his body heat.

"You have always been my first love," he cooed. "There will be more, but you are my queen. You will sit on my right hand and rule with me."

I'd forgotten that Joel was called by God to reintroduce polygamy to a world of sinners. I pictured myself with him, ruling a small kingdom in the mountains of Southern Utah. I saw my children and my sister-wives and their children. I pictured all of us—Joel's parents and their ten children, and their spouses and children, too—doing God's work, multiplying and replenishing the earth, outcasts in the desert living in caves or dormitory-like homes.

"No," I said after a moment, pushing Joel away. "I can't. This won't work."

Joel threw my hand down so suddenly that it smacked against the cold bench before I even realized it was falling. I grabbed my stinging hand to suck the cracked, bleeding knuckles. The coldness in his voice sent chills through my body as he declared, "You still won't submit!"

I suddenly wanted to take my statement back. I wanted him to hold me again. Instead, I told myself, *Just hold out. The pain will fade.* My insides twisted in turmoil until I thought I'd burst. But then, just as I'd prophesied, the pain began to fade. Wordlessly, I followed Joel back down the trail to his car. After he'd cranked the heat on, but before shifting into reverse, he looked at me and asked, "What was it we felt when we prayed about getting married?"

"I don't know."

"You're rejecting God's will," Joel said. "You will not be exalted."

I opened my mouth but nothing came out, so I gazed out the window at the ducks and the dirty snow. Time slowed and I was tired. "Just take me home," I said.

Near the end of February, I returned from work to find a yellow rose on my doorstep. The accompanying card said, "I'm sorry for everything. Please take me back. Love, Joel."

I put the rose in the garbage can, but two minutes later fished it back out and poked it into a bud vase. The petals drooped and then, one-by-one, they detached themselves from the stem and fluttered lifeless to the ground. The leaves and stem yellowed, withered, and hardened. Finally, the water thickened and the stem molded.

On a Monday night in March, I answered the phone. "I still love you," Joel spurted into my ear.

"OK," I said into the blank space he left.

"But if you're not going to marry me, I have to move on." All I wanted was for him to move on, so why did the words hurt so much? "I need you to tell me it's never going to happen between us. Tell me that."

"It's never going to happen between us," I repeated, feeling hollow.

"Good," Joel said. "Because I'm engaged."

"What?" I gasped.

"I didn't mean to," Joel stammered. "Her name is Melinda. She's blonde and perfect and, well, she loves me for who I am. She's younger than you, too, so she's not so set in her ways." A train derailed and wrecked somewhere inside of me and there were no survivors. "Not only that," Joel continued. "She accepts lymphnogenesis and she needs me. She needs me." I was quiet, so

Joel went on. "See, she's been on meds for schizophrenia and I'm helping her change her life around. She's just . . . perfect for me and perfect for lymphnogenesis."

"Joel?" a girl's voice echoed into the phone. "Who are you talking to?"

"Alysa."

"Why are you talking to her?" Melinda asked. "You said you loved me."

"I do love you," Joel insisted.

I hung up and decided not to tell anyone the news.

When the semester ended, I moved back home. At the dinner table two days later, my little brother blared out over a pan of green peas, "Joel's engaged."

His words had removed a very thin floodgate. I screamed and tears flooded down my cheeks as I ran to hide among piles of dirty clothes in the laundry room. The violence of my outburst left my family speechless.

Moving back into my parents' house felt like trying to breathe through a plastic grocery bag. Even though I was almost twenty-one, I had to adhere to my dad's every whim while living under his roof. My hope to forge a good relationship with my father soon dissolved.

"Can I borrow the car to go shopping?" I'd ask.

"I don't think so," he'd say. "I don't know if I can trust you to make decisions."

One bad dating decision had apparently ruined my ability to think, so despite chafing at the rules, I began to doubt myself and to feel thankful my parents would still make good decisions for me, because I couldn't do it myself. I did want some stability and safety, but my dad didn't see it that way. To him, it was a selfish move and I was freeloading. I was used to him berating my mother, but months away from home made the same treatment directed at me seem foreign and I resisted.

One evening my dad returned to find the family sitting around the dinner table and he exploded. "Belly-uppers! I work all day, and all you kids do is lie around and stuff your faces. When are you going to contribute around here?"

I was taking sixteen credit hours of classes and working twenty-five hours a week. Add two hours of travel time on the city bus, and I was busier than my father was. His nearsightedness angered me, and I looked him in the eye from across the room, undaunted. I stood up. "How do you know what we did all day? You were at work."

Without warning he charged at me, bringing his hand down hard against my face. The force of his hand surprised me and I remembered his strength. He could pin me down with one arm. I bolted downstairs to the bedroom I borrowed from my dad and stuffed some clothes and school books into my backpack. When I crossed the hardwood floor to the back door, I could see my dad heaping food onto his plate.

I grabbed my shoes and banged out the back door, sure of only one thing—that I was a legal adult and I was going to leave. I slipped my shoes on but didn't stoop to tie them until I was a safe distance from home. The sun's setting rays stabbed my eyes, so I turned my back to them and ran toward a bus stop. A bus was climbing the hill when I got to Center Street. The ride was blurred. My face stung from the blow, and I couldn't think past that final look on my dad's face. I got off at the university and wandered aimlessly, trying to add up the events that equaled my error and the subsequent punishment. I'd spoken my mind. That was it.

My plan was to walk the streets until daylight and then go to class. I hadn't thought further than that. But as I wandered in the darkness, I came face to face with Christine and tears began to fall. "My dad hit me," I told her. "I think I should have stayed with Joel." In my mind, that was the only solution that made sense. I hated my dad and I hated Joel. At the same time, I loved both. And they both showed their love in the same way. I couldn't remember why I wasn't with Joel.

Christine led me down the street to her apartment. Once inside, I reached for the phone. "I need to talk to Joel," I said. "I made a mistake. Maybe it's not too late. Maybe he still loves me."

She put her phone into a drawer. "You're not calling him," she said firmly. Christine had a mild personality and her sternness made me stop in my tracks.

"Maybe you're right. I can't think."

"Let's go for a walk," Christine suggested. It was eleven p.m., not the safest time to be on the streets. "You're not safe near the phone," she said. "I don't care what's out there. It's better than you being in here with the phone."

Over a pumpkin pie shake at a run-down malt stand, I poured my soul out to Christine. She listened silently, stony-faced, though her eyes flashed when something I said angered her. Finally, when I couldn't talk anymore, Christine put her hand on top of mine and said, "You need to get out of here." I suspected the same thing, though I hadn't yet put it into words. The idea of leaving everything I knew frightened me more than going back home or marrying Joel. Preserving my own life seemed dangerous enough to kill me.

When I returned home the following day, my dad was pulling weeds from the flower gardens in the front yard. It was a half-mile walk from the bus stop to the house, and I was tired when I arrived. My dad nodded at me as I approached. I met his eyes and went into his house.

In July, Joel brought me an invitation to his wedding. I didn't invite him inside. I opened the envelope on the porch and looked at the picture of him and Melinda. As Joel had said, Melinda looked blonde and perfect. Joel smiled out from where he stood behind her. They were standing at the duck pond where Joel always took me. The same place he'd taken me just weeks before he proposed to Melinda. I put the photo back into the envelope.

"Do you ever think of me?" Joel asked. The dull porch light illuminated his hopeful face.

"Sometimes," I lied. I actually still thought about him all the time. Shards of conversations drifted in and out of my consciousness throughout the day. He was my last thought before going to sleep and my first thought waking up. Before I did anything, I'd think, *What would Joel want me to do?*

"I still love you," he said.

"You're getting married!" I exclaimed.

"I know. But I look at her and sometimes just wish it was you. I don't want to marry her if there's a possibility you might take me back."

"No." Then I left Joel standing on the front porch while I rushed down to my room to gather up everything he ever gave me. I grabbed two stuffed animals he won for me at an amusement park duck hunt and a handful of ticket stubs from the movies we saw together. I also lifted a cardboard box filled with dried flowers and then went back upstairs. After shoving my armful of relationship paraphernalia into Joel's arms, I shut the door. Then I sat on the floor and tore the smiling picture of Joel and his perfect fiancée into a thousand pieces.

That was the day I stopped crying.

Joel's wedding was set for the middle of August and, as it grew closer, I delved deeper into my work and studies. I picked up extra shifts at work and revised homework assignments until I eliminated any minutes available for free thought. When my mind started down the road toward Joel's pending marriage, I redirected it toward filling silverware containers faster or writing and rewriting papers until they were perfect. The result was a larger paycheck and a 4.0 GPA, but I also developed a series of strange health conditions.

Toward the end of July, the pupil of my right eye dilated and the tear duct dried out. For three weeks I had to wear dark glasses. The muscles in my neck also seized up and cut off the blood supply to my hands. The left side of my face went numb. During the worst of it, I longed for Dr. Adams to lymphasize the poisons from my body and I missed the cult taking control of, and responsibility for, my life.

I woke up stiff, sad and disoriented the day Joel got married. I'd turned around in my sleep. Pain seized my heart and I played with the idea of stopping the wedding. Instead, I borrowed my mom's sewing scissors and sat on the floor of the laundry room chopping at my hair. I found a strange satisfaction in butchering my one feature I thought was beautiful. I slashed at it until it hung traumatized in quivering, lifeless clumps.

9

Utah seemed like such a pleasant place to live until I discovered that I could get on a plane and fly away.

I never thought I could leave the security of home. When I thought of my future, I never saw myself with a career. I saw myself snuggled with husband and kids into a tiny starter home somewhere close to my parents. My parents must have dreamed of that as well. Growing up, I had trouble with slumber parties and spending a week at girl's camp. Moving alone across the country was not something I was destined to do. Leaving was the biggest battle I've ever faced.

When I left Joel and the cult, I felt my spirit had been extinguished like a tiny candle flame in a typhoon. Deep unresolved pain racked my body, and the rare moments when the pain was absent, a void took its place. I spent the winter barely conscious, going through the motions of having a life while I slowly wasted away. Each morning I pulled myself from my tangled covers and smothered my face with makeup to hide the dark circles under my eyes. My clothes hung off me. I didn't eat, didn't sleep, and I'd forgotten how to smile. I was little more than a forgotten dried leaf still clinging to a tree long after the rest of the leaves fell and blew away.

The cult went on without me but I didn't continue on my own. My identity had been swallowed up in its rules, regulations, doctrines and mind games; without them, I couldn't function. I was alone, broken and awake while the city slept, dreading the shock of reentering reality after sleep. I plodded through the days, my feet sticking in the thick mud of loneliness. Like quicksand, once I stepped into it, I couldn't pull myself free.

One dark evening, my mom sent me to the store to buy a matting board for one of her projects. "Get a nice white or off-white," she said.

Poster boards and mats in all colors lined the walls of the basement craft store. I walked the length of the room to the neutral colors—black, gray, beige, white and off-white. I crouched at the end of the rack and read the names of the colors posted beneath the possible choices: white, off-white and egg-shell.

White, off-white and egg-shell. I eventually eliminated white because its glaring purity made me nervous.

"Off-white or egg-shell," I said out loud. I sat cross-legged in front of the display, staring at one and then the other. "Off-white or egg-shell." The tension rose. There was barely a difference. I wondered why the manufacturer even bothered to make the distinction. Still, like standing before the soda machine with my grandma and two quarters, or in front of a table of food—some of which could send you to hell—I was afraid of making the wrong choice. I became frantic and tears slipped down my cheeks. The tension escalated into panic.

An hour after I entered the store, I left in tears, empty-handed.

I was close to finishing my journalism degree at Brigham Young University when I decided to take my ten-week internship as far from home as possible. It was the beginning of my nomadic lifestyle. In June, I catapulted myself into what I called my geographic cure and a new land called Massachusetts, with little planning and no safety net once I got there. It was two a.m. when my plane landed in Hartford, Connecticut. A man I'd corresponded with by e-mail picked me up and deposited me in Northampton on the doorstep of a two-story yellow house.

A childlike young man opened the door and told me my room was upstairs. Fortunately, it was furnished. After stashing my two suitcases, I went back downstairs to formally introduce myself to nineteen-year-old Nissan, who was busily devouring everything in the kitchen.

"Wanna smoke some pot?" he asked.

I decided pot must be some kind of illegal drug. Nissan was probably going to hell. "No thanks," I said instinctively.

Nissan settled down into an overstuffed chair in the front room, his pot cigarette between the fingers of his left hand and the TV remote in his right. We watched music videos on MTV. I'd heard of the channel before, how all its performers were sinners. At three a.m., "Sifl and Ollie" came on and I made my way upstairs.

As I climbed the rickety wooden steps, I felt I could fly. I was more than two thousand miles from anything familiar. Alone in the queen-sized bed in the yellow house, I wondered how I'd entered such a foreign and free environment just by stepping on an airplane. I wondered about Northampton and Nissan smoking pot downstairs. But the newness of life was comforting. I actually felt happy. I didn't even lock my bedroom door that night.

Morning burst into the room through windows on two sides of the house. Flimsy curtains barely filtered the mid-morning glow. My familiar pain was eerily absent. My head floated above me in the room, surveying the dirty wooden floor, the bruised bureau and bed, a floor-length mirror in the corner and finally, the brown-haired girl lying sideways in a queen-sized bed, smiling.

I met my three other roommates that day. Matt was a student at the University of Massachusetts who donated to the Free Tibet cause every chance he got. He also had a theory that everyone came to Northampton to find their way, but then they moved on.

"What are you here for?" Matt asked me.

"Words," I said.

I was going to explain how my heart danced when I wrote and how finding the truth was the only thing really worth living for, but Matt didn't need the explanation. He nodded. "Yes," he said. "I can see that."

My other two roommates were Omar, a student from India hoping to gain citizenship, and Abby, a recent college graduate who was engaged to her boss at the local health food store. Living in the co-ed house was grounds for me to be expelled from BYU. I think the honor code office would rather have had me living in a cardboard box than with three men.

My sole contact in Northampton was the news editor of *The Hampshire Examiner*, Dan Preiss. There were twelve of us that summer, twelve aspiring journalists cautiously feeling our way around the newspaper office. I was different from the others. "Usually we like to recruit from the local colleges. We've never taken interns from as far away as Utah," Dan told me on my first day. Northampton sits in Western Massachusetts in the Pioneer Valley, which is home to five colleges—Smith, Mount Holyoke, Amherst, Hampshire and the University of Massachusetts-Amherst. The other interns were all upperclassmen at one of these.

"But we figured we'd take a chance on you," Dan continued. "We've never had someone from Utah." Every time he said the word *Utah* out loud, people looked up from their computers or notepads and eyed me curiously. I wanted to buy a T-shirt that said something clever about being from Utah and still being a human being.

On Friday night, our whole group was having dinner at a fancy Japanese restaurant in downtown Northampton. Everyone was already there when I arrived, but they'd waited to order. I took the soft leather chair designated for me, with Dan on my right and the managing editor at the head of the table. Some people talked quietly and others looked bored. I watched other customers make quiet conversation while eating delicately with thin chopsticks. The faces of one couple in the corner were aglow with the flames of a platter they shared.

The restaurant was called Ichiban, specializing in fine sushi. I looked at the menu, trying to sound out the dishes in my head. As the waiter, a slim, good-looking Japanese man in a tuxedo, circled our table taking orders, I panicked. Before I was ready, his eyes fell on me and with pencil poised he raised his eyebrows in my direction.

"Um," I stuttered, hating myself. "I'll have the same thing as Dan." My face reddened but no one seemed to notice. The waiter jotted down my order on his pad and moved on. I breathed out and tried to smile.

When they arrived, the colorful patterns of sushi took my breath away. I took a pair of chopsticks and handed on the basket to the boy next to me. Then I looked down at my food. Bright green avocado wrapped itself next to dull pink, surrounded by the off-white rice. Wisps of pink ginger framed the plate, and a tiny cup of green wasabi sat off to the side. I wanted to put the whole thing into my pocket to take home to my mom, to show her the simple beauty of it all. I carefully watched the other interns position their chopsticks and dip pieces of sushi into soy sauce. No one cut the large pieces first—that seemed impolite.

I picked up a knife and tried to slice a piece of sushi in half. The rice spilled over the seaweed that held it together and the tiny beautiful painting collapsed. A waiter, watching me from across the room, shook his head and motioned for me to eat the piece whole, in one bite. I moved on to another, using the chopsticks like gigantic tweezers. I dipped the sushi liberally into the green wasabi and then crammed the whole thing into my mouth.

My tongue caught on fire and the green ooze seared the roof of my mouth. Things went into slow motion around me as I forced the half-masticated food down my throat. I imagined I'd never be able to taste again, but I mulled the raw fish and rice around with my tongue nonchalantly anyway, pretending I ate fire all the time.

I was so green that Dan finally assigned me to follow other reporters around and learn about what he called "East Coast Liberals." So I spent that summer experiencing equal portions of sushi, lesbian poetry, Zen Buddhism and strip poker. I watched myself that summer as if from above as I broke through the fog of my innocence like a butterfly from its cocoon.

Leaving Utah was the second best decision I ever made.

When I'd left BYU, I was a twenty-one-year-old maid whose prime dating years were over; I was a failure. When I arrived in Massachusetts, I discovered an entire world at my feet and that I could be anything I wanted. The first thing I learned was that marriage isn't essential for happiness. The second thing I learned was that I had a lot of self-discovery ahead of me. In Utah, my every movement had been monitored and questioned for many years. So even 2,300 miles from anyone I knew, I still ducked my head when I walked, wondered if what I was doing was acceptable, and refrained from looking people in the eye. But mirrors were friendlier on the East Coast. Northampton was a city that looked for intellectual beauty and scorned false perfection, especially when it came out of a bottle. I stopped smearing my face with makeup and felt wings growing.

I met Emily my third day there. She was two years younger than I was but she was infinitely wiser. "Emily," she said to me as she held out a hand of greeting. "That's M-L-E."

She signed her name the same way she pronounced it. Capital M, capital L, capital E. She didn't have a last name. "It's the only thing my dad ever gave me and I don't want it," she explained.

I felt a strange frantic jealousy of Emily. I also wanted my name reduced to letters, and to dismiss my father as easily as she had hers. I watched Emily dance confidently through life without so much as a backward glance, while I still tripped over my shoelaces. She didn't waste words or energy on insignificant things. When she decided to divorce her family, she did it and never thought about it again. When people made small talk and asked where she was from, she'd smile and say, "I dropped out of a cornstalk." I almost believed she had.

Emily wore faded bell bottoms and big loose T-shirts with a pocket in front or advertisements for some fund raiser or amateur performance. She never wore a bra and she was usually barefoot, except when she was at one of her two jobs. She worked part-time at the ice cream parlor and part-time at a curio shop. At the shop, she wore a dress over her jeans and casually scooped her long hair into a messy bun. Emily never prioritized appearance; her goal in life was comfort. That is, except on Friday nights.

Friday nights, Emily and I danced in muggy ballrooms—many of them joined at the hip with bars, like conjoined twins. With the rotten smell of hops on their breath, men spun me around and around until the soft lamps in the corners blended into a string of dull Christmas lights and I had to go outside to catch my breath. The Latinos were all shorter than I was but eager to dance with me. To them I was beautiful, and that was all that mattered. I drifted from one sweaty-palmed man to the next, enjoying the attention as much as the thrill of moving to foreign music.

Emily gyrated with the most expert male dancers, their bodies melting together and turning the ballroom into a kaleidoscope of color. She wore a low-cut and short dress that showed off her long legs and pretty feet in high heels. As she twirled, her animated face illuminated the room.

The bars closed at one a.m. but the ballroom remained crowded for at least an hour longer. By the time I followed the dancers into the hot summer air at two or three in the morning, the soles of my feet were callused and my knees ached from stooping—an awkward habit I picked up to try to look shorter. Towering over the Latinos made me feel like a baby giraffe.

Emily slipped her shoes off as she left the building and massaged the soles of her feet against the gravel of the parking lot. Sometimes she stopped at a Dunkin' Donuts on the way to my house. Sometimes she drove me home in silence, the beautiful Spanish tunes lingering in the air between us and the sweet smell of perspiration drying on our skin. She kissed me on the cheek in front of the old yellow house I called home. Then she disappeared into the early morning light.

Emily was at least two of the things I'd assumed would mean burning for all eternity: a feminist and a communist. But she was the envy of every girl and the object of every man's affection. I was too tall, too gawky, too uncoordinated, too *me* when she was around, but she never seemed to notice. Emily's feminist side surfaced at unexpected times. Early one Saturday morning as she drove the silent streets of Northampton to drop me at my house, a man driving a pickup truck pulled in front of her and honked. Another man got out, obviously drunk, and draped himself through the passenger-side window, calling out, "Hey, baby!"

Without hesitating, Emily punched the gas pedal and plowed into the truck.

I spent weekday evenings wandering from shop to shop, inhaling the odors of ice cream, cappuccinos, bakeries, cigar smoke, exhaust— the smells of a city that was vivid and alive. Often I skipped down the five stone steps into an underground cafe called The Fire and Water. Every night a local musician or band performed, or seasoned poets, silver-haired and dignified. They played for masses of vegan college students. Sometimes an indignant graduate student or young college professor lectured about composting, global warming, or chemotherapy. Other times beauty school dropouts graced the performance space dressed in patchwork, hair twisted into long dreadlocks, reciting angst-ridden, rhythmic poetry. It didn't really matter what was happening there; it was all new to me. New and baffling but real, and I gulped it down like someone dying of thirst would chug water.

At night, I sprawled out on my queen-sized bed, enjoying the luxury of space and the sweet residue of marijuana that clung perpetually to the walls. Sometimes Omar or Nissan smoked on the porch in the silence of a humid night, and the smoke wafted through the floor of my room and then lingered for a time before swirling out the open windows into the hushed street. The curtains moved soundlessly in the breeze, and every so often I could hear the brakes of a semi as it exited the freeway. I slept lightly that summer, always alert for something new and beautiful.

Saturdays I window shopped or lay on the grass at Smith College with a book of John Steinbeck stories or poems by Sylvia Plath. Joggers circled the track and slim, muscular elderly men smashed green tennis balls back and forth, their tan legs shiny with perspiration. The more bookish people sprawled on grass and colored blankets with books and bottles of mineral water. I never spoke to these people—these Saturday friends—but I knew we were kin lazing the day away on the same acre of grass.

I bumped into the same people Saturday nights at the movies. The two theaters in town competed for the intellectual crowds who gathered to view independent films—the kind of movie that I had to pay attention to the whole time. And even then, I'd walk away with a dozen questions about the point of life.

Halfway through my internship I conducted an interview with a quadriplegic musician who taught at the University of Massachusetts. An accident ten years earlier had left him that way. When he spoke, a microphone pinned to his shirt amplified his throaty grunts, projecting them into the room. His lips barely moved.

When I knocked on his half-open office door, he greeted me with his robot voice. "Hello. Come in, come in." I couldn't remember a warmer greeting. Subtle movements of his head allowed the man to maneuver around in an electric wheelchair. I took a chair in the corner, poised with pen and paper.

The man spoke as I wrote furiously in my notebook. I wanted to concentrate on something other than the man's handicaps. "I was headed for a world-class career as a trumpeter. Then the accident." I glanced up in time to see a half-grimace on his otherwise expressionless face. "My students researched the instrument and my mobility, and they built this."

The man moved forward to a crazy contraption nestled on metal in the middle of the room. A piece of fishing line connected the trumpet to a pole that stood five or six feet tall. When the man was in place, he put his lips around the trumpet and used his fingertips to control more fishing lines that hooked to the instrument's buttons. I listened in stunned disbelief as he pumped out "Amazing Grace" using only the ends of his fingers and the air in his cheeks. When he finished I clapped in spite of myself, then hung my head, embarrassed at my outburst.

The man didn't mind. He nodded his head in a mock bow, and then backed up in his wheelchair to see me again. "Music is the only thing I ever cared about," he said with his magnified robot voice. "When I lost the use of my limbs, I wanted to die. How can God take away a man's only passion? I was angry at God, the world, myself. . . . But now, this miracle. I don't need my arms or legs. I'm whole with this machine."

During my early reporting endeavors, I always waited for a silent cue from the interviewee that he was done. "I guess that's all I have to say about that," the musician said. "I hope you do my instrument justice in print."

On the bus ride home, I thought about what he'd said. What could I do without and still live with passion? Then I realized I wasn't handicapped, nor was I living with passion. I got off the bus at the next stop and decided to walk home.

I kissed Jeremy on the Connecticut River Bridge late one evening in July. I'd known him for two hours. His lips tasted like burnt sugar and butter ice cream, and his tongue tasted like cigarettes. The combination was bittersweet, a reminiscing of the evening. I'd met Jeremy on Main Street and, on an impulse, he asked me to join him for ice cream.

He talked about literary contributions by James Joyce and quoted Goethe and Shakespeare. I argued for American literature, quoting Thoreau and Emerson. Jeremy talked about jazz and folk musicians. I protested with lyrics by the Beatles and Alanis Morissette. Jeremy shared his research into the innards of computers, and I tried to find words to tell him about my passion for the arts. The sun drowned itself in the river while the blues and greens of fireflies flickered near the water's surface. A cool breeze roused humid air from the pavement, and Jeremy and I were silent for too long. Then he kissed me.

When I stood up straight, I could see directly into Jeremy's eyes and I knew what he was thinking: It was a kiss stolen on a bridge under a full moon, a moment of passion that wasn't meant to go further. It was a kiss of affection and innocence, two strangers experiencing a temporary bond.

After the kiss, Jeremy leaned back against the railing of the bridge and lit up another cigarette. He exhaled through his nose, the swirls of smoke puddling for a split second below his nostrils before floating upward and out of sight. "You're cute," he said. "I like that."

It was the best compliment I'd ever received and for a moment I was in love with Jeremy. I leaned into his body and he put his arms around me. For a moment I wanted to extend the moment, maybe even into a lifetime. But I let it go. Anything more would have ruined it.

I kissed Jeremy again before leaving him in his car outside my yellow house. Then I said good-bye.

That experience encapsulated my time in Northampton. Two and a half months ended quickly. I wore a sleeveless dress to work on the last day. The co-workers I'd spent lazy summer afternoons with chirped their good-byes and good-lucks as I gathered my office souvenirs and exited. I glanced back once, but the evening sun burning into the glass of the door revealed only my reflection—a skinny, clumsy, awkward girl. But I didn't care. I had belonged there.

Matt and Omar met me at the front door of the yellow house. "It's your last day," Omar said. "Let's celebrate. I'm taking you to Burger King."

I clambered into the back of Omar's car. He drove the mile and a half for two Whoppers. Then he paused in front of Stop and Shop so Matt could grab a quick vegetarian meal. On our way back up the hill, Omar pulled over to let Abby hop in, and then we all gathered on our porch to perch on the rickety rails for one last haphazard family meal. Only Nissan was missing. My cheeks ached from smiling.

Later, Omar drove Matt and me to Springfield, where he wanted to say good-bye in style. "You can't go back to Utah without experiencing the world." For two hours we danced and schmoozed in a bar called The Ogre. Men drifted in and out of my arms as I swayed through the night. Men pulled out chairs for me, guided me to and from the dance floor, refused to let me sit alone. The men seemed to become one being—a faceless male creature devoted to making my stay at the bar more comfortable.

Matt pulled me from the creature's arms at one a.m. "We're going home," he said. "I'm tired."

I followed my housemates to the parking lot. Omar bought a hotdog from a street vendor, drowned it in mustard, and munched it as he steered the car toward the freeway. "Who sells hot dogs in the middle of the night?" I wondered out loud.

Omar and Matt exchanged a look. "Welcome to the world," Omar said.

I left the world the next day.

After cramming my belongings back into two suitcases, sweeping my tiny upstairs bedroom, and grabbing my toothbrush from the bathroom, I found Matt on the front porch. It was a Saturday morning in late August. "We should have spent more time sitting on the porch," he mused. He heaved my heavy suitcases to the sidewalk and perched next to me again on the steps. "People are too busy to sit on the porch but they keep building them anyway. We really should have sat out here more often."

I nodded in agreement, picturing the enormous concrete porches studded with lawn chairs and intricate dining arrangements that front many homes in Utah. I couldn't remember ever seeing people on any of those porches. Maybe the furniture was designed only for decoration and couldn't be sat on. I caressed the worn slanted wood of the porch, the flaking paint sticking under my fingernails. I leaned back against an old armchair that had been rotting on the porch all summer, and my hand brushed against something metal poking from beneath it. I closed my fingers around it and brought it up to my face. It was the curly-cue five that used to hang on the front of the building—half of the number that designated the yellow house as 45 Olive Street. I put the number into my pocket for luck.

A yellow taxi turned onto Olive Street and blinked its headlights at me. I waved to the driver. Matt picked up my suitcases and heaved them into the trunk. Then he gave me a big hug. "Sit on the porch for me sometime," he said. I started to get into the cab but he called out, "Wait!"

He ran back into the house and returned a moment later with a huge red dictionary. "Take this with you," he said. "To remember the words."

Two hours later I boarded a homebound plane and sat throughout the trip with a dictionary on my lap, smiling.

10

The plane delivering me and my two suitcases back to Utah hovered on a fragment of upwind over the runway. I wished, suddenly and earnestly, that it would crash. Instead, the tires met pavement with a smooth whishing sound and the plane pulled up to a gate long before I was ready. As I walked off the plane, I saw my dad's face hovering four inches above my mom's in the small crowd. Their features were familiar in the hazy kind of way a person recognizes her own face in a mirror she unexpectedly comes across.

Everything was wrong again.

I'd stretched beautiful wings I never guessed I had and I was just beginning to learn to soar, to see the world from a bigger perspective. If moving to the East Coast evoked an emerging butterfly, returning to Utah meant cramming that butterfly back into its cocoon with the blunt end of a butter knife. My first night in Utah I stood next to my twin-sized bed—the box springs, mattress and headboard I'd had since I was three—and felt the wings being torn from my body.

After lugging the suitcases to my room and dropping them on the floor, I returned to the kitchen, where I made myself a cup of raspberry tea and pulled out a new journal. Usually the smell of new paper intoxicated me but now the 8.5 x 11 sheets loomed ominously, judging the touch of black ink before I even raised my pen. "Write," I instructed my hand. "If you can write, you can hold on to it."

I couldn't do it. Only two hours in Utah and I was already losing the beautiful new thing inside. Just being in my father's house felt like I was trying to jam my adult feet into a pair of childhood shoes, shoes I'd maybe worn to take some important steps but that in no way fit any longer. I could recognize my dad's footsteps anywhere, and when the soft pad of his slipper-clad feet echoed on the wooden tiles, I didn't need to look up. I closed my blank book, uncrumpled my hand from the pen and sipped my tea.

"What are you drinking?" my dad asked.

"Herbal tea."

"We don't drink tea," he stated flatly, approaching the table.

I curled my tongue into a tube and inserted it in the hot liquid, slurping. "It's herbal," I said.

"It's time for you to go to bed," he countered.

"It's only ten thirty," I said to the table, the defiance draining from my voice.

I waited as my dad got a drink of water and strolled back down the hallway to his room, and then I opened the back door to sit on the porch, my blank journal resting on my knees. The air was different in Utah. It was thinner, cooler, less substantial, like I couldn't breathe in enough of it to satisfy my lungs. I sat barefoot on the porch for a long time, listening to grasshoppers bounce across the dusk-shaded lawn. The cold cement under me sent shivers darting through my body; goose bumps prickled on my arms, standing the hairs on their ends. I missed the blues and greens of fireflies, the smell of tiki lamps, frogs and crickets in the distance and glasses clinking together at outside cafes. I missed the free-standing sink and bathtub of my Northampton apartment and the way the entire house slowly slanted toward the right. I missed sitting on Omar's swivel chair at one end of the kitchen and letting gravity force the chair to the opposite corner. I was so lonely even for the smell of marijuana that I wanted to cry.

My return coincided with the disappearance of a local teenage girl. I watched from the edge of my consciousness as news anchors relayed, over and over, Elizabeth Smart's abduction by knife-point from her bedroom. Among the suspects was a drifter Elizabeth's father had hired for a day or two to complete jobs around their house. Something about the blonde-haired, blue-eyed girl's disappearance seemed oddly familiar to me—the way she was wakened from innocent slumber and forced from her home. I ignored the whispering resonance. Nothing about Utah would be familiar to me. It was not my home.

My second day back in Utah was a Sunday. I accompanied my parents to church, where we sat on a pew in the back. A young man with dreadlocks jutting in every direction occupied the pew in front of us. I didn't notice him until my parents began whispering.

"Disrespectful," my dad said.

My mom asked, "How can he come to church like that?"

Dreadlocks had become so familiar to me by then that I hadn't even seen them. Most worshippers wore brand-name clothing, ties, sunglasses, perfect hair, and flawless peach makeup that looked like it would crack if the wearer experienced any emotion. I gazed at the dreadlocks for comfort throughout the service.

On Monday I went back to classes and back to work in the cafeteria. Something about delivering dishwasher-hot spoons, forks and knives into the greedy hands of nineteen-year-old boys felt degrading. I scuffled my feet as if to give voice to the reluctance swimming through my body. I'd become spoiled. Ten weeks of a professional job made menial labor humiliating.

After my shift I changed out of the white button-down shirt and maroon apron, and then hopped on a city bus to campus. As I trudged the familiar sidewalks, I avoided making eye contact with anyone. I looked through them instead, focusing on chins or foreheads to give the illusion I was connected to the world. But all my energy went to holding on to the tiny piece of beauty I still had inside.

Joel's voice echoed in my head from two years prior: "If I can't see the white of your eyes below your pupils, there's something wrong with you. People can tell you're not happy if your eyes are sagging in their sockets." Joel was always studying my eyes to determine if I was appropriately cheerful. He wouldn't even acknowledge me if I looked at all depressed. So the sadder I felt, the harder I strained to make my eyes look happy.

I stopped at the bookstore my first day back, intending to purchase my textbooks. I squeezed in along the crowded corridors searching for course and section numbers, gathering books, packets of handouts and syllabi. Then I opened my checkbook. The balance was $5.46. The trip home had wiped out my finances. When the cashier looked away, I tucked my stack of books on a shelf. I bought a paperback philosophy book instead. I didn't really need the books for the first day anyway; I could buy them when I got my first paycheck.

I never went back to the store.

I decided if I didn't unpack, I wasn't really home. I chose to rummage through piles of clothes still sitting lifeless in my suitcases instead of folding them and putting them away. The clothes I wore in Northampton represented my summer of freedom and they, like me, rejected assimilation with their counterparts in the closet. In a way, it was funny how quickly I lost ground. In the space of about seventy-two hours I was reduced to lint. During the first week, I sifted through heaps of clothes on the floor every morning searching for something to wear. By the end of the second week, all my clothes were dirty. I didn't see any point in washing them, so I wore the same thing every day. Nothing around me was changing so I didn't bother to change either.

Nights lying awake under my childhood blankets were unbearable. I missed the pink and white checked sheets I'd stretched across my bed in Northampton. Instead of waking up early to watch the sun creep across the floor or to listen for the morning birds, I succumbed to a sleepy absence of feeling every morning.

As everything in my life diminished, the protrusion in my forehead grew. Every day it stuck out farther until it was the only thing I could see. After a month in Utah, I began to avoid mirrors. Then, in a 180-degree spin, I started seeking them out, stopping at several different bathrooms between classes, hunting down car windows and any other reflective surface to examine my profile. The only rest I got from my forehead crisis was at work. A baseball cap was a mandatory part of the uniform and I pulled mine down low.

After work though, and sometimes for hours at a time, I examined the protrusion. I stood under a light and watched how the shadows contoured around it, causing it to bulge and grow, to obliterate my other features. One step backward or forward could ease the severity of the shadows, and then I could almost endure my reflection, so I became intensely aware of the lighting in every room and never positioned myself underneath a light. "Be careful where you stand," Joel had always told me. I heard his voice wherever I went and sought out dark corners or dimly lit rooms.

I finally consulted another plastic surgeon, but his solutions, too, were costly or temporary, so I resorted to the only thing over which I had control. For an hour each day, I bludgeoned the deformity in my head with the dull end of a hammer.

I knew that my salvation would rest again on my ability to get out of Utah. I played with the idea of telling my parents I had a job, and then moving back to the one place I felt beautiful. I contacted my internship adviser at the *Examiner* to ask about possible jobs and then I decided to buy a car.

Since I was eighteen, my dad had pestered me to buy a car but I'd resisted, having seen the financial burden it put on my older brother. My dad ran his own bank and he encouraged us to invest our money with him. But we found it nearly impossible to make withdrawals, especially if my dad didn't agree with the purchase. Until I was eighteen, I earned an allowance of less than a dollar per week, and that money went directly into my dad's bank. The formula for allowance was a nickel per year of age per week, or 85¢ per week when I was seventeen. I made $2.60 during my first year of life and $44.20 the year I was seventeen.

My dad wanted his bank to fund my purchase of a car. In return, I'd pay monthly installments until it was paid for. The burden of owing my father $12,476.14 was immense. My dad wrote down the exact cost of the car to the penny, and reminded me of it several times the week after I bought it. Until the car was officially mine, I had to OK every trip in 'his' car. It was easier to continue taking the bus than to ask my dad's permission to drive, so that's what I did. Every morning I walked past the car in the driveway and hiked the half-mile to a bus stop.

In October, my family went on vacation to Park City. I drove up the canyon with two of my younger sisters. I couldn't bear to look at the brilliant autumn trees on the mountain because I was so ugly. I spent the weekend in the rented condo avoiding mirrors and eye contact with my family.

"Can you see the bump now?" I'd ask, turning my head slightly to one side or the other.

"No," my sisters or mother would shout. "There's nothing there!"

"What about my nose?"

I spiraled downhill, digging myself into a hole of self-loathing until I couldn't stand to be inside my own head. I struck the hammer against my forehead relentlessly, two or three hundred times in a sitting, until my head throbbed and I couldn't see straight, willing the bone structure to collapse. Then I used a small, hand-held mirror reflecting against the large bathroom mirror to examine the bump from all angles. It didn't shrink. Instead, the bluish-purple bruising bloated it. I'd pull my hair over my eyes or jam a hat onto my head and slink away. More than once, I also held the sharp end of a paring knife against my nose, ready to perform plastic surgery on myself.

Joel's opposing demands rattled around in my head until I was exhausted. He enforced one set of standards in his house and a completely opposite set in public. "You need to wear your hair up more often," he commanded. "Around me anyway. But don't fix it up when we're around other men."

But then when we were in public he ignored me, choosing to flirt with other—more heavily made-up—girls. I was to be desirable only for him, and he was to find me desirable only when it was convenient. I also had to wear clothes that covered my arms and legs when we were in public, but in private Joel wanted to see more skin.

Even with Joel out of my life, my ugliness was still a thought process akin to the bump on my forehead. I stopped trying to appear OK, succumbing to my depression. I stopped combing my hair and let it hang limply around my pale face. I decided I'd finish out my final semester and then give up.

At the end of November, however, hope appeared. I got an email from Dan Preiss inviting me back to Massachusetts to take a job. It gave me the courage I needed to trek through the last month of classes. I walked through my final month of Utah like I was walking on splintered glass, the hope so fragile that I feared I'd break it by celebrating.

Because I hadn't really unpacked, preparing to leave was an easy task. I left two days after Christmas, all my things in the car and my dad in the passenger seat. Two hours into the drive though, I forfeited the driver's seat; he was more comfortable there.

Conversation with my dad was never an easy thing. I can't remember ever talking directly to him the first twelve years of my life, though I remember always being terrified of him. Confined to the same six feet of living space for a four-day drive was not relaxing. When we finally arrived in Massachusetts, we weren't talking at all.

I'd managed to secure an apartment before moving. My dad accompanied me to the doorstep but refused to go any farther. I carried up my things to a tiny third-story apartment I was sharing with a man and his dog. My dad waited outside. Record-deep snow was falling and the sky darkened by six p.m. As night approached I became increasingly anxious. Planes were grounded and my dad was forced to postpone his flight home until the next day.

Suddenly, unexpected and empty hours were thrust upon us. We walked the streets once familiar to me, but now the freedom of summer was embedded in thigh-deep snow and for the first time since I'd left there, I doubted. The absence of college students left a void on the streets, but plenty of seats at local restaurants. I decided to treat my dad to a sushi dinner, but he ordered chicken instead. We boarded at one final hotel for the night rather than brave the fetid haunt that was my new home, and my dad left the following morning.

I slept the afternoon away in my new bedroom and then put on my snow boots to wade through the snow along Main Street. It was New Year's Eve and the dark street looked deserted, the town closed. But window displays called out from behind glass, and I sensed the town's magic restive in the frozen air. I walked to the ancient building that housed the library, continued up the hill to Smith College, then turned and half-walked, half-slid down the hill to my house. It was nearly midnight and the house was empty. I unscrewed two of the light bulbs in my room to soften the light, swept the hardwood floor and started unpacking. As the clock ticked down to midnight, the sounds of celebration wafted through thin walls and into my room from the bar next door. I opened the door to listen as drunken voices sang "Auld Lang Syne." Glasses knocked clumsily together. I smiled and shut the door. I was home.

I started work January second. Still hiding my face behind a curtain of hair, I marched into my first day as a professional journalist. The lights in the building were harsher than I remembered and I felt young and inadequate. Dan presented me with paperwork to fill out—taxes, bank information, in-case-of-emergency contacts—and I spent the day signing away my life to a job I was no longer confident I could do. But I sat at my desk and wrote, or interviewed over the phone. Dan bought a video recorder and asked me to start taping my interviews so we could post video clips on the website with our print stories. I was calm, quiet and organized and I got a raise after three months.

My first big assignment involved a murder trial. A nurse named Kristen Gilbert was on trial for killing her patients at a VA Medical Center. Her goal was to cause heart attacks in her patients and then revive them, to make herself a hero for a security guard she wanted to impress. But some of them died and Kristen was charged with four counts of murder and found guilty. Then sentencing deliberations began. My job was to hang around the federal courthouse and catch the prosecutor and defense lawyer for comments after the jury reached a verdict.

Everywhere I went, people discussed the death penalty. "She killed at least four people," some argued. "She should die, too." Others claimed the law has no right to end a person's life, no matter what they did. Although Kristen narrowly got life in prison, I kept imagining her reaction if told she'd get the injection. For weeks, I woke every night to Kristen's white somber face looming in front of me.

As time went on, Joel's face replaced Kristen's. I saw his disgusted expression when I argued with him or ate meat. I saw his disappointment when I failed to be beautiful. More and more though, I saw the look on his face when I told him I'd never marry him. Sometimes I woke in a panic, bathed in sweat and unable to breathe. Every morning I had to lie awake in bed for hours until I found the courage to face the world. I'd stumble into the office at nine or ten a.m., always equipped with a disaster or breaking-story excuse.

It probably didn't help that my roommate was unemployed and slept all day. All night, Jesse sat in an armchair with his sick dog, watching TV, smoking marijuana, and filling a mixing bowl with ashes. Sometimes he made phone calls, and I heard him use words like psychiatrist, father, and malpractice.

In February I noticed that my food supply was depleting on a nightly basis. I'd wake in the morning with nothing for breakfast or to pack for lunch. I also noticed subtle changes in my room, like someone was rummaging through my things when I was gone. Then one night at the beginning of March, I woke to a fight. I backed up into the far corner of my room to the sounds of fists colliding with skin and bodies colliding with walls.

"It's over," Jesse seethed. "I don't want anything to do with you."

The other man spoke softly, trying to cool Jesse down. "Come here. Let me get the blood from your lip."

I moved out the following weekend.

I held down my job at the paper for a year, but then I quit. I'm not sure why. I had no source of income or new job prospects, but I did have the peace of mind that accompanied not being forced to appear in public every day. That peace of mind lasted for a week. Then, in a paranoid frenzy, I began to scour the area for a job. The Northampton School District hired me as a substitute teacher, but standing in front of dozens of scrutinizing eyes was too much.

My bank account depleted quickly, and as I lay in bed at one or two in the afternoon, I'd replay scenes from the cult. Its members were waiting for final instructions on how to find the Dream Mine, a buried stash of ancient treasure. The Dream Mine was located in the southern end of Utah County, but God was waiting for his chosen servant before he revealed the exact location. The gold and jewels dated to nearly six hundred years before Christ, and they could support God's chosen people for a thousand years while their evil counterparts destroyed themselves and the earth.

"I had a dream last night," Joel told me once. "The time is approaching. I saw the Dream Mine. The entrance was near a river flowing from a rock."

It frightened me that Joel's cognitive skills functioned at a level that could believe these things. I asked, "Do you really believe that?"

"Do you really think God would have given us this science without also providing a way for us to take care of ourselves?"

It was a good point. If God was behind the science, as I believed he was, he would never leave us to starve. If I had only married Joel, I would have saved myself a lot of pain. I'd be in Utah, taken care of by a large incestuous family and reaping the benefits of the Dream Mine.

During the next four months, I held the same number of jobs. I was a waitress at a greasy diner until I got fired for sleeping in. I was a custodian until I got fired for not going to work. I was a filer at a doctor's office until I quit. Finally, I decided to apply for professional jobs, but I lacked the energy to author a simple resumé. So I'd sleep until noon and then wander the streets half-looking for Help Wanted signs. Some evenings I looked in the newspaper, but that was depressing because it reminded me of the steady job I'd quit for no apparent reason.

In April, after I'd been unemployed for four months, my dad called. "Your grandpa died this evening."

My grandpa was the source of my earliest memory. I was two years old when my family moved from New Mexico to Utah. As soon as we were in town, my dad swooped me off my feet and sat me down on Grandpa's lap in a recliner next to the fireplace. I had no idea who the man was but I knew he loved me. I'd often returned to that memory for comfort.

Before I could answer my dad, the phone slipped from my hand to the floor. I retrieved it and asked, "Are you still there?"

"Yes. He died of congested heart failure a couple of hours ago." I had never witnessed my dad express any emotion except anger, but I was still surprised at the lack of feeling in his voice. I decided to be as stalwart and unfeeling as he was, determined not to cry until my dad did. "You'll come to the funeral," my dad continued. "It's on Thursday."

"I have to work . . ." I started, but I was too tired to lie.

"I'll get on the Internet and find you a flight."

My grandpa was a staple in his environment, deeply and widely respected. Only two sets of eyes remained dry during his funeral service: my dad's and mine. My dad presented a eulogy of his father's life and mourners sobbed audibly. But I chewed on my tongue and pinched the insides of my elbows. Even when I looked into my grandmother's eyes, which reflected the loss of her companion of more than fifty years, I didn't cry. Even when I looked into the casket and saw my grandpa's chalky face and lifeless hands, still chapped from decades of labor, I didn't cry. And even when my dad, for two or three seconds, threatened to lose his composure, I didn't lose mine. As he paid tribute to the most important man in his life, I wanted more than anything for my dad to show he was a human being capable of being touched. But he didn't. He finished the eulogy dry-eyed and sat down. And suddenly I couldn't feel either.

That's when I knew I'd never heal.

I flew back to Massachusetts the next day. My dad dropped me at the airport and as I handed my suitcase to a sky hop, my dad called out the car window, "Remember, you owe me $700 for the plane ticket."

When the plane touched down, I decided to dye my hair black. I used the last of my savings for the dye and then started packing my belongings. When my food supply ran out, I moved back to my parents' house.

The drive back across the country to Utah was long and strange. Somewhere in the middle of Nebraska the muscles in my neck tensed up, and they never relaxed. As I approached Utah, I drove slower and slower until, when I reached Elysium Drive, my tires were moving too slowly to scale the speed bumps. Moving back into my dad's house meant, of course, that I ate when he wanted me to eat, slept when he said it was time for bed, and said whatever he wanted to hear. I even tried to have thoughts he'd find appropriate.

Every day my dad berated me for not working, but even the local Kmart rejected my application. I decided to protest fashion and civilization in general by dressing in dirty T-shirts and baggy jeans, looking the epitome of failure. Then I encountered Joel in the mall.

"Alysa!" I turned around expecting some former classmate, married with several toddlers in tow. I didn't even recognize the stocky, graying man. "Alysa, it's me!" When he smiled I recognized the gap between his front teeth.

Joel's thoughts showed readily on his face as he looked me up and down. He snickered, "You look good."

I wanted to say something that would explain my appearance, my failure, my presence in a city I swore I'd never return to, but I came up blank. "Thanks," I finally said.

Spinning on his heel, Joel said, "See you around?"

"OK." As I walked away, I glanced back and caught Joel glancing simultaneously at me with a smug look of satisfaction plastered across his face.

Something died in me during the two and a half months I spent back in Utah, and I knew I needed the geographic cure again. After sending resumés to practically every newspaper in the country, I accepted a job at a small community paper in southern Arizona. I felt like I was preparing to die, so the sleepy town seemed the appropriate place to be.

I was running from a nameless black something, a deep unrest. I knew it wasn't Joel or the cult anymore. It wasn't hit men following me at discreet distances and staking out my house, or foreign Mafia wearing dark sunglasses and carrying concealed weapons under black trench coats. It would have been easier if my enemy were that solid.

I arrived at my new town in a two vehicle caravan—my Toyota Corolla with my mom, and my dad following in his Ford Ranger with my bed and a bookshelf in the truck bed. After two days of travel we read the sign, "Welcome to Grant, a good place to live, work and visit." It was 110 degrees. Phoenix and Tucson, the closest things to civilization as I knew it, were hours away.

Grant looked like the kind of place people drive through without stopping, the kind of town locals never leave because the task of driving through endless miles of sand, rock, and desert shrub is too daunting. Still, I would have slept on the street to get away from Utah.

I didn't know yet that Grant was home to cattle poachers, child molesters, drug dealers, and wife beaters. I didn't know about the cowboy poets who rode through town with guitars, the bonfires that lit up winter nights or the security a small town could afford. I also didn't know how easy it was to become an enemy of that sense of security. I had told myself this was a career move and that I was going to Grant for my big break. My voice would be heard in the small town, and my ladder to *The New York Times* or *The Chicago Tribune* would all start with a by-line in *The Grant Gazette*.

In actuality, Grant was at the end of my emotional road. When I got there, I was prepared to kill myself. Every moment, waking or sleeping, I was drowning in pain.

As we drove through town, dark clouds crowded the sky and the wind whipped through sparse trees, filling the air with thick red dust and moving the hinged parts of colorful lawn ornaments. The houses were painted garish shades of pink, purple and blue that contrasted sharply with the natural desert landscape. The poorest residents tried to disguise their run-down trailer homes with flags, streamers and obsolete road signs. The smaller the house, the more plastic junk was heaped around it.

I pulled into a gas station parking lot. My dad pulled up next to me and leaned his head out. Beads of sweat dripped down his face. "What next?" he asked in irritation. The last two hundred miles, descending from the mountains on hairpin roads, had been excruciating.

I found a pay phone and dialed the only local number I knew—the cell phone of a doctor who had advertised an apartment online. Dust was flying everywhere. I covered my eyes with one hand as Dr. Gonzalez gave me directions to the corner apartment. I found it easily, surrounded by a short dilapidated stone wall and not looking promising. As I got out of my car, a tall bearded man moved toward me, holding out a hand. "Hi. Alysa, right?"

My dad called a hello from his truck but made no effort to get out. A flash of lightning lit the air, followed by a huge crash of thunder, and I ducked impulsively. Dr. Gonzalez chuckled. "It's a desert monsoon. You'll get used to it."

I followed him across the parking lot to a battered door. He jiggled a key, then gave the door a sharp kick. As it burst open, he stood aside and motioned for me to enter. My mom followed. I quickly took in a barren room with dirty and faded walls. Abandoned socks and dishes suggested the last resident left in a hurry. A toaster oven in the kitchen took up most of the counter space and an accordion door opened into a grimy bathroom.

Back in the front room, Dr. Gonzalez talked over the thunder. "If you have a sofa bed, you can fold it up every day and use this for a living room as well."

Without a word, I walked out into the rain and approached my dad. "You didn't come in to see."

"I don't need to see some grungy apartment," he said. "I figure it's good enough for you. You'll settle for anything."

I yelled out to the doctor before heading for my car, "I'll call you tomorrow."

Plopping into my driver's seat, I looked desperately at my mom. "What am I supposed to do?" She didn't answer.

My dad flashed his brights and I followed him onto the highway and then to a motel. He got a room with two double beds and promptly lay down on one of them, ignoring me, my mom, and my possessions getting drenched in the back of his truck. I went out to tuck the edges of a packing blanket around my mattress. The world was a sickly pale green as the storm raged under scrutiny of the streetlights. Horizontal rain and blowing sand stung my face and made my eyes water.

My dad didn't say a word all night. He feigned sleep as I walked by softly to use the bathroom. As I lay in bed, my mom cried softly into her pillow. My stomach rumbled with hunger but I rolled over to face the wall and wait for sleep.

The first thing I did in the morning was to find a copy of the local classifieds and use the motel phone. The only question I asked of every landlord was, "Can I move in today?" Halfway down the rental list, I found a man willing to let me move in immediately. "I got one," I told my parents, and we hit the streets.

In my twenty-four years, I'd never seen a town so overwhelmingly bleak. Some yards sported beds of sand while others were overgrown with cacti and wild resin bush. Still others were dominated by slabs of cement, or had gravel paths weaving among cacti and huge boulders. I wondered if the houses or the boulders were there first. As I drove, I tried to keep track of various places. The police department, county sheriff's office, courthouse, and library were clustered in the center of town. Small shops decorated with Kokopelli cluttered the streets, advertising Indian beads, crafts, music, and Western wear.

My new place turned out to be a desert-colored adobe house with a green roof, and it was within walking distance of the newspaper office. Its walls were two feet thick, made of straw caked with gray-yellow mud. My front yard was about six feet by four feet, boxed in on three sides by concrete and on the fourth by a fence. The house itself was wedged into the block between an auto repair shop and a set of train tracks.

The interior of the house seemed bigger than it actually was because of its emptiness. My possessions would barely make a dent in the space. The ceilings stretched ten feet above the earth-colored floor. The front door opened into the living room and a chest-high wall divided the kitchen from a tiny dining room at the rear. A hallway leading to the bedroom and bathroom branched off on the left. I walked through the house, turning on lights and trying not to think about the dismal echoing sound my footsteps made on the faux-stone tiles.

As my dad moved my wet bed into the house, I followed my new landlord to City Hall to pay for utilities and register for a mail box. By the time I returned, all my possessions were inside. I stood awkwardly among my things, holding a teddy bear like a frightened child.

After a quick hug, my dad pulled my mom toward the truck and I urged, "Don't leave! I don't know anyone yet."

"You'll figure it out," my dad said. My mom, crying again, lingered with her good-bye before they drove off.

I recalled the sign on the highway and repeated to myself, "A good place to live, work and visit."

Pain greeted me when I woke my first morning in Grant and looked out the window. The town was still brown, barren and stiflingly hot, still scattered with long strips of parched land and littered by glass from shot-out windows of abandoned gas stations. Waves of anxiety bathed me in sweat, so I lay staring up at the yellow, bulging ceiling that reminded me of the inside of a wasp's nest.

With a groan I finally pulled myself out of bed and selected an unwrinkled khaki skirt and a short-sleeved, button-down denim shirt—not too dressy, not too casual. Positioning myself in front of the mirror, the morning sunshine outlined my features, making me look clumsy, unpolished and inadequate. I put on too much eye makeup trying to make myself look older and more experienced; maybe then I'd feel that way.

I've always had a young face. I had a journalism professor in college who told me that as a reporter my face would either be the cause of my eventual downfall or my secret weapon. "You've got to get in there and make them think you're just a dumb, curious kid playing reporter," he told me. "Ask a lot of dumb questions, get them to tell you everything, then spin around and slap them in the face with your story."

A secret weapon sounded good to me, but during college I resented having a wholesome innocent face. I wanted more than anything to appear worldly and knowledgeable. During inspired adolescent phases, I'd dyed my hair black and smoked with the wrong crowd on the other side of the fence, but as far as real life experience went, I got through college without having any. I considered myself more experienced when I reached Arizona, but that didn't stop my adolescent reflection from staring back at me from the bathroom mirror. When I gave up trying to look older, I decided to walk to work to calm my nerves. Even at nine in the morning the heat was unbearable.

The *Gazette* was housed in a renovated trailer on Highway 30 near the eastern edge of town. Additions were tacked on at erratic angles. I sat down in the waiting area, listening to the receptionist argue with a young sunburned man in cutoff shorts and a backwards baseball cap. He was complaining about his bedridden grandmother's subscription. "She only reads the obituaries, so she shouldn't have to pay for the whole paper."

The receptionist said, "We don't sell the paper by sections. It's only fifty cents a day. What else can you buy for fifty cents these days?"

The man reluctantly paid for the full paper—delivered to the front porch, please—and let himself out angrily, making the glass rattle and the bell above the door rock violently for several seconds.

The receptionist shook her head and gave me a smile. I admired her long gray-white hair, braided and twisted into a bun. Her face was pleasant and didn't look old enough to be fringed with white hair. "You get all kinds. I'm Pat, and you must be the new reporter?"

"I guess so."

"Where are you from?" Pat asked.

"I grew up in Utah, but I'm never going back." Even as I spoke, I could hear the sullen, pouting child in my voice. It was a ridiculous thing to say out loud. My face grew hot with shame but Pat didn't seem to notice.

"I was born and raised in Grant." I detected a familiar bitterness and something almost wistful in her voice, but Pat went on quickly, "Grant takes people a while to warm up to, but they will. Just don't leave before you give it a fair chance, is all I'm saying."

Before I could ask Pat what she meant, another irate customer stormed in. I became restless, alternately studying the barren landscape out the windows and the clock ticking loudly on the wall. It was nine forty a.m. Pat was still busy, so I wandered toward the "Editorial Staff Only" door that was slightly ajar. Inside was a desk in each corner, all facing inward, and a floor littered with papers, notepads, folders, and various office paraphernalia. None of the furnishing in the office matched and it seemed likely they were picked up at the local Salvation Army. There were no windows.

A man at one of the desks stared at his computer, typing furiously with his two index fingers. He gave me a brief glance but his eyes were glazed over in concentration, and he went back to his work. A police scanner beeped and hummed as it spun through the channels, occasionally picking up the voices of officers as they called in license plate numbers or discussed lunch menus.

In the far corner was a closed door with a solemn nameplate engraved "Managing Editor." His name was Reginald Thomas Jefferson. I'd talked to him twice over the phone in the previous week—once when he offered me the job, and a second time when we negotiated pay. Reginald Thomas Jefferson was a name that commanded respect. I hoped he'd be large, black, and outspoken, dedicated to serving the public and its constitutional rights to information. I was so convinced by this mental picture that when the door swung open, I gasped in disappointment.

He was easily six-foot-five, but his shoulders slumped over a beer belly, shortening his height by several inches and creating the most unusual body shape I'd ever seen. His posture caused him to wobble as he walked. His pants were six inches too short and a flimsy knitted shirt hung open at the neck, revealing pallid skin. Undisciplined eyebrows thrust themselves out over the tops of thick grimy glasses, and a lopsided Van Dyke mustache drooped over his moist pink lips. Greasy black hair tinged with gray was slicked back with a liberal amount of pomade.

As he stuck out his hand, I noticed large turquoise and silver rings jammed onto all of his fingers. I wondered if he could even bend them. I took his hand, smiled and introduced myself. "Alysa Phillips," I said, surprised at the confidence in my voice. I was actually starting to get tired of my own name.

"Reginald Jefferson," my boss said, "but call me Reggie." His voice was a perfect match for his body. It was neither professional nor masculine. In fact, as I looked at him, I realized that every detail about him challenged all I'd hoped for in an editor.

"Let me give you a quick tour of the building," he said. We walked through the editorial room first, and Reggie introduced me to the reporter I'd seen before. "This is Bruce," he said. "He covers county government and the Bureau of Land Management."

Bruce still had the glazed look in his eyes as he stood to shake my hand. He mumbled a welcome and went back to his story. "The sports reporter sits here and the lifestyles editor, Renee, is over there," Reggie continued, pointing out two of the other desks in the room.

Then he moved to the last one. "And this is your desk. You cover the sheriff's office, the junior college, and the town of Grant." My desk was easily twice the size of any other desk in the room and reminded me vaguely of the spaceship command station in a science fiction movie.

Reggie said we'd finish the tour later since it was almost time for the weekly editorial meeting in the publisher's office. So he steered me toward another room and told me to take a seat. There were seven of us. The only other woman in the room, who I guessed to be Renee, was heavyset and in her early thirties with long, naturally curly hair and an orange skin glow that was probably from a bottle. She seemed eclectic but glamorous and motioned for me to sit next to her. "Thank goodness you're here," she breathed as soon as I sat down, leaning in to put her hand on my arm like we were old friends. "This much testosterone can't be good for a woman."

The publisher, Glen, was a thin intense man, bald except for a rim of brown-gray hair lining his dome of skin. I learned later that he always rubbed his head fiercely in frustration or excitement, and that he was always frustrated or excited about something—an armed robber, a hit-and-run accident, a brush fire, a Democrat coming to town, or a Little Miss beauty pageant. Glen grew even more frustrated and excited when the local radio stations picked up on the latest news before we did.

My first day at *Grant Gazette* was an initiation into this reality. Glen opened the meeting with, "We've been scooped!" Local stations had been covering the growing homeless population and stacks of angry letters about the problem covered his desk. What were we going to do about it? Everyone began to stare at their hands, shift through papers or furiously pretend to take notes. I quickly learned that this ritual was so we wouldn't have to face the disappointment in Glen's eyes. Letting our readers down was one thing; letting down the paper and Glen was something different altogether. "We have a solemn duty to provide Benton and Lapis Counties with news," he pounded into us at every Wednesday meeting. As reporters, we shared an unspoken need to gain—and to keep—Glen's approval. That atmosphere seemed eerily familiar.

"We've been scooped!" It was a statement that probably should have motivated me. Instead, it added a final brick to the load I was carrying. I went home and cried.

II

I decided to make it through one week in Arizona before killing myself. That way it could at least be said that I tried. Then I decided a week was too long. I'd survive one day. I'd smile at the right people and laugh at the right times, and then park my car straight in its parking space in front of my adobe house. I'd turn the lights off and slit my wrists. Or I'd tidy up the house and then drive my car off a cliff. Or I'd just drive and drive until I ran out of gas, and then wander around the desert until I collapsed.

One day is a long time. One day contains 1,440 minutes. One week is seven times that. I finally decided to survive one minute at a time. That was bearable.

I didn't know what was wrong with me when I got to Arizona. I thought I'd leave my darkness in Utah, but everywhere I turned I found it. I barely slept my entire first week. The muscles in my neck and back were so tight I couldn't find a comfortable position. Since I couldn't relax lying down, I spent nights sitting in my bed keeping time by listening for the hourly cargo trains. When the early light of dawn crept across my stone floor, I slept, but two hours later, I'd wake to a gripping panic attack. They greeted me every morning, threatening to choke the air from my lungs.

I lay in bed gasping, pushing silent screams out my throat until I could cough and roll out of bed. Only then would I be able to cry, as if the pain was great enough to stifle natural emotion.

My arrival in Arizona reminded me of a family trip to Disneyland when I was fourteen. The Space Mountain ride broke down while we were on it, and the overhead lights suddenly beamed on to illuminate the flimsy gyrating track, and stabilizing rods, on which our miniature space shuttle perched. The high-speed, futuristic, laser-flashing adventure was revealed as a stupid gymnasium-sized room full of metal tracks and strings of lights.

I had thought even the life of a small town reporter might be glamorous. But there I was, and there my life was, illuminated in the ugly light. Once that light went on, mud pies didn't look like chocolate anymore; ice cream was full of calories; people died when they got old; and sometimes children were robbed of their innocence and the chance to lead normal lives.

James seemed to represent the possibility of seeing that ugly reality and refusing it. The bearded transient, who spent his days on curbs by the mall weaving roses from palm leaves, was my first story assignment. His name, James Allen, was an alias he'd chosen when he took to street life. He'd accept donations of any size, including bus tickets. Every morning at precisely nine, James arrived to stake out a spot selected to intercept as many slow-moving cars as possible. He sat cross-legged all day, unobtrusively offering his roses to anyone who rolled down a car window. At exactly five p.m., James strapped on his backpack to make his way north of town, leaving only trampled weeds or a handful of wilting palm leaves on the side of the road. Somewhere across the river, he kept a campsite stocked with potatoes, beans, and rice. He never revealed exactly where it was, but I supposed he was near the natural hot springs.

His naturally dreaded hair and worn tunic testified that he belonged on the street, but the question the community raised was whether he belonged in the more upscale Oroya Valley. As Glen had informed us, letters had been pouring in to the *Gazette* from concerned tax-paying citizens who wanted the homeless cleared from their streets and their minds. I approached James where he sat on a bedroll next to a cardboard sign reading, "Handmade palm flowers. Spread love. Donations gratefully accepted." The majority of passing drivers gave him dirty looks and others called out, "Get a real job," but his facial expression remained one of complete serenity.

"Can I join you?" I asked. I towered over him, feeling awkward and overdressed.

Without a word, James pulled a horse blanket from his pack and spread it on the ground next to him. Then he bent his head down again to concentrate on his flower.

"I'm Alysa," I offered as I sat, wrapping my long skirt around my ankles. "I'm a reporter for the *Gazette* writing about the homeless population. Some people aren't happy with the situation, especially when they're trying to shop." I wanted James to know I wasn't numbered among those people, but I wasn't sure how to begin.

Although he couldn't have been more than thirty, James's face was much older. His two front teeth were crooked and half rotten and his skin was parched from sun and wind. He looked like he'd seen too much of the world, but he smiled pleasantly. "I'm a seeker of wisdom and a student of knowledge," he said. "I mind nobody's business but my own. Everything I own I can carry in my backpack or in my head."

His fingers didn't stop weaving while he spoke. They were chapped and rubbed roughly against the palm leaves with a scraping sound. "Homeless only means you don't own," James continued, apparently pleased to have such a rapt audience. "Buying and owning is a trap. First you think you need a house, so you buy a house. Then you have to buy furniture for the house, and insurance and utilities. It never ends. Those who own will always be afraid of people like me."

"But don't you ever want to own things?" I pressed. "Wouldn't you rather work for a living instead of surviving on donations?" Even as I asked these questions, I realized that I dreaded going back to the office. I hated daily chores and monthly bills.

A car stopped and a young girl held a bill out the window. James stood to replace the bill with a rose. "God bless," he said and then sat down again. "One of these days I'm going to follow Bob Dylan around or rewrite the Bible. Until then, this life has enough glamour for me. People are always telling me they wish they could do this. But there's nothing stopping them."

As I watched James's face, his features turned into David's. I saw him and Elidah asking for small donations—enough for a bus fare or a cup of hot soup to warm their fingers. "God doesn't want us to have money," David often said. "Money paves the path to greed and destruction." He also preached that the wealthy needed to witness the chasm between their lusty lifestyles and that of the street-dweller. It was good for them, he said, to see him bend over the embers of a gutter fire or scavenge through garbage cans.

David and Elidah spent their winter months boarding with families kind or naive enough to open their doors. People were especially generous during the Christmas holidays. David and Elidah often posed as Joseph and Mary on their way to Bethlehem; people love that kind of thing. David and Elidah would come home with pockets full of clinking change, but they wouldn't want more than that.

May and Dr. Adams didn't believe in currency either. Cold hard cash was the purest form of evil, Dr. Adams often said, the basis of every quarrel and all bloodshed. Plastic money didn't carry the same consequences. "The government has created a people dependant on currency. It, therefore, will pay the ultimate price." Dr. Adams taught that in the last days all unpaid bills would have to be settled by the corrupt government.

Although we weren't yet dressed in robes and scarves like David and Elidah, that day was always drawing nearer. David wanted Dr. Adams to set aside his worldly things and join him in his walk of faith. He preached at Dr. Adams, "The peoples of the earth stumble and grope in darkness at noonday, and the humble followers of

Christ suffer and mourn under the heavy hand of oppression, murder, secret crafts and arts, of secret governments and societies. False traditions and churches subject the whole earth to the iron yoke of bondage, misery and death. You are still in bondage. Let go of your belongings and follow me." In exchange for forfeiting our worldly goods, David would grant us complete forgiveness. Our sins would be white as snow, he promised.

As I looked at James that day, I regretted my decision of four years earlier not to make that leap David offered to us, that decision not to be cleansed. James's fingers kept moving, but his expression changed from serenity to concern. "Hey," he said. "Are you OK? You look pale."

I stared, lost in my reveries, as James's features morphed from David's back into his own. He was James, not David. I was in Arizona, not Utah. In rising panic, I stood up and began backing away, then turned and ran toward my car with James shouting after me, "Are you OK? Hey! What happened?" I didn't breathe easily until I was safely inside my car with all the doors locked.

"Ma'am?" A police officer was knocking on my car window. "Are you OK?"

I cracked the window open an inch. "I'm fine."

"Are you sure?" the officer persisted. "I saw you run to your car. What are you running from?"

"Nothing. I'm fine."

The officer scanned the parking lot, looked at me suspiciously and then shrugged. "OK," he said. "Have yourself a nice day."

I was terrified of policemen. The only time I was ever close to one was when I was watching Joel or one of his brothers get arrested, a common occurrence in the Adams family. I watched knife fights, plugged my ears during screaming and yelling, nursed various wounds, and stayed up all hours waiting for a chance to escape the house's chaos. That chance rarely came before the police did. The violence always happened in slow motion for me, and my memories of these times are hazy.

One of the worst fights happened one humid evening in June during a glow-in-the-dark parade at dusk. Floats and streamers of fluorescent pink, yellow and green stood out against the night sky. Children chased after handfuls of thrown candy or ran up to shake a clown's hand. Even the music seemed to glow in the dark. Joel and I zoomed around groups of people on our rollerblades, trying to keep our cotton candy from blowing off their paper sticks. We raced toward the city park and staked out a spot near the swings to wait for the fireworks.

"Joel!" someone called out as I fidgeted around. The blades made finding a comfortable sitting position on the grass nearly impossible. High-stepping across the lawn in rollerblades of their own were two of Joel's brothers and their wives.

"Hey! Come over here!" Joel hollered. "Alysa, scoot over so Matt and Reuben can sit down."

I moved to the edge of the growing group, wondering idly where James and Kristi were. Like them, Reuben and Hannah lived at the Adams house, though the two wives hated each other. The brothers had renovated their childhood bedrooms into dormitory-like dwellings. Instead of growing emptier as their children married, Dr. Adams and May's home grew more and more crowded. Matt and his wife Laura lived across town in an apartment of their own, though they frequented the house.

I lost myself in the fireworks for half an hour, until I felt a tug on my sleeve. Joel and his brothers stood above me. "Let's go," Joel said. "We want to avoid the traffic. We can see the grand finale from my house." I struggled to my feet though everything below my ankles was numb. Following them, I tripped and tumbled several times before the sensation of pins and needles subsided. But Joel and I quickly bladed the eight blocks to his house, beating the others.

As we bounced through the door, trying to unhook our rollerblades at the same time, we heard Kristi yelling from the couch for James to bring her some ice cream. "You can't have sugar," he yelled back from the kitchen. "You'll screw up the baby."

I'd learned not to interrupt arguments in the Adams house. I glanced at Joel and we skirted the living room to finish easing off our rollerblades on the stairs. The front door banged open again as the two other couples spilled through the doorway, tangled together and laughing, the girls sporting glow-in-the-dark bracelets.

"I could have taken you if it weren't for these lame-ass skates," Matt told Reuben.

"Right," Reuben shot back. "It's equipment failure. I beat you and you know it. Just admit it."

Matt tossed his skates into a corner and jumped down the eight steps to the basement, landing on the red shag carpet in front of the TV. He pulled out joysticks and a mess of wires from a cabinet as he flipped the TV on. "Hey, I'll take you in a game of Command and Conquer," he challenged Reuben.

"You're on!" Reuben catapulted himself downstairs next to Matt. Hannah and Laura rolled their eyes at each other and moved toward the kitchen together.

Suddenly Matt's voice thundered through the house. "Who's the bitch that messed with my game station?" The hush in the wake of his voice was unsettling. Matt bounded back up the stairs into the living room and stopped only inches from Kristi, yelling, "You trashed my system!"

Kristi put her arms in front of her face and began to cry. Infuriated, Matt turned toward the kitchen, nearly bumping into James, who was on his way to the living room. "Your stupid wife has been in my stuff again," Matt shouted.

The two men were so close that if it weren't for their defensive stances, they could have been about to embrace. James was the

163

shorter of the two and moved slower, but he was stockier and quicker to lose his temper. He stretched an arm behind him, groping the kitchen counter until his hand found a butcher knife. When he wielded it in front of him, Matt backed up, hands in the air. James still advanced. "What'd you call my wife?" he demanded.

"She's a whore," Matt said, one eye on the menacing blade. "You could've done better. Why'd you settle for a wench like her?"

Kristi spat, "Look who's talking! You're lucky Laura stays with you. Did you tell her what you and Lindsey did in Reuben's bed?" Matt turned toward Kristi with a hand poised to slap her.

We all knew about Lindsey. Matt had an affair with her while married to his first wife, and she got pregnant. Matt refused to divorce his wife and marry her, saying instead that he wanted Lindsey as a sister-wife. She was furious and the baby was stillborn. Matt took Lindsey to court and tried to sue her for the death of their child, claiming that she made herself sick and killed the baby on purpose. He lost the case and Lindsey disappeared.

With a controlled effort, Matt lowered his hand, leaving a void where we expected the sound of flesh on flesh. Kristi snickered. Matt suddenly shoved Kristi, who fell headfirst down the flight of stairs. She curled up at the bottom moaning, hands on her abdomen.

James looked at his wife and then turned on Matt, his face red with fury, screaming, "You killed my baby!" His knuckles were white from gripping the knife, and the blade flashed as he lunged toward Matt.

"Good riddance!" Matt shot back as he ducked from the blade. "The only thing worse than that cow is her baby."

James lunged again while Matt raised his hands into a Kung Fu stance and began circling his brother.

Laura screamed, "I'm calling the police!" In her haste she knocked the phone from its cradle and had to crawl among the recliners in front of the TV to retrieve it. The three tones as she pressed 9-1-1 rang through the house.

When the two officers arrived five minutes later, things had calmed down. James had put the knife away, and everyone stood around awkwardly. I hadn't moved at all. I was still sitting on the stairs, but my socks were neatly rolled down on my ankles and my rollerblades stood symmetrically next to me on the carpet. I'd arranged and rearranged them repeatedly, thinking that if only I was organized enough, I could withdraw from the chaos around me. I tried to blend into the wallpaper, wanting desperately to be anywhere else, but I didn't have my shoes and I couldn't get out the front door without passing James and Matt.

When the officers stepped through the partly opened door, I saw that the sky was black. No one spoke for a minute, but then everyone began at once. One officer watched carefully as the other pulled a notepad from his breast pocket and started talking. "Who called 9-1-1?" he asked. Laura waved at the cop. "You, tell me what happened," he demanded.

"James got jealous and pulled a knife on Matt," she said innocently.

"You whore!" James roared, lunging at her.

The officer dropped his notepad and put a hand on James's chest. "This is a warning, sir," he said. "No more outbursts."

He retrieved his notepad and turned back to Laura. The other officer put his hands on James's shoulders. "Take it easy, buddy," he soothed.

Laura stuck her tongue out at James, who lashed out, elbowing the cop in the stomach. The cop tightened his grip on James's shoulders as he bent to catch his breath. James turned with his fist aimed at the officer's mouth. In an instant he was on the floor. The officer had a knee in his back and yanked his hands behind him, securing them in handcuffs.

"That's enough of that," he said through clenched teeth. James struggled on the ground until the officer pulled him to his feet and hauled him toward the door. At the same time, he called for backup from a radio hanging by a cord from his shoulder.

Matt told the remaining officer in a steady voice, "He has an anger management problem."

As he glared at Matt, the cop said, "I'm not through with you." He shut his notepad and shot a look of disgust around the room, then helped wrestle James out the door and into the patrol car. Out the open door, I could see all the neighbors watching from their front porches. It reminded me of something I'd seen on Jerry Springer—trashy women fighting over their no-good men. *I'm part of this now,* I thought. *This is going to be my family.*

I never returned to the mall to speak to James Allen but I did frequently deal with his kin. The Oroya Valley was a magnet for homeless people. With so many natural hot springs and land available for free camping, it was an ideal spot for the vagrant crowd to congregate. In time, I got used to their religious meanderings and preachings, but I never got used to their sexual aggressiveness. Homeless men in the Oroya Valley wanted two things—a hot meal and copulation. Every time I passed one, he inevitably asked for both. A tin cup held the day's income, but he was constantly ready to grab his backpack and bedroll and head into the desert for a quick romp.

Dr. Adams was always taking me aside to offer sexual enlightenment to me; I think he knew I had a deep fear of sex and took it upon himself to prepare me for life in the cult. "God made us man and woman for an eternal purpose," he taught. "He made us unique, yet as compatible as puzzle pieces. Men were created to be in power and we were created to be satisfied by more than one woman. Biologically, one woman cannot meet all of a man's sexual needs, so God instituted plural marriage."

At some level that made sense. The only thing Joel ever talked about was sex. The only thing James, Matt, and Reuben ever talked about was sex. How could one woman keep up with all that demand? Besides, women were created to give birth. "Once you are pregnant," Dr. Adams explained, "Joel will have to go elsewhere for sexual fulfillment. You can't expect to satisfy him while you're nourishing his child. That's why there are more righteous, faithful women than there are men."

Dale Hanlin seemed to confirm Dr. Adams's teachings on the needs of men. He had called me at the *Gazette* because he'd been fired from the local community college after thirty years. He claimed the firing was due to his appearance and he invited me to his house to conduct an interview. His wife Liz sat with us. Sporting waist-length, greasy gray hair and a stiff handlebar mustache, it's true that Dale didn't fit the stereotype of a small-town college. "I was wrongfully terminated," he said over and over while the sweet smoke from his pipe made me woozy.

Within ten minutes, instead of hearing about the college, I was being tutored about Dale's strange desert cult. What is it, I wondered, that turns a rational human being into someone who relies on revelation from an unknown God to dictate his actions? What is it that entices a person to seek spiritual guidance through drugs or sex or records played backward?

Dale puttered around his house talking as overgrown orchids tinged the room with a green light. His tune was a familiar one. During the two hours I spent in his living room, breathing in the sweet marijuana, he spoke about the body being a temple and God wanting us to use our bodies to create beautiful art. "Sex is a creative thing," he said. "Especially between more than two people."

The cult's circle of worshippers, of course, was a state-wide group of adult swingers who never exchanged names or phone numbers. All business was conducted through email and no two nights were ever the same. The only rule outside of sworn secrecy was that art was best created when three or more artists collaborated.

I was beginning to suspect that I'd be unlikely to find a good story for the paper there, but I was waiting for a signal that Dale was done with the interview. Then he paused, looking me over, and said, "You seem to be artistically inclined. Would you like to experiment with Liz and me?"

I pictured the three of us naked in Dale's bed making art for each other and wanted to vomit. I said, "I'm here as a reporter. How could you ask me something like that?"

"There's just something about you," Dale said. "I don't know, a look in your eyes, the way you carry yourself . . . something that calls to me." I'd heard that before. In fact, Joel had said the same thing. There was something about me that solicited the insane, the unstable, and the religiously perverse.

Dale tried to reassure me, "It's all confidential. No one will ever know who or what you are, outside of the circle. If we like the music we make together, I can sign you up." Dale was practically pulling me toward his bedroom by that point. "If it's as beautiful as I think it will be, we can do it again. We can be partners and offer our goods elsewhere."

I separated myself from Dale's grip and sidled toward the front door, racking my brain for a neutral way of leaving the house without hurting his feelings. But unable to come up with anything, I finally decided my top priority was to leave. "I have another interview," I said. "I have to go."

"I'll call you later," Dale promised as I bolted out the front door.

At home later that night, I tried to process what had happened, studying my face in the bathroom mirror for a clue to what people saw as an invitation. My white young face stared back at me until the shapes didn't make sense and the bump in my forehead bulged forward. Then I took a knife and made three small parallel cuts on the inside of my left wrist. It had been more than a year since I'd last cut myself, and reintroducing the blade to my skin simultaneously produced thrill and a sense of guilt.

The knife sliced easily into my skin. I had to control the force to keep from cutting too deep. Like an alcoholic who sips a beer after years of being sober, the old desire flooded back into me. I wanted to cut through the tissues and veins, expose the layers of skin and taste the blood. I put the knife into the sink and went to bed trembling, leaving the blood to dry into three straight lines, like tally marks during a game of tic-tac-toe.

Cutting was a game I'd missed, and the notches carved into my skin beckoned me back for another round. I would go slowly, I decided. I would cut only when I needed to, and this time I would make sure no one found out.

12

In Southeast Arizona the sun rises and sets on men and women who give their lives to farming, ranching, or mining. Its shifting seasons can be calculated by watching changes in the cotton fields. Winter is marked by squares of hard, gray land covered with the dying remains of last year's crop and separated by fences, ditches, and roads. During early spring, farmers begin tilling and turning the fresh red-brown soil to form long furrows. Throughout summer water seeps through the furrows on a strict schedule determined by county water rights laws. The plants that survive the fierce heat produce dozens of prickly balls in the fall. Cotton blows all over the county, sticking to shrubs, tires and window screens. It's the closest thing to snow residents of Grant will ever see.

The ranchers are up with the sun every day, mucking, feeding, and tending to their livestock. Nearby ranches lure retired folks from all over the country—people with more time than money, who want to live the last years of their lives in the Sonoran climate. They generally care for goats, horses, cattle, and birds. More serious ranchers breed cattle and horses and wear Stetson hats as they prod their herds from field to field, counting heads and watching for signs of deadly viruses. Commercial ranches dot the land and draw vacationers who grew up with a vague desire to live on a farm, or who want to play out fantasies of being a cowboy in the old West.

To a miner, sunlight doesn't matter. Miners from Grant rise in the middle of the night to carpool to a mine near the New Mexico border. The mine never closes and workers spend their ten-hour shifts in underground darkness. They work four days underground and then get three days of light, and the copper is extracted in a continuous flow into train cars to be shipped all over the world.

There's a fourth industry in Grant, too, though it's not spoken of as much—state and federal correctional institutions. Both prisons are overcapacity with inmates. A fifth and correlative industry is breaking the law to earn room and board at the facilities. The reporter I was replacing apparently knew that life well.

"Joe worked at the *Gazette* for almost twelve years," Renee told me during my first slow afternoon. She was listening to the police scanner and I was waiting for a call. Glen and Reggie had taken a late lunch and the editorial room was empty. "He was in and out of jail all the time for dealing meth."

I asked in amazement, "And he kept his job?"

Renee shrugged. "He was a good reporter. Well, except when he was gone for months at a time. Then I had to pick up his beats."

"What finally happened?"

"I'm not sure." Renee pushed off from her desk and rolled her chair toward me. She lowered her voice. "All I know is that Reggie spent a lot of time last month at the courthouse looking through police logs. There were a lot of drug busts reported but few arrests. The nearest I can tell, Joe had struck a deal with the sheriff's office. He wrote what they wanted him to write and he and his friends were exempt from arrest."

I didn't have to fake my naiveté. I asked, "What do you mean, writing what they wanted him to write?"

Renee looked at me. "Not all cops are good cops." Wheeling her chair back toward her desk, she added, "Sometimes it pays to cover your butt, on either side of the law. I think Joe found that out fast." Almost as an afterthought she said, "You're going to have a tough job replacing Joe on the sheriff's beat. That relationship was twelve years strong."

171

Bad relationships between reporters and law enforcement are historic, and that wasn't something I was interested in changing. My first professional encounter came shortly after the conversation with Renee. Monday morning started with a fax coming in from the sheriff's office, followed seconds later by a phone call patched through to my desk. My phone rang as Reggie approached me, slapping the fax down in front of me. "This is your beat," he said. "Looks like it could be breaking news."

He swiveled on one foot and walked back to his office, but still peered at me through the dirty window that separated his office from ours. Mondays were set aside for putting the newspaper together and only breaking news was allowed into the office. When I picked up the phone, a voice announced into my ear, "This is Undersheriff Stan Brindamour. The sheriff wants to see you immediately. Bring the press release he just faxed."

I nervously grabbed my notebook and camera and headed out for the sheriff's office. In the reception area, a woman with frizzy red hair sprouting from her head in all directions sat behind a bullet-proof window. She slid the window open a crack. "Can I help you?"

I stuttered, "I'm here to see the sheriff."

"You're from the *Gazette*?" Without waiting for an answer, she said, "The sheriff's in the basement, next to the jail. He's expecting you."

There were two doors in the basement, one of them metal and barred. I knocked on the other one and an officer let me in and guided me to the end of a short hallway, knocked on the door, opened it and stuck his head in. "The reporter from the *Gazette* is here," he said before turning to me. "Go ahead, they're ready."

The bareness of the small room surprised me. There were no windows and the only furnishings were an old desk and a few scattered chairs. Two large muscular men sat with their feet propped on the desk, but both stood when I entered.

"I'm Sheriff Mark Moneza," the heavier one said, "and this is

172

Undersheriff Stan Brindamour. Thanks for coming."

The sheriff, who wore the star-shaped badge on his vest, talked from only one corner of his mouth, which hid beneath a droopy mustache. As I later learned, Sheriff Moneza was recovering from Bell's Palsy and the entire left side of his face was paralyzed. Stan Brindamour was shorter and thinner, but no less muscular. The sheriff motioned for me to sit and Mr. Brindamour pulled out a tape recorder and a stack of papers.

"We had a good relationship with your predecessor, Joe, and we hope to continue that with you," Sheriff Moneza said in a tone of authority. "I need the paper's help to catch a cattle poacher. I want to offer a reward of $2,500 to anyone with information leading to the arrest of the responsible party."

I nodded, opened my notebook and began writing.

"In two instances, nine cows were shot and killed last week," the sheriff said when I'd finished. "I've assigned Stan here to the investigation." He leaned back in his chair when he spoke, pressing his index fingers into a point that prodded his upper lip between sentences.

"Most of the cattle have gunshot wounds to the abdomen and chest, but at least one rancher reported wounds to the head," the sheriff continued. "Last night a rancher called in and said four cows and one calf had been shot to death on his ranch on Brooks Road. Seventy-eight spent .22-caliber casings and three live rounds were found near the cows."

I wrote furiously before looking up. "Where's Brooks Road?"

"East of Grant, past the state prison," Mr. Brindamour said. "But that wasn't the only ranch hit this week." His feet dug into the floor and his face gradually reddened in anger as the sheriff began to speak.

"Another rancher reported two dead cows last week," the sheriff said. "One cow had been dead three or four days when he found it. It had numerous gunshot holes in the torso. The other cow was found in the middle of a nearby water hole."

Mr. Brindamour broke in, his voice loud with anger. "A .22 doesn't kill immediately. Injured cows often move toward water and wander for days before they die." He pounded the desk with a clenched fist. "These are random acts of violence against defenseless animals."

I avoided his eyes and scribbled in my notebook. "What kind of charges would come against a poacher?"

Sheriff Moneza was still calm. "Illegal killing of livestock is a felony offense," he said. "An individual convicted of the crime can be sentenced to two and a half years in prison and a fine of three times the value of the cattle."

"What kind of a person would kill livestock?" I asked.

Mr. Brindamour leapt to his feet and practically yelled, "This is the work of a sick, malicious person. We will bring this person to justice."

During his outburst, I'd unconsciously moved my chair back until it bumped against the wall. I waited for the air to settle and then brought the interview to a close. "Thank you for your time," I mumbled, inching toward the door.

"No, thank you for coming, and for doing the article," Sheriff Moneza said sincerely. "I think this can be the beginning of a good relationship." Mr. Brindamour nodded his agreement and opened the door for me.

I looked back just before I left the building. The two men were still standing outside the door watching me. I waved awkwardly before the door slammed shut behind me.

I once watched a young cow die. The humiliated animal was shot to death after a rodeo in Utah. Thick red blood oozed from the bullet hole as the calf lay dying in the dust behind the barn. For months afterwards, I saw that hole and the worn and bewildered look of the calf every time I closed my eyes.

I'd gone to the rodeo with Joel after we were engaged. It was his father's idea; he bought the tickets and accompanied us. It was the first time I'd been so close to large animals. Dr. Adams also brought May along. She drifted around the grounds like a ghost with vacant eyes, startling people with her sudden appearances and disappearances. "Watch the animals," she said in her small raspy voice as we took our front-row seats. "You can learn a lot from the way they act."

The energy of the restless livestock mixed with the hunger of the crowd, causing a general air of anticipation. The rodeo started just before sundown with music blaring from speakers mounted on poles. Girls in short skirts and sashes that glittered with rhinestones and sequins rode bareback into the arena. The horses' hooves kicked up mud and manure as they paraded around, stimulated by deafening applause and the sting of the girls' spurs on their flanks.

All I knew about rodeos came from magazine advertisements, which usually showed a man in boots and spurs, hand wrapped around the leather of the reins. He hung on with one hand atop a bucking bronco. The other hand was always straight up in the air, symbolizing victory over the animal's will. Despite my unfamiliarity with rodeo, the mood was contagious. I found myself on my feet with the rest of the crowd, cheering riders on as they introduced the evening's agenda.

"First event, bull riding," a man called over the loudspeaker.

With a clang, a metal gate opened and a snorting animal wedged itself into a metal stall. A tall, calm rider mounted its shoulders while it was held unmoving. A bell rang and the gate in front of the bull disappeared. The rider dug his heals into the bull's sides and they shot out into the muddy arena. I held my breath for the next eight seconds. Man and beast moved as one, hurtling, thrusting, and gyrating in some crazily choreographed dance. The man's body turned into rubber as he moved with the bull, his face a mask of determination and terror.

Then it was over. The man lost his grip and launched from the bull's shoulders through the air and into the muck with a thud. He got to his feet slowly. The bull panted and the stands rang with whistling and stomping. A young boy entered the arena to guide the exhausted bull back to its stall. The other cowboys welcomed the rider with high-fives and pats on the back as he stiffly scaled the fence and took his seat. I watched him wipe his sweat and dirt onto his jeans and imitated him, wiping my own sweaty palms against my thighs, surprised at the relief I felt.

"That was great, wasn't it?" Joel yelled. He was on his feet, clapping, and his eyes shone with excitement.

Before I had a chance to respond, the next rider was ready, the bell rang, and everything started over. Entranced, I couldn't pull my eyes from the scene in front of me. The rodeo was exciting and gruesome at the same time. I wanted to hide under the bleachers and wait for the noise to stop, for the sounds of heaving, squealing animals to end, but I couldn't stop watching. It was as if the very act of watching kept everything in balance. I was almost sure that if I didn't keep my eyes on the action, something terrible would happen.

As daylight faded, humming halogen bulbs flickered on. Shadows to add depth to the faces in the crowd were eerily absent in the false light, adding to my sense of unease. Pairs of riders were roping cattle. The first rider aimed his rope for the head and the second roped the hind legs, pulling them out from under the calf. For an instant, the calf was strung above the ground between the ropes, and then it slid into the mud. The event was nearly over when the gate opened in front of a particularly feisty calf. A bell rang and it bolted from its stall. Riders and horses stood restlessly, awaiting their signal.

"Come on, come on," Joel chanted in time with the rest of the crowd. The metal bleachers were a drum for the steady rhythm of stomping feet. The very air seemed to surge with energy.

"It's not fair," I tried to tell Joel. "They're giving that calf a sense of freedom only to rope and humiliate it." Joel paid no attention to me.

A second bell rang. The riders took off in pursuit, ropes spiraling through the air above them. Without warning, the calf ground to a halt and then headed straight for the riders. Caught off guard, the first rider reined his horse to a stop and clumsily hurtled his rope toward the calf's head. It landed harmlessly in the mud. Then— startlingly—the calf charged. In a single violent effort, it rammed into the horse's left front leg. The arena was silent. The liquid sound of flesh colliding with flesh was almost tangible as the animals collapsed into each other.

Everything happened in slow motion. The horse toppled into the mud, the rider still perched on top. The calf cried as it wobbled to its feet and then stumbled around dizzily. The crowd was on its feet with a single, multitudinous gasp, booing the animals and calling encouragement to the rider as he disentangled himself from the knot of broken limbs.

The halogen light transformed the arena into a dream world. Natural colors were washed out and everything shone with larger-than-life translucence. I stared at the people around me, searching for something real, for an explanation behind the raw bawling sound of the injured calf. My heart made that same sound and it began to echo in my head. Faint, I grabbed at Joel's hand.

That was the first time I knew something was wrong. He looked at me with a mixture of pity and disgust. His eyes, instead of offering compassion, grew full of hunger. I dropped his hand. "I'll be back," I said. "I need some air." I staggered through the crowd and out of the arena.

Steadying myself with one hand on the fence, I made my way toward the back. Once there, I ran until I couldn't hear the noise of the crowd or the crying of the calf. I ran half a mile before I stopped, gasping for breath, at a small cluster of barns where restless livestock snorted and pawed the ground. That's when I noticed I was crying, too. I wiped angrily at my eyes and turned toward the distant light of the arena. Joel was approaching, silhouetted against the night. When he reached me, he pulled me into his arms. I let him lead me into the looming darkness of the nearest barn.

"I followed you," he stated obviously.

I looked into his eyes and saw that the hungry look was gone, but I didn't recognize what was in its place. I pulled back.

Joel asked softly, "You know why the calf acted that way, don't you?" When I was quiet he continued, "It's because cows are red meat. They're violent by nature and have to be forced into submission." When he talked his face became animated and he seemed distant, almost like he was back in the arena tying down a calf himself. I took a step backward, but his grip tightened around me.

He asked harshly, "Have you been eating red meat?" I could feel his warm breath on my cheek. Goose bumps pricked up on my arms and I struggled against his grasp. "Answer my question," he demanded.

"I . . . I don't know what you mean," I stammered.

My ignorance infuriated him. "Red meat makes people violent, too," he said. "Then someone has to force them to submit."

He clenched my wrists and twisted them sharply. I whimpered in pain as he forced me first to my knees, and then pushed my head down to the ground, positioning his knee between my shoulder blades. I cowered beneath him. My heart was beating so hard I could taste its blood. The cool, loose dirt was soft on my cheek. The thick smell of manure and the cooling night air filled my nostrils. It was a smell that, at any other time, might have been sweet.

With one hand around my neck and the other tangled in my hair, Joel flipped my body over. I let myself go limp like a rag doll in the hands of a spoiled child. With his hands encircling my arms, Joel pinned me again to the dirt. Then he dug his fingernails into the softness of the insides of my wrists as he lowered himself on top of me. The air rushed from my stomach in a gasp, startling me. I stopped breathing.

Joel pressed his mouth, cold and hard, over mine. His lips were familiar but his violent kiss was one of deep, unsatisfied hunger. He forced his tongue into my mouth. I choked and turned away. He moved his hands callously across my body, teasing and caressing my skin. I lay still. *So this is how it's going to happen,* I thought. *If I don't do something, he's going to rape me.*

But I couldn't make my mouth move. Instead, I thought about our wedding plans. I remembered the sound my wedding dress made as it brushed the floor while I twirled in front of the boutique mirror and later, when I modeled it for my father. I pictured myself with Joel, hand-in-hand in the years ahead. I saw myself greeting him when he returned from work, falling asleep in his arms, waking with my head resting on his chest. I thought about our children and the tender way we'd raise them.

A twig snapped. Even in the softness of the dirt and hay outside the barn, the footstep was audible. As suddenly as it had started, the violence was over. As Joel yanked me to my feet, he said into my ear, "I'm no better than you if I take you this way."

My hands stung and I rubbed my wrists to start the blood flowing again. I staggered, and then followed Joel to the door of the barn. He didn't touch me. A man was guiding a truck with a trailer as it backed toward the barn. In the trailer, the injured horse lay silent and dejected on its side, his broken leg sticking unnaturally into the air. The bone protruded through the skin and shone white in the moonlight. The horse's other legs convulsed irregularly, clattering against the trailer bed. The smell of blood stung my nostrils.

On the opposite side of the trailer was the calf, bound together with cord. It whimpered, kicking at the side of the trailer, hooves scraping metal.

The truck eased to a stop just feet from where Joel and I stood in the darkness of the barn, and the horse raised its head. Its eyes were vacant like it was already dead, or had at least resigned itself to its fate. The night was suddenly alive as four or five men appeared and circled the trailer. Some had flashlights and all seemed eager for blood. One jumped onto the trailer and started nudging the horse and the calf with the toe of his boot. The impact made soft, sickening thuds, and the men joked about the injured animals.

"He moves slower than your mother did last night," one of them called to the man on the trailer.

"Shut up, Ned," the man snarled, kicking the horse again. It raised its head and tore at the slippery metal with its feet as it pushed itself off the bed and into the dirt.

The driver got out of the truck with a rifle. I recognized him as the horse's rider. I'd last seen him in a twisted heap in the middle of the arena. The man slammed the cab door and walked to the back of the truck. "Hurry up, Dick," he called to the man on the trailer.

"Sure, boss," Dick said. He nudged the horse in the dirt one last time and went back for the calf.

The boss cocked his rifle and took aim at an imaginary target in the distance. "Pow," he said, jerking his head back. "Right between the eyes." Then he aimed at the horse and shot it twice in the head. The sound of the shot bounced off the back of the barn wall and hit me in the back, reverberating in my head. I put my hands over my ears too late and watched in horror as blood filled the holes in the horse's head and spilled to the ground. His eyes had been closed and he hadn't moved. He'd given up before he'd even had a chance.

The calf was next. Two men picked it up by its feet, still bound together, and laid it struggling and crying against the dead horse. Its eyes, wide and fearful, flickered in the glare from the flashlights as the man took aim. "Come on, give it to the bastard," someone said.

My hands still over my ears, I watched the man aim the barrel right between the calf's eyes, watched like someone watches a train wreck, unable to take my eyes off the crazy half-lit scene. The moment stretched on and on until I was sure the man had changed his mind. Then he shot, hitting the calf right where he'd aimed. The bawling stopped mid-squeal like an interrupted sentence. Thick blood oozed from the wound like toothpaste in a heavy, coagulated string, but the eyes stayed open, staring at me.

"Bastard," the man said, and he kicked the dead calf. "He cost me a horse and the chance to go to state." He kicked the calf again, harder. The men piled silently back into the truck without a single backward glance at the carnage. They left the dead animals sprawled out in the open like little boys leaving their broken, forgotten toys.

Joel still hadn't touched me. I stared at the dead calf as its eyes started to glaze over, and wondered idly what its last thought had been. Joel finally nudged me and motioned with his head toward the arena. The blues, reds and greens of fireworks were lighting up the black air. I hadn't noticed. The cheeriness of the arena was a rude and confusing contrast as I followed my boyfriend to his car.

Later that night I lowered myself into the bathtub. Ugly black, blue, red and green bruises were forming on my arms and my hips. I could still feel Joel's rough hands moving across my bare skin, his taste in my mouth. I gagged, wanting to scrub until the dirty, betrayed layer of skin peeled off, until I could no longer feel Joel on me or even remember lying under his gaze.

I picked up a razor and pressed my finger to it. A bright red drop of blood formed next to my fingernail and trickled down to my wrist. I put the blade against the inside of that wrist, on the spot where Joel had dug his fingers into the soft flesh. Then I pushed in.

I read once that when a person bleeds in the bathtub, the water turns pink. It must take a lot of blood to make pink water. All I got was a sick shade of orange. I watched the blood fill the thin red cut, then bubble and spill over the side. I turned my arm from side to side, making the rivulets of pain cascade over my hand, dripping off the points of my fingers into the water. When I got tired of watching, I grabbed a wad of toilet paper and pressed it to my wrist to make the bleeding stop. Then I put a Band-Aid over it and went to bed.

13

One mistake I made in Grant was living alone. Although I didn't really have any choice in the matter, my living situation became something of a final step toward insanity. Too much empty space surrounded me, and with nothing for company except my own thoughts, my demons grew. Like harmless hand puppets magnified by candlelight until the shadows rage in colossal proportions on opposing walls, my thoughts and emotions became fiends towering over me in my empty house.

Too much space had a claustrophobic effect on me. With the high, slightly domed ceilings of the adobe house, my monsters multiplied, crowding me. I started spending a lot of time in the grocery store a block from my house. Walking the fluorescent aisles and bumping elbows with other shoppers gave me the illusion that I wasn't alone. I made grocery lists every day, limiting what I bought so I'd have something to put on my list the next day. Those nightly visits became the first stable ground I found in Arizona.

At night when I couldn't sleep, I sometimes crept from my bed and dialed the number for the *The Hampshire Examiner* in Massachusetts. I craved the grainy sound of the secretary's recorded voice as she announced that the office was closed, but I could leave a message for any of the departments by pressing its corresponding number. Then she read a list of employees and I cried. Even unfamiliar names caused my heart to tremble with loneliness. Since starting the cutting again, I lost control, frequently slicing dozens of times up and down the inside of my arm until finally the outer pain reflected the inner pain. Then I'd toss the blood-lined blade into the kitchen sink on my way to the bathroom to bandage the wounds.

Before I could kill myself, I met Neil Sicora. He entered my life twice in a strange, coincidental twist that forged a crucial turning point. Neil was the kind of person either born with a kindred spirit, or one who'd done so much damage to the human race that he constantly had to give back to alleviate his own guilt. Either way, Neil entered my life when I was spinning dizzily ever closer to the cliff, and he pulled me to relative safety.

I first met him when I went to the state prison to interview the warden about rising inmate populations. Neil worked as information technology specialist at the prison. The door to his office opened into a busy hallway in the administration building, just inside the rows of chain link fences topped with wicked spirals of barbed wire. The warden was on a conference call when I arrived so Neil pulled me into his untidy office. A plaque that read "Computer Geek" sat on his dinged-up desktop.

Though I'd just met him, he asked from across his desk, "What are you running from? I've been working with inmates for twenty years and I recognize fear when I see it. You have that deer-in-headlights look about you."

"I'm not running," I said, and I meant it. It hadn't yet occurred to me that I was using geography to escape.

"Where are you going?" he asked. "I mean, what are your future plans?"

In the void left by Neil's question, I realized I had no future plans; my goal when I moved to Grant was to survive, nothing more. I had no short-term goals and I had no long-term goals. I was so busy surviving every minute that I forgot about the rest of my life.

A head covered with shiny black curls poked into the room. It was the warden. "You from the newspaper?" he jabbed at me.

184

"Yes."

"Come in," he said, motioning with a beefy arm for me to follow. The door swung shut behind us and a thick carpet met my feet. The interior of the warden's office was lavish, and his demeanor almost theatrical. He belonged in that office and he knew it. He waved me into a stuffy chair across a highly polished desk. I knew I'd see my reflection in it, so I didn't look down. Then the warden eased himself into an armchair opposite me, squeezing his frame into a space that looked entirely too small. He clasped thick sausage fingers together into a ball on the desk, leaving oil on the polished top. I figured his secretary would be in to wipe it clean again after I left.

"Let's talk about the inmate problem," he said. "Afterward, if you want, I'll take you on a tour."

Bailing Joel and his brothers out of the county jail was the closest I'd gotten to seeing the inside of a prison. Joel got arrested for traffic violations, refusing to pay sales tax, and arguing. His brothers were arrested for assault and bribery, and Dr. Adams was arrested for fraud and tax violations. I had my hands full bailing everyone out.

Joel always accused me of flirting with policemen when I went to bail them out. "That cop wanted you," he'd taunt in a mean jealous voice when I presented an officer with a stack of crisp bills. "What did you do, screw him while I was in jail? I get locked up for two days and you're having sex with everything in pants!"

I wished I'd had the nerve to leave Joel in there at least once. But when I ran out of money, I started getting cash advances on my credit cards to help bail them out.

I watched Joel rack up tens of thousands on his credit cards. When he reached the limit on one, he'd simply apply for another. He had more than a dozen of the plastic rectangles spurting from his wallet. "Buy now, pay later," he sang.

I rarely saw my parents spend money, and when they did it was in a restricted and cautious way. Watching Joel frivolously spend his imaginary money was thrilling. I envied him. So when my six-dollars-an-hour job didn't supply enough money, and Joel insisted I use credit cards as well, I did. I was still trying to pay them off in Arizona. I later learned that when Joel's debt finally caught up with him, he declared bankruptcy and joined the Army, leaving his wife and child to fend for themselves. His father, on the other hand, tried to defend his monetary approach in court. It was one of the last things he did.

I was curious to see the inside of the prison—curious about the conditions in which Joel might have survived if I'd had the courage to turn him in. As I toured the prison at the warden's elbow, I imagined Joel in an orange jumpsuit lounging on a cot. A tiny locker at the foot of his bed contained his few belongings, and a TV was his only company. The facility was for minimum security prisoners—white collar criminals, drug offenders, and inmates finishing the last months of longer sentences. I wondered where rapists were kept.

"We are definitely overcrowded and understaffed," the warden was saying. "We have nearly five thousand inmates, and not nearly enough correctional officers to maintain the level of safety we need."

The cots, two to a cubicle, spanned the length of the dormitories. Forty or fifty inmates bunked in each room in the units, and most seemed upbeat. Several of them threw out low cat calls as I walked through their living quarters. When I edged closer to the warden, he smiled and teased, "They don't bite." Several inmates laughed. Embarrassed, I backed off. "Hey, I didn't mean you had to do that," the warden said chuckling. I took out my notebook and pretended to write.

At home that evening, I double-checked the dead bolt on my front door. Then I shut myself into the back bedroom, locking that door, too. Then I went into the closet and closed that door. It seemed I couldn't get enough closed doors between myself and the memory of the orange-clad inmates leering at me. I thought I saw Joel's face among the crowd, and I pushed myself into the far corner of the closet, wrapping my arms around my legs.

My shoulder and neck muscles screamed and my fingers began to go numb. When the left side of my face started to throb and I knew I was losing the battle, I stretched out on the floor and cried until I fell asleep. I woke exhausted, and the exhaustion grew during the day until I could barely stand without wavering. I went home early and crawled into bed, willing myself to sleep before the silence and emptiness of my apartment overwhelmed me.

The next morning, my legs wouldn't move and the room spun every time I turned my head. I stumbled into the kitchen and called the office. "I'm sick," I told Reggie when he answered.

"What's wrong? If you're not dying, I need you in the office."

Despair bogged me down. I wasn't dying but I could barely move. If I didn't get to work, I might lose my job. If I couldn't pay rent, I'd have to go back to Utah. Dread swam in a cold lump from my stomach up to my throat. I swallowed it. "I'm dizzy," I explained. "I'm sick to my stomach and I'm really tired."

"Get in to the doctor," Reggie instructed. "I need you to bring me a doctor's note if you want to take time off."

The diagnosis was stress. "Take a couple of days off," the doctor said. "Get your feet back on the ground before you try to go back to work." He wrote on his prescription pad, "Please excuse Alysa from work. She's sick." He ripped the page from his pad and handed it to me. The simplicity of the whole thing depressed me. He wrote seven words that relieved my responsibility to the *Gazette* and granted me safety. I began to cry.

The doctor yanked a tissue from a box near the sink and handed it to me. He was a tall, thin man with sandy brown hair. He was young—about ten years older than I was—and he seemed genuinely concerned. I couldn't look him in the eye. "Are you OK?" he asked when I was done crying.

I sniffled and tried to look him in the eye again. Failing, I looked down at my lap. I knew that once I took the step I was about to take, nothing would be the same. "Can I show you something without you getting grossed out?" I asked.

"Sure," the doctor said, rolling back on his stool. "Nothing grosses me out anymore."

I rolled up my sleeve and slid my watch off. I hesitated and then thrust my wrist, palm-up, at the doctor, simultaneously turning my head away.

"Hmmmm," he said.

I looked at him. "Gross, huh?"

"I've seen worse," he said casually. Then he sat up straight and folded his arms in front of him. "The good news is that you're cutting horizontally. Against the grain, to put it crudely. The chances of you dying from this are very small." He let that sink in, and then added, "But we can't have you doing this."

I'd never before admitted to cutting out loud. I hadn't even said it to myself. Somehow involving someone else made it real. There was no turning back. "I'm a cutter," I said, feeling the words as they left my mouth and trying them on for size. They fit, but I needed to shift around nervously to keep them from being too true. "I'm a cutter," I said again. My shoulders shook with sobs and I buried my head in my hands. "What do I do?" I asked.

I felt the way I'd felt when I visited the doctor's office at four. During a rough game with my brothers, they'd piled on top of me and sprained my arm. A nurse had tried to tie a sling around the damaged limb but, scared of the way the sling felt, I screamed hysterically until she took it off. In a way, I thought that if I cried hard enough, the cutting would go away. As my sniffles slowed though, I recognized that I was twenty years older and if I was going to get better, I'd have to tie the sling on myself.

"I can give you some names of therapists," the doctor was saying.

188

"I want you to make an appointment with one of them and come back and see me in a couple weeks."

He handed me another tissue as he ushered me from the office. By the time I got to my car, I was the frightened four-year-old again and I didn't need a sling.

A daily routine at the newspaper, though haphazard, helped. Dragging a razor across my skin every night helped, too. I didn't think about the act; to do so would create guilt. I repeatedly cut and bandaged my arm from a sort of nether dimension, creating and maintaining a dangerous sort of stability—one that ironically relied on bleeding to keep myself alive.

As the days shortened and the first crisp autumn breeze lifted my skirts though, the cuts got deeper and the cutting sessions more intense. Overcoming the morning panic attacks and getting out of bed gradually got harder. Then, one Thursday morning in November, I didn't get up at all. I felt my body sink into the center of the mattress and for a minute I thought I'd fall all the way through. The feeling passed and I was lying on top of the bed again, but the panic came in ever more violent waves. At the peak of each cycle I felt my chest diving downward.

Finally, I rolled over and slid out from under the covers. Chafing my knees on the cold stone floor, I clambered into a sitting position and then rocked, hugging my injured knees and wheezing as the pain left my body in giant wrenching sobs. Through bleary eyes, I peered at the clock radio. Its red digits read 11:42. I was four hours late to work. I laid my head against the cold floor and watched the sideways numbers shuffle time away. At 12:32 I wandered, still in my pajamas, into the kitchen. The four or five kitchen knives I used to slice my wrist were dirty and standing point-down in a sink full of dirty water.

I opened the back door, the one that led to the auto shop next door, scanning the ground for something sharp. A broken beer bottle caught my eye so I grabbed a sliver of glass and the cap, which sported sharp bends of metal. It took a couple of dry runs to figure out the correct angle but once I mastered it, I hit pay dirt. Thick blood oozed from my arm to mingle with the brown-yellow residue from the dirty glass.

After I was bandaged up and dressed for work, the filthy piece of glass started to bother me. *I've given myself tetanus,* I thought. *I've inadvertently committed some form of delayed-effect suicide.* My concern escalated once I got to the office. Something about interacting with normal people forced me to view my own behavior as ridiculous. I decided it was time to follow the doctor's advice and call a therapist.

After I regurgitated my life's story, the therapist told me, "You need to have a relationship with God. You're searching for something greater than yourself—a God, if you will—yet you're rejecting the God your parents introduced you to. Why is God so important?"

"If there's nothing out there, no grand scheme, why the hell am I still alive?" I demanded.

"I'm not saying there's anything wrong with not wanting to be alone in the universe," the man said, his calmness infuriating me. "We'll work on your abuse and trust issues in my office, but in the meantime why don't you visit some of the churches around here?"

I'd met Joel in a church and since then I'd been wary of anybody who frequented churches. Still, the therapist was right—I wanted my life to have some kind of meaning and church was as good a place to look for that meaning as any. I started going to appease the therapist, but I continued to go so I wouldn't be alone. When a person lives alone, weekends can be torture. I broke up the monotony of my own thoughts by going to church and discovered a subculture of lonely people who did the same thing. Dozens of single people—though mostly old, life-weary people—frequented church buildings searching more for fragile ties with other human beings than for spiritual enlightenment.

One such woman introduced herself on a late Sunday evening as we knelt side-by-side at a bench in the Assembly of God chapel. Her hands were clasped together and she leaned across the velvet cushion to whisper to me, "Are you a runaway?"

I'm not sure why, but I whispered back, "Yes." Then I realized I *was* a runaway. I'd been running across the country for three years.

"You shouldn't do that," the woman said.

She approached me again the following Sunday. I couldn't think of any better way to spend my Sunday nights. Besides, I was intrigued with the guitar and accordion music and the enormous, soulful man who sang gospel songs until he was overcome with the spirit and passed out. The second time she talked to me, the woman extended her hand in greeting. Short fleshy stubs were all that remained of several of her fingers. I took her hand, exquisitely conscious of the abbreviated digits rubbing against my skin. I got goose bumps and a wave of nausea flushed over me.

From out of nowhere, I heard Joel's voice snarling, "If you touch my computer again, I'm going to cut your fingers off." I'd only pushed the wrong button or extended a cord too far. I dropped the woman's hand like it was a scorpion.

"Oh," she said, noticing my expression. "My fingers. My ex-husband used to beat me. He used a hammer to smash my hands when I messed up the dinner or forgot to wash or iron his clothes. Or just whenever I made him angry."

"What?" I gasped.

Her face was rueful when she looked at me. "That's why he's my *ex*-husband."

Then I was running. I bolted from the chapel, leaving worshippers staring after me, silently looking to each other for explanation. I ran down the highway toward my house, forgetting my car entirely. I ran through the red dirt and gravel on the shoulder until I had to stop, bending over and gasping for air. Then I ran again. I ran until I reached my house and then I threw open the door and fell to the ground, sobbing.

The next morning I demanded answers from my therapist. I was pacing the hardwood floor, afraid to stop moving. "Why?" I screamed. "Why do men treat women like that? Why do they marry for love and then beat her up?"

When the man didn't answer, I continued my tirade. "Do they have to prove their manhood? That they're stronger than women? Why the hell do so many men treat their wives like crap?"

"I don't have an answer for that, Alysa," the therapist started. "There are so many factors that contribute . . ."

I'd had enough. "I could just start beating on you," I said. I imagined my fists connecting with the flesh and muscle of the man in front of me. It would feel good.

He said calmly, "Then you could plan on spending the rest of the week in jail."

"Two people are in love," I yelled. "Then the man beats the woman so badly she has to get her fingers amputated? What kind of relationship is that?"

The therapist let me pace and vent for half an hour, but then he asked me to go home. "Schedule another appointment when you've calmed down," he instructed, opening the door for me. I never went back.

The anguish at night worsened. I'd had nightmares while I was with Joel about losing all my fingers, but the dreams had stopped and I'd forgotten their terror. After the incident with the abused woman, the nightmares came back. I'd wake disoriented in the middle of the night, drenched in sweat, searching for the appendages I was sure were missing. I couldn't sleep again until I'd counted all my fingers and assured myself they were still attached.

I never returned to the Assembly of God church, but Sundays were too long without anything to do, so I continued to look. When I entered a new church building one Sunday morning, I saw Neil Sicora for the second time. He was near the lectern at the front of the chapel. Our eyes locked and I decided to stay. After the service, he greeted me. "It's good to see you again. I was wondering how you were doing."

I began talking to Neil regularly—once or twice a week at church and whenever I could find him at the prison. He soon promised to be available for me day or night. When he offered me the scrap of paper with his home phone number, work phone number, and pager number, I quipped, "Wow, now I'll know where you are all the time."

Neil looked at me sternly. "You'll need those numbers," he promised.

He was right. As soon as I knew a person would be on the other end of the line whenever the pain threatened to drown me, I capitalized on it. Every time I began to crave the cold metal of a blade or the warm blood streaming from a self-created wound, I called Neil.

Over the months, as we grew closer, Neil started pushing buttons he knew would cause me to think. "Alysa," he said on the phone one Friday evening, "You're cutting your own skin and only causing yourself more pain."

As obvious as his words were, I couldn't believe them. It was the first time I *emotionally* understood that what I was doing wasn't normal. I'd pretend sometimes that everyone cut their arms to stay alive. We could hide the marks under our sleeves or jewelry and forget about them.

"I've contacted authorities in your home town," Neil continued.

"If there's abuse going on in that place, it needs to stop. There's no reason other people up there should experience the same things you have."

I dropped the phone.

"Hello?" I heard from the receiver. "Hello?"

I picked up the phone again. "You already talked to them? You already told them what I said?"

"Alysa," Neil said gently. "You're not the only victim. There are other people up there being hurt, and if we don't say something we could even have a mass suicide on our hands."

Numb, I opened the cupboard above the sink where I kept the glass dishes. I picked up a mug and dropped it to the floor. It smashed. I picked up another one and, with more force, sent it tumbling after the first.

"Alysa, that whole community is crazy. It's abusive. Joel *raped* you for God's sake." That was even harder to hear. Good girls don't get raped. Something else must have happened to me. I didn't know what, but it wasn't rape.

I heard Joel's voice replay in my mind: "If you try to leave me, I'll rape you every day until you get pregnant. Then you'll have to marry me." I put the phone down, picked up a plate and smashed it. Pieces of jagged glass skittered across the floor, getting lost in corners and under furniture. One by one, I broke every dish in the kitchen.

My hatred toward the cult only lasted for ten minutes before it turned inward. I hated myself for staying with Joel for so long, for allowing the cult to brainwash me, for not being strong enough to break away. I banged my wrists against the edges of the counters, the rhythm keeping me sane. But it wasn't enough. I could still feel between the bangs, so I sped it up, emitting wails of pain as I flung the insides of my wrists against every hard surface I could find.

Neil was still on the phone when I finished. "Are you there?" he asked gently, and I started to cry.

"I think you should move in with my family," he said. "We'll rearrange and have a room for you by the beginning of next month."

I spent the morning of my first day on Dry Basin Road watching the woman across the street from Neil's house move out. She and her husband had fought for a long time and she'd finally had enough. Mr. Ward, as I came to know him, watched her move out as well, standing clumsily off to the side as she carried out boxes and stacked them into her station wagon. After she drove off with a load, Mr. Ward sat on the porch with his head in his hands.

Suddenly it was Joel sitting there as the woman he loved drove away—as I drove away. Joel was lost without me. He gave everything to me and I'd walked out on him. For a hysterical half-minute, I wanted to dial his phone number and apologize. But it was five years too late. A week or so before he got married, Joel told me, "Sometimes I look at Melinda and think I can't love her. It's like I still love you, even though I'm marrying her. Do you think that's bad?"

I understood what he was asking, but even as I ached for the comparative stability his lifestyle offered me, I kept my mouth shut. In my mind I was the victim, the only one hurting. Watching from the other side, across the road from the Wards' house, I began to doubt myself again. When Mrs. Ward left the final time, I watched until Mr. Ward finally went back into the house. Then I decided to go for a walk, heading west toward Highway 63.

Suddenly I wasn't on Dry Basin Road anymore. I was on Elysium Drive and my mom held my hand as I skipped along the sidewalk. When I came to the end of the road, I crouched in the dust to search for the apple. But there was no apple—no plump, juicy apple, and no rotting, shriveling apple either. Not even stem or seeds. Back alone in Arizona, I swallowed my disappointment, pretending I knew all along that the apple wasn't there. I was an adult and my mom wasn't going to hold my hand now. I sat in the dirt on the side of the road for a long time before walking back to my new living quarters.

My arrival on Dry Basin Road coincided with the rapid health decline of Neil's aging parents. Although Neil hated his parents, he spent his adult life in the same converted trailer home in which he grew up, sleeping in the same bedroom where he likely was conceived. His parents lived next door. Every morning and every evening, Neil walked the forty steps from his front door to his parents'. He helped them in and out of bed, in and out of the shower, and in and out of the car for weekly doctor appointments. I was careful to avoid Neil whenever he returned from next door, because he'd invariably experience every emotion from guilt and pain to rage.

He stumbled into the house late one evening on the brink of tears. "My father just tried to kill me," he said. "I told him he couldn't drive, so he told me he wanted to kill me and took swings at me."

My friendship with Neil faltered when I moved into his house. His intimate knowledge of all my coping methods left me feeling like I had no defense. In a way, living under the canopy of Neil's knowledge and rules reminded me of lying in bed when I was seven or eight. My mom had tied a ribbon to my bed post that attached to a helium-filled balloon. The balloon cast a shadow from the night light—two or three times its size on the opposite wall—and as it hovered there, I imagined it was my mother watching to make sure I didn't put my thumb into my mouth. For years my parents had tried every threat and bribe to get me to stop sucking my thumb, but it wasn't until I thought my mom was standing over my bed all night that I finally stopped.

When Neil was home I walked the halls of his house lightly, fearful of upsetting him, imagining his presence always directly behind me like the helium-filled balloon. I was quiet and stayed mostly to myself, spending hours alone in my room reading, or listening to music through headphones so I wouldn't disturb the rest of the household. Neil's wife, Halley, was kind and friendly, and their two teen kids, Jane and Troy, seemed to accept the stranger in their midst as they went about their own lives, but I felt like a parasitic intruder. I paid Neil $200 a month and I was free to join his family at dinner. But I could only pick at my food, afraid. It was as if showing a human weakness like hunger was too intimate a display for Neil to witness. As a result, I began to lose weight I couldn't afford to lose.

The value of waking up to the sound of other people in the house, though, was immeasurable. The familiar panic greeted me the second I woke, but it vanished when the teapot began to steam in the kitchen or someone cranked on the faucet in the shower. On bad mornings, however, the panic was stronger than I was, stronger even than the sounds of four other people getting ready for the day. On those days, Neil held my hand while I cried enough pain away to get ready for work.

"I can't do it," I'd cry into my lap, sitting on the living room floor with Halley on one side and Neil on the other. Neil would grip my hand as I squeezed back on the only thing that convinced me I was still in the physical world.

"Just breathe," he coached. "In and out, in and out."

I'd follow his instructions, crouched tiny and terrorized in front of him, until the panic began to drain from my body. When the attacks were finally over, I'd feel stupid of course. I'd grin at Neil and Halley's concerned faces, joking, "Well, that was fun. Now I have to get to work." They didn't understand what I was going through but they were there, and that's all I needed.

On the other hand, the Sicoras' five children thought they understood and, as it turned out, didn't want me in their parents' house. Carrie was the worst. The first time I met her, I barely had time to take her in—she was short and stocky but pretty—before she laid into me. She lived with her husband of two years in the northern part of the state, and she was visiting her parents during a long weekend. "I know you're jealous of me, of my place in this family, and I know you have a thing for my dad," she accused me, loudly enough for the neighbors to hear. "You're not welcome here. My dad doesn't need another woman in the house to distract him. You're destroying the best thing he ever had." I sat quietly, not making eye contact, trying to remind myself that the woman berating me was a year younger than I was.

She later demanded of her father, "What is Alysa doing in your house anyway? She's twenty-four freaking years old, not a child. She can take care of herself." She had a point. But somehow I couldn't imagine how normal adults functioned by themselves. I had no idea how they could get up in the morning and go to work, or return home in the evening and amuse themselves before retiring. It was a life that eluded my wildest imagination.

In my defense, Neil asked his eldest daughter, "What if you were alone? What if you were in a new place and didn't know anyone?"

"If she can't handle it, she should go home," Carrie countered. "Maybe she really can't cut it as an adult and that's sad, but she has no right being in your house."

"It's my house and I'll decide who lives here."

Even after she returned to her husband in Flagstaff, Carrie called on a weekly basis to make sure things hadn't gotten out of hand. Neil told me, "Don't worry about what my kids think. I want you here and Halley wants you here. That's all that matters."

I decided to believe him. My only other option was to go back to square one—living alone and barely breathing. I tried to ignore the complaints from Neil's children.

Though shaky at times, living with Neil offered enough of a foundation to begin healing. I also made a friend when I interviewed her about the non-profit spay and neuter clinic she operated. Gloria was sixty-seven and topped with wild silver hair. She plunged from her house as I parked my car at the end of her long driveway and called out from between lips smeared with hot pink lipstick, "Hello!" When I got closer, I saw that several of her teeth were also covered with the gooey wax.

Gloria lived ten miles south of town in a house that looked seasick. She'd painted turquoise spots on the brown rambler and decorated it inside and out with knickknacks, lawn ornaments and piles of items that could only be described as junk. I couldn't help but stare at the house in amazement, trying to take in all its baubles—bicycle tires converted into pixie-sized Ferris wheels in a strawberry patch; beheaded ceramic gnomes lying in chaotic positions like a bomb had gone off while they worked in their diamond mine; a heavy bronze bust with Sigmund Freud emblazoned under it.

Over the front door a sign proclaimed "Crislerville." When Gloria saw me eyeing it, she said, "I declared this my own country. That way, I don't have to associate with the humanoids. I prefer animals anyway." I followed her inside, through a dining room where medieval curtains and wall hangings accented a dark table with wooden plates, goblets and platters.

The next room was bright with color and light from floor-to-ceiling windows. "Have a seat," Gloria instructed, motioning toward an ancient-looking couch. "And meet Sugar," she added as a little mutt nuzzled against my leg. I perched on the edge of the couch and pulled my note pad out, poised to write. But Gloria wanted to entertain. "Can I get you some ice tea or lemonade?"

"Lemonade, please," I said. I'd learned to always accept refreshments; refusing to be served made a lot of people—especially elderly women—suspicious. Gloria limped to the kitchen before hobbling back with a tall glass of pink lemonade and some ice tea.

"My darn hip," she explained. A short coffee table stood between us, and she balanced her glass on the edge of a pile of *National Geographics*. "I injured it more than ten years ago and it still hurts me to walk around. I was living in Colorado at the time, with my husband, and I fell. He had some kind of freak midlife crisis and left me for a girl half his age."

She was lost in her own memories for a few moments before continuing. "Anyway, after he ran away, the doctor told me to move to a warmer climate." I had a bad feeling that Gloria was about to discuss all her physical ailments and I made a mental note never to interview a reclusive woman again. But then she remembered me. "Let's talk about the animal problem in this county," she said. "And how no one here knows anything about taking care of their pets."

I took the cap off my pen, but the atmosphere was conducive to drifting off into daydreams or memories, which I did throughout the entire visit.

Gloria said, "Basically the only reason we have stray cats running all over, and packs of wild dogs, is because no one will spay or neuter their animals. People out here have the old rancher's way of looking at everything. They think neutering a dog or cat takes away his manhood. So then they mate with everything that moves and we get the kind of animal problem we've got."

I thought about the day Joel took me to the dog pound, wanting to show me the dogs scheduled to be euthanized the next day. Three or four sad-eyed dogs stared back at me through the bars, communicating a despair I couldn't understand. It was as if they knew.

Every outing with Joel turned into some sort of religious parable. Surrounded by whining dogs, Joel said that unrighteous people were like the caged animals. "If the people refuse to follow direction, refuse to be trained, they will be put to death." The analogy was a bit of a stretch but it also made some sense. If the dogs would have been precious in the eyes of their owners, they wouldn't be on death row. And the way to be valued is through obedience.

A big yellow Vizsla was yapping at Joel, trying to grab the elbow of his leather jacket in its teeth. "How much to adopt him?" Joel asked the animal control officer.

The woman said, "Sixty dollars covers the license."

Joel peeled off the bills from a wad in his pocket, asking, "When can we take him?"

"Right now, if you want." She snapped a leash on the band around the dog's neck.

The big dog jumped on Joel, putting his paws up on his shoulders and introducing himself by washing Joel's face with his tongue. "We'll call you Lucky," Joel said.

As we left, I glanced back at the death row dogs. One small dark mutt I'd been petting stared at me through her one good eye. Our eyes met and I thought something passed between us.

Joel had refused to have Lucky neutered.

Gloria coughed and I forced my thoughts back to the interview. She was saying, "One unneutered dog can produce hundreds of puppies a year and most of those, if caught, will be put to sleep. It's all about educating people."

I connected back to the Adamses again. This time, Matt was preaching about the absurdities people believed just because they came from a college professor's mouth, or from a book published by some university press. "Take the world for example," he said. "For hundreds of years, people have believed it's round, but that's just a trick played on our minds by the government. I've received revelation saying the ancient prophets actually knew more than people claim to know now. The prophets knew the world was flat." Even as my brain spun with amazement that Matt could believe the earth was flat, I knew that I only believed the earth was round because a grade-school teacher had told me so. But I had no proof. God hadn't told me either way.

Again, I had to force my mind back to Gloria's living room. "The animal problem reminds me of my ex-husband," she said from her own faraway place. "Even before he ran off, he was screwing younger women. Like he had to prove something to himself."

I didn't know what to say. But I recalled a friend who'd brought her Barbie dolls over to my house to show me exactly how a baby came to be. "Then Barbie takes care of the baby and Ken goes to find another Barbie—one without a baby," she concluded. Later I learned that when she was six, her mother had packed her and her siblings into the car and treated them to a vacation in Disneyland. It was the best week she ever had. But when she returned home, my friend discovered that her father had moved out. He'd gotten himself a new Barbie.

I started spending much of my spare time at Gloria's house. Although Grant was small, its prejudices were large. The majority of its residents lived there because their roots were deep. "Who do you belong to?" people always asked me, wondering why I was walking their streets and breathing their air if my mother's mother's mother hadn't walked the same streets. Instead of explaining, I chose to avoid town altogether.

Gloria's house was at the end of a rugged dirt road. If I hadn't known her house would emerge from a thicket of Mesquite trees after I'd traveled a mile down the washboard road, I never would have believed anyone lived there.

Gloria was the first truly bitter woman I met, and I was attracted to her shameless hatred of men. Once a month she threw a medieval feast, lighting two thick candles and bringing platters of bread and meat in from the kitchen. With the company of the three other women she allowed into her life, she ate from the wooden plates on the dining table and yelled profanities.

After dinner, Gloria led us into the small sitting room that opened from her bedroom. There she played a videotape of John

Denver in concert, and the women swooned. Their warped sense of decency was attractive to me. The women shared a friendship more than a decade strong and, although I was lost in their conversations, I lingered at Gloria's house until midnight.

I decided to stay at Gloria's house when Carrie visited her parents. She showed up on a Thursday evening without warning, her bags packed for the weekend. I simply gathered up my own things and left. Neil didn't question my disappearance and I didn't offer an explanation. When I showed up on her doorstep carrying a pillow, Gloria gave me the sitting room with a fold-out couch.

Strange things happened at Gloria's house. The county ignored everything outside the city limits, so a certain level of lawlessness existed. Gloria woke early every morning to feed the wild animals that crept into her back yard. Javelinas, deer, raccoons, and skunks visited her daily for leftovers or seeds. One morning I woke to her yelling at something or someone in the yard. "Get out of here, you pervert!" she screamed.

I decided the target of her anger must be a person, so I slid out of bed to look out the window. A man clothed in nothing but a pair of women's pantyhose was streaking across the yard. From his direction, I guessed he'd been helping himself to her hot spring. When Gloria returned, she said, "My squatter was here again."

"You have a squatter?"

"When I moved into this house twenty years ago, I walked around my land and decided what to do with everything. Then this guy shows up and builds a fence—a fence out of dead refrigerators—and squats."

I giggled, picturing the gutted-out fridges in a row that protected the man from Gloria.

"You laugh," Gloria said. "But it's terrible. The county says there's this law that makes it illegal to evict someone if there's been a fence for a certain number of years."

"So what happened this morning?"

"He shows up every once in a while," she said. "One time I woke up because he was in the house looking for waffles. Sometimes he tries to use my pool. Today he was just running around in nylons."

I went to work that day feeling richer for knowing a person with a squatter—and a squatter who declared his independence with a row of refrigerators at that.

When Christmas rolled around and Neil's family stormed his house, I again retreated to Gloria's. But my timing was all wrong. Gloria's dog, Sugar, was lying at the foot of her bed gasping for air, and Gloria was wringing her hands and sobbing. When she saw me, she declared simply, "Sugar's dying." And there we sat—Gloria and I on Christmas Day—watching her best friend die while John Denver sang from the persistent videotape in the other room.

Although it helped to have Gloria as a friend, I didn't realize how much I relied on Neil until he went out of town. He and Halley went on vacation for a week and, less than twenty-four hours after they left, I had a nervous breakdown. They left early one Monday morning and by eight that night, I was in bad shape. My pulse raced at 125 beats per minute. Dizzy and nauseated, I couldn't get out of bed the following morning. I played with the idea of packing my car and running away.

At ten a.m., Reggie called. "I'm sick," I said lamely. Then, remembering protocol, I added, "And I have a doctor's appointment this afternoon." After hanging up, I called the doctor's office.

He asked, "How are your visits with the therapist going?"

"Badly. They went badly. He scared me."

"So I assume you're not seeing him?"

"I didn't trust him," I said. "I couldn't talk to him."

"You're living with a family now, right?" he asked. "That seems to be helping. You seem happier. Let me see your wrists."

I complied. Tiny red marks stood out that I'd made the night before. I explained, "That's because Neil and Halley are out of town. I got scared."

"You do realize that you're twenty-four years old and that this behavior isn't normal?" the doctor asked. "I might expect reactions from a child, but not from a grown woman."

"I know," I said. "I'm working on it." I didn't know what "it" was, but it seemed the kind of thing the doctor wanted to hear.

He prescribed a medication for dizziness and wrote a note excusing me from work. Then he said, "You can't leave until you promise two things. I want you to look me in the eye and promise you're not going to hurt yourself. I also want you to promise you won't run away."

I thought about leaving the safety of the doctor's office and I was frantic. I didn't know if I could promise not to hurt myself. "What if I can't?"

"I'll send you to the emergency room," the doctor said.

"OK," I said, feeling very tired. "I promise."

The doctor persisted. "You promise what?"

"I promise not to run away, and I promise not to hurt myself." I stood up to go, though I didn't know where I was going.

Before he opened the door, the doctor slapped the inside of my wrist hard enough to make the cuts throb. "Don't do this," he said.

14

An anonymous e-mail informed me that a fourth-grade teacher was being suspended on allegations of sexual misconduct with students. I wrote back with a request for a phone call, guaranteeing anonymity. "All I know is that my daughter brought home a letter," the woman told me on the phone. "There are two fourth-grade classes, and my daughter is in the other one."

"What's the teacher's name?" I asked.

"Edwin Clayton Moore. Don't quote me on anything."

I banged my head on the desk and asked, "What about the letter? Can I get a copy of that?"

The letter, dated the beginning of February, was short and direct. All it said was that Mr. Moore was suspended until some allegations of misconduct were cleared up. I had my work cut out for me. My first stop was the police department, which had a staff much too small. The phone number went directly to an answering machine and the three full-time officers only returned calls if they were having a slow day. I stopped by the double-wide trailer it shared with the Justice of the Peace Precinct 1. A sign was posted on the door: "We are away from the office. If this is an emergency, dial 9-1-1." Of course there wasn't a phone in sight. I decided I'd have better luck driving around and looking for someone.

I caught up with the chief on Highway 50, where he was monitoring traffic going through a construction zone. As I pulled up next to him, he leaned out the driver's side window expectantly and a look of recognition crossed his face. He seemed amused.

I said boldly, "I'm looking for information about the elementary teacher facing charges of molestation."

"Sorry, but that case isn't available to talk about at this point."

"So it's true," I said slyly. "He *is* being charged for molestation."

The chief was caught off guard. "Uh," he stumbled. "We got some reports of suspicious behavior that we're investigating."

"Are there charges?" I probed.

"Off the record," the chief said, "yes. But you'll have to get the details somewhere else."

I smiled. "Sorry to bother you."

The facts I had were sparse, but I went back to the office to write. I stared at the mocking computer screen for several minutes before typing, "Allegations of misconduct led to the dismissal of a fourth-grade teacher at Saguaro Elementary School."

Then I wandered to the front of the office with a quarter for the candy machine, twisting the knob slowly as the gears began working to measure out my M&Ms. Popping the small handful into my mouth, I walked over to check my inbox.

As I brushed past her desk, Pat asked, "Having a good day?"

"I just need to wander."

I mulled over the few facts I had. Writing the story would open up a can of worms and I wasn't sure I was ready to face the repercussions. Even a town as peaceful as Grant can turn vicious, and I had a feeling that was about to happen. I went back to my desk to call the superintendent of the school district.

"I don't think this is news," he said curtly. "It's just sensationalism, and I'd rather you didn't print anything about it." Frustrated and hurt, I decided I'd have to develop a thicker skin to survive as a reporter.

The police chief arrived later that afternoon with a manila envelope for me, stuffed with interviews and police reports from the case. "I've blacked out the names of victims because they're minors and because it's a sexual assault case. But the rest is all here. Good luck."

In his haste, the chief missed some names with his black marker. My heart stopped for a couple seconds when I saw the name of Neil's niece. I'd met her a few weeks before, when I'd awkwardly tagged along with the Sicoras to a relative's house. My gut told me something was wrong with the girl when I met her. She was aggressive and secretive, yet anxious for attention. I'd respected her space and didn't try to decipher what her behavior was practically shouting at me. I'd seen part of myself in her eyes and I'd ignored it.

I was sick reading the reports. One nine-year-old girl knew things no girl should know. No way could she be lying in that interview. Even reading around the black spots, I became engrossed in the repulsive story. She was the first to come forward. Her mother had noticed a change in her behavior and asked about it. The child burst into tears and said her teacher had been touching her for a month. She was alone in the classroom with her teacher after school, the report stated. Moore locked the door and drew the blinds, then tickled the girl and put his hands down her pants. My stomach lurched as I imagined the teacher's hands probing into my own secret and delicate places.

The girl told officers that Moore often hugged his students and stood behind them to give back rubs while they worked. I began to imagine myself in the interview room, and I watched the girl tell investigators about the teacher. "I was special," she said. "He let me sit at the special table in front of the classroom and help him grade assignments."

"Were you the only special one?"

"No. He had other special friends. Three or four of them. But he liked me the best."

"When you say that he touched you under your clothes," the investigator continued, "can you show me where he touched you?" He put a doll on the desk.

Tears welled up in the girl's eyes and she quickly looked around the room before answering. "Here," she said, pointing between the doll's legs.

"Are you sure he touched you under your clothes?" the officer asked.

Rolling her eyes, the girl said again, "Yes."

"Did he touch you under your underwear?" the officer asked.

Still at the age when underwear is funny, the girl giggled, but I could still see the pain in her eyes as she answered, "Yes."

I stopped reading and looked up. I had no idea how long I'd been reading, but in that time the newsroom had become surreal. Bruce was typing noisily in his corner, headphones strapped to his ears. He had the volume up so loud that I could hear the bass thumping from across the room. Everything in the room was in order, but I was scared. I put the papers down and walked to the middle of the room to look out the front window. I don't know what I was looking for, but when I saw the empty front office and the vacant sidewalk out front, I felt better. I went back to my desk and picked up the reports again.

The second victim's story was easier to read but I still felt like a little kid with a dirty secret, or a teenager hoarding dirty magazines in my room. I was ashamed of the material spread before me. Pieces of me identified with the victim and then disappeared into the black letters on the page. A headache settled over my right eye and I knew I was losing but I continued to read, silently urging the victims to divulge every detail to the investigators.

One report summed up all the pages in a single sentence: "Mr. Moore is facing two counts of child molestation and two counts of attempted child molestation." I couldn't understand how so many inhuman acts, so many particular details these children would carry for life, could amount to a single generic sentence.

I wrote my story echoing the dispassionate tone of the police reports, spelling out the facts without emotion. But there was no doubt in my mind that Mr. Moore was guilty. He represented to me every man who had ever hurt a child or a woman, and I wanted him to pay.

The article finished with Moore's bond, which was set at $10,000.

A month later, I attended the pre-trial hearing. Vivid dreams of black creeping things had haunted me the night before and I woke bathed in sweat. Sluggish and hesitant, I arrived at the courthouse minutes before the hearing started. Something wasn't right when I entered. An impression or a premonition met me at the door and I had to pause to catch my breath. Scanning the room, I recognized Moore by the darkness that exuded from his body. Even from behind, the evil seemed to balloon around him.

Then I was reminded of Joel's brother and the only other time I'd been in front of a judge. A subpoena had arrived in the hands of a lawyer on my doorstep, six months after Joel married his blonde version of me. Kristi was filing for divorce and child custody and I was ordered to testify about James assaulting her. I'd arrived at the courthouse by bus. It was snowing. The judge had asked me to recount the incident in question.

Everything but my physical self left the courtroom and my gargoyle voice took over. The drone of it was the only thing I heard. I tried to pay attention to what it said, but I was so tired. "Kristi and I were going out," I heard myself say. "We were going to have dinner and then see a movie. James was staying home with the baby."

Less than ten minutes after Kristi picked me up, James had called to ask what she was doing. Kristi barked into the phone, "I told you already. No, you can't come. It's girls' night. We have to talk about girl things." After listening briefly, she shouted, "No, James, we're not going out with guys." Hanging up, Kristi punched on the gas. "Stupid bastard!"

I just stared ahead, pretending I hadn't heard anything. I already knew how the thinking went. Away from the house, women might fall prey to other men; there was no guarantee they'd ever come back. Men, on the other hand, could openly wander to scan the horizon for sister-wives.

Thirty seconds later, the phone rang again. "James," Kristi spat. "What do you want?" The next instant she was jabbing the car around in traffic, tires squealing and gears protesting. "We're coming back to the house," she said, and then hung up and tossed the phone into the backseat.

James was waiting on the driveway and he wrenched open the back door before the car had even stopped. He jumped into the backseat and tapped Kristi on her head. "Drive," he instructed.

"What are you doing?" she asked, shifting and backing out of the driveway.

James countered, "Where are you two going?"

"We already talked about this, James," Kristi said, her voice rising to a whine. "We're not meeting other men. We're not having wild monkey sex in the back of the car, and we're not sitting at home jacking off because we're too lame to have a social life."

That last bit was too much and I imagined the color rising in James's neck, as I'd seen so many times before. When he finally struck Kristi, I felt I'd been anticipating it for decades. He shoved her head forward.

"Bitch," he ejected, droplets of spit spraying from his mouth.

Kristi burst into tears and screamed, "Don't you dare touch me again!" She lashed out blindly, one pink plastic fingernail making contact with James's cheek. A drop of blood trickled from the wound. With her other hand, Kristi continued to steer. Instinctively, I clenched my seat belt and prepared for the inevitable metal-on-metal crunch.

I turned my head just in time to see James thrash Kristi on the back of the head. Both hands clasped together rigidly, he punched her neck twice. The resulting force sent Kristi's head bashing into the steering wheel. Dazed, she thrust her foot on the brake and swerved violently into the curb. James's head slammed against the headrest as the car came to a sudden lopsided stop.

"Get out of my car," Kristi screamed. She reached back and

shoved James's door open. James put one foot on the ground to get out and then changed his mind. Shifting his weight, he leaned back toward the car.

"*You* get out," he demanded. "The car is in *my* name. *You* get out."

I hugged my chest as Kristi punched the gas pedal and the car shot out into traffic, James dangling from the back door. She changed lanes several times, cutting madly through traffic. "Stop the car!" James was yelling. "You're going to kill me!"

Then I couldn't hear him anymore. I couldn't hear Kristi crying and cursing either. All I heard was the gruesome sound cars make when they collide. The metal cages people use to transport themselves around at high speeds seem so invincible, until two of them try to occupy the same space.

I knew the wreck was coming long before it did. I heard it like a reverse echo. By the time Kristi finally lost control, ramming into a BMW on the seven-lane highway, I was already thinking about something else.

I stayed in the crushed car watching the police cars arrive. Their flashing reds reminded me of lights strung on a tree so I played back Christmas memories from my childhood, watching them like I'd watch a movie of my own life. I remembered myself as a tiny barefoot toddler, quivering in anticipation as I waited with my brothers for Christmas morning; the stockings stuffed with oranges and bright presents under the tree; wrapping paper strewn about the floor as the aroma of cinnamon and baking bread wafted in from the kitchen; cuddling between my parents for an afternoon nap in front of the tree.

I sat in the crumpled front seat of Kristi's car watching as James was strapped to a stretcher and inserted into the back of the ambulance. I imagined he was a pair of socks I was pushing into an enormous bureau drawer. Kristi sat on a stretcher of her own, paramedics dabbing blood from her face. Then I thought maybe I was dead. Why else would I still be in the car?

I learned later that I hadn't even been in the car at all. I'd jumped unhurt from the car right after the accident and watched the scene from the sidewalk. I sat on the concrete waiting as the lights from police cars and ambulance dimmed, and the tow truck came and went after that, until someone remembered me and drove me home.

I told all this to the judge in the tiny courtroom, my voice getting lost in the space between my seat and his. I didn't recognize my voice but I kept talking because I was more afraid of the silence. My mind kept going back to the Christmas lights I'd seen that night, and to the out-of-place sense of safety I'd found sitting among the battered cars. Then I was done. The judge told me to step down and I obeyed, feeling I'd lost some time and wondering how to get it back.

A migraine began in the base of my neck as I walked out of the courthouse, and then its strobe lights pulsated behind my eyes. Kristi's mom dropped me off at my house, and I waded through fresh snow to the front door. Without bothering to untie my shoes, I fell onto my bed and succumbed to the headache.

Later, I sat on the floor of the shower, gazing stupidly at the water spiraling down the drain. The only thing I felt was the sharp droplets of water as they collided with the top of my head and back. Then I was cutting my wrist with a Bic razor. It was too easy. One quick tug at the right angle and two perfect, parallel lines of blood appeared. The bright red joined to a tornado of clear water as the drain sucked it in. It was beautiful.

Maybe it was because that time had been lost that it kept returning to me. At any rate, I thought about those Christmas lights again from my hard wooden chair in the Grant County Courthouse. I sat in the back, away from the rows of family and friends of the alleged victims. I stood up and sat down at all the right times, in sync with the rest of the people in the courtroom, but my mind was somewhere else.

Mr. Moore stood in front of the judge. "How does the defendant plead?"

"Not guilty," Moore's lawyer answered.

The judge warned, "Do you understand that if you choose to enter a not guilty plea, the state may file additional charges against you?" Moore understood.

The judge scheduled the first day of trial and dismissed Moore with a wave of his hand, disgust clouding his face. Moore turned and shot a pitiful expression around the courtroom before leaving with his wife. He'd met bail, so he was free to go. I closed my eyes and his hollow eyes stared back at me, his face shifting into Joel's face, then Dr. Adams's face, and David's face, and Russ's face, and thousands of other faces belonging to predatory men. When I opened my eyes, my hands were in fists.

Back outside, the brightness of the winter sun reminded me that I was on deadline. I rushed to the office and pounded out a story: an alleged sexual predator loose in a town of two thousand people. I couldn't think about anything else. "If Moore doesn't change his plea," I wrote, "the alleged victims, ages nine and ten, will have to take the stand."

That night I woke in a cold sweat, dread weighing me down. I went to the kitchen for a glass of water and the furniture was unfamiliar. I stumbled around looking for my mother. It wasn't until I reached the kitchen faucet that I realized I wasn't in my parents' house. I was at the Sicoras'. I wasn't a child anymore. I was an adult, an adult with responsibilities and expectations. Panicking, I imagined myself back in time five years. Joel's arms encircled me, and I was safe. But Joel was also the source of my fear. I could never quite figure that part out. I reassured myself that I wasn't a victim anymore. I was a reporter and I was going to write the truth. I trudged down the hall to my room and hugged a teddy bear until the fear left.

The day the newspaper came out, I started receiving threats. I arrived at work early to find two voice messages already on my machine. One voice, obviously drunk, boomed from my phone, "You're ruining Mr. Moore's life. You're probably the stupidest person on earth. I hope you have a hard time sleeping at night because you'll be held accountable for what you've done. I hope you go to hell."

In the next message, a woman's voice blurted out, "Asshole! I don't understand how you call yourself a reporter. You're a tabloid hypocrite and you're going to burn for eternity for what you're doing."

I punched at the buttons on the phone, anxious to shut the voices up. Then I called my doctor's office and made an appointment for stress.

When he saw me, he tugged at my sleeve. "Let me see it," he demanded. I rotated my arm and a dozen cuts of various depths stared up at him. "You've got to stop this," he said, but I knew he didn't mean it.

He took out his tablet and wrote a prescription for the antidepressant Wellbutrin. "Take this once a day," he instructed. "Come back in a week. And stop cutting yourself." I left the office with no intention of filling the prescription but by the time I reached my car, I'd changed my mind.

The trial wasn't scheduled to begin for a month, so I was surprised to find a message on my machine a couple days later from the county attorney: "Mr. Moore has agreed to settle. He appears in court at ten a.m." I looked at my watch to discover I had seven minutes to get to the courthouse. I sped to Main Street and took the stairs to the top floor three at a time. Moore and his lawyer were standing side by side in front of the judge when I eased the door open and sat down. The mother of one of the victims glanced back at me and held eye contact for a couple seconds.

"In Arizona versus Edwin Clayton Moore, in the case of three felony charges of child molestation and attempted child molestation, how do you plead?" the judge asked.

Moore's lawyer answered, "No contest."

"Thank you," I whispered into the air.

"Do you understand that these pleas carry severe consequences, including time in the state correctional institution and two terms of lifetime sex offender status?" the judge asked.

Leaning into the microphone, Moore said, "Yes, your honor." I cringed at the sound of the man's voice and wondered at how easily I could hate him.

Except for the soft click of the stenographer's fingers hitting the keys, the courtroom was silent. The judge scheduled Moore's sentencing for two weeks and pounded his gavel in dismissal. A sheriff's deputy cinched a pair of handcuffs around Moore's wrists and led him from the room.

I forced my way through the small mob of spectators who were hugging and congratulating each other. I needed air. In the hallway, I found myself face-to-face with Moore's wife, her eyes red-rimmed but dry. The press pass I wore around my neck suddenly felt like a Nazi symbol and I lowered my eyes as the woman passed by.

The county attorney met me on the front steps. He said, "Moore did well to settle when he did." I just looked at him numbly as he continued. "Further investigations revealed that he was fired from his last job for the same allegations. His former superintendent only gave him a verbal reprimand so the incident wouldn't mar his professional record. I'm just wondering how many other victims he has."

The attorney gazed out over the town as he talked. "And the really sad thing is that all his victims are statistics now. They're much more likely to fall victim again. It's hard to say no to predators after you've been victimized, no matter how strong you think you are."

216

Neil's daughter and I were putting together a jigsaw puzzle on the kitchen table, and Neil and Halley were singing in the living room. The CNN channel kept Jane and me company from the big screen TV, and the broadcasters' voices had became so familiar that I didn't even hear them anymore. That evening in March though, the words the anchor said cannoned through the familiar chatter: "Elizabeth Smart found alive and well with two drifters in Salt Lake City." It had been nine months since the fourteen-year-old had been kidnapped from her bedroom. I glanced up at the screen to see a man's clear blue eyes peering out from behind clumps of long brown hair. His white robes were gray from wear and the skin on his face looked taut from malnutrition.

Jane asked, "Alysa, don't you know some drifters in Utah?"

"Yes, but that's not them." I went back to the puzzle.

By the following morning, everyone was talking about Elizabeth Smart. People were curious about what she'd gone through during those nine months. As I made my way through the busy office to my desk, one overheard phrase hung in the air. "Religious kidnapper," someone had said, though I couldn't remember who. All I knew was that I suddenly needed a closer look at the perpetrator.

I logged on to my computer and brought up a story. Staring venerably at me from the screen was David, with Elidah looking stiffly at the camera from a couple of inches behind him. Another shot showed them cleaned up—freshly showered and still wet—in the baggy yellow jail uniforms assigned to them. Elidah looked frightened, but David eyed the camera with an expression that suggested satisfaction. He'd known the world would come against him, and his arrest was the beginning of a great unfolding.

I felt the blood drain from my face and stumbled, grabbing the wall for support. My mouth half open, I tried to say something, but then realized that would require a lot of explaining. So I shut my mouth and sat back down. Maybe I'd been mistaken? I looked at my monitor again, and the faces staring back were as familiar as my mother's.

"Alysa, are you OK?" Renee was coming toward me. That's when I realized I was standing by my desk, though I couldn't remember rising. I swayed and Renee braced my fall, helping me to the floor. I put my head down and breathed in deep.

"You screamed," Renee explained later. "I looked up and your face was gray."

That entire day, I tripped on my own feet while my head floated above me like a balloon attached to my neck with a flimsy string. The world was too bright, too real, for me to focus. I called Neil from work in the early afternoon. "I need to talk to you."

"What about?"

"I'm not sure," I said.

I corralled Neil and Halley into the living room that evening and began. "The people who kidnapped Elizabeth Smart . . ." I faltered and started again. "Remember when I told you about that man and his wife who were part of the cult?"

Eventually, Neil made sense out of my words. "You have to call the police," he said. "Tell them about the other members still out there. This is your chance for vindication."

I didn't want vindication. All I wanted was to go to sleep. But before I could go to bed, my dad called. "Isn't that interesting? David and what's-her-name were behind the kidnapping."

"Elidah. Her name is Elidah." I suddenly hated my father for not considering how I might feel.

"You need to get in touch with the police up here," he said. "I'll call them and give them your name and phone number."

I numbly wandered back into the living room, where Neil and Halley intently watched photos flashing on the TV, Elizabeth Smart before and after the kidnapping juxtaposed by mug shots of David and Elidah. Every ten minutes, the station replayed a video of Elizabeth's father crying into a microphone. "We just never gave up hope," he kept saying.

Reporters updated the story with photos of the crude shacks and tents in which they'd lived. "Brian David Mitchell probably raped Elizabeth here, in this makeshift shelter, just miles behind her family's house," a reporter said. In the background I could see a pile of sticks thrown together over a small gully, the crudest of places to be raped. That was the first time I'd heard David's real name. "Mitchell and his wife, Wanda Barzee, are being charged with aggravated kidnapping and sexual assault," the reporter continued.

The station showed a close-up of Mitchell the day he was arrested. He and his wife had been stopped on the street, where they acted as peddlers in downtown Salt Lake. The two robed figures seemed so harmless. "I am chosen of God," David said, his eyes boring into my soul from the other side of the screen. I shivered.

His arms pinned behind his back, David continued to stare at the camera, ignorant of or impassive to his pending downfall. His voice softened into its gentle preaching nature. "And God will not be mocked. Repent ye of all your idolatries and your abominations, for the Lord God will bring to utter shame and execration all those who exalt themselves. Wherefore, great and marvelous shall be the destruction of the wicked. I am a servant of God. You can hurt my physical body but you cannot damage my soul."

A police officer finished frisking David and then stowed him in the back seat of a patrol car. Elidah was escorted to another car. Like innocent children, the two familiar figures allowed themselves to be taken to jail.

Then Dr. Adams appeared, larger than life. The anchor called him a natural healer, a naturopath, and said he was being interviewed for information on the making of a monster. His face covered with peach makeup and a lapel microphone pinned to his ironed suit coat, Dr. Adams smiled into the camera. "Brian David Mitchell and his wife lived with me in 1998, while they built a handcart on my back porch. We had religious differences. He became too extreme and I asked him to leave." The reporter thanked and dismissed him. He hadn't noticed the similarities that seemed so obvious to me. He let Dr. Adams walk away to continue David's work.

I don't remember waking up the next morning. The world was sloppy and two-dimensional, like the sky during twilight when it's neither night nor day. At first I thought I was drunk. Then I thought I might be dead. But I couldn't explain the carpet or the silence banging on my ears. As my brain freed itself from the fog, the incidents of the day before played on my eyelids like a movie. And then came incidents from when I was in the cult, and with Joel.

I knew what I had to do. Still in my pajamas, I padded down the hall to the kitchen. The house was empty, which meant it must be a weekday. I grabbed a glass from the cupboard and filled it with lukewarm water, grinning at the irony of all the poisons swimming out from the tap. Back in my room, I shut the door and then mechanically put a pill on my tongue and washed it down. I waited for a moment and then swallowed another. I took another, then another. I hoped they might resurrect whatever feeling I had left. Then I started swallowing them by the handful until the container was empty.

For good measure I decided to drink a cup of ammonia as well.

Then I sat on the floor in silence, waiting for something to happen. When nothing did, I dressed and drove to work. The commotion of other people going about business as usual jogged me out of my stupor, and made me realize I'd stupidly ingested an entire bottle of antidepressants. I did an Internet search and discovered that an overdose of Wellbutrin may cause seizures or death. I suddenly had trouble swallowing. Had I really ingested an entire bottle? It seemed silly from where I was sitting among other people.

I quickly walked to the tiny staff bathroom, locked the door and sat on the floor. I wasn't completely sure whether I'd taken the pills or only dreamed it. Finally, when my hands began to get numb, I decided to throw up. I poked at my uvula a couple of times and dry heaved into the toilet. Acid pooled on the back of my throat and saliva dripped from my hands. I switched fingers and prodded at my tonsils, then scraped at them with a fingernail. I dry heaved again, and then warmth rushed from my stomach, pouring into the ceramic bowl. I counted four or five partially dissolved pills. I scraped at my throat until I counted several more pills floating in wads of mucus. Then I was done.

I decided to go home for a while and take a nap. Curling into a ball on my bed, I immediately fell asleep. When I woke an hour later, I couldn't move my fingers. I brought them in front of my face and saw the veins sticking out. My knuckles were stuck, half-bent and rigid, skeletal under my skin. Then I noticed I was shaking and couldn't breathe. I forced myself to breathe slowly and deliberately for a minute, then got to my feet and stumbled to the phone, which lay where I left it on the cold kitchen floor.

I poked at the numbers with a clumsy finger: 9-1-1.

"What is the nature of your emergency?"

Numb lips blurred my response. "I took too many pills."

"Stay on the line," she said. "Someone is coming. Were the pills prescription medication?"

"Yes."

"How many did you take?"

"I don't know," I said. "Five are left, maybe." My lips weren't quite as numb and I began to feel stupid. Maybe I hadn't killed myself.

"I need you to stay with me," the operator prompted. "Are you there?"

"I'm here," I said, sighing. Blood was flowing into my fingers again, and my heart rate was slowing down. It was only a panic attack, not a seizure. I wanted to tell the operator I was all right but I was too tired. I laid my head on the cold tiles and propped the phone against my ear.

"Are you there?" the operator asked again. I didn't answer. A tear found its way out of the corner of my eye, and I watched it dangle for a second before it fell. Another one took its place.

I heard the operator calling, "Hello, hello?" But I thought I was dreaming again. I hung up.

Heavy footsteps clomped on the front porch, and someone rapped on the door. I looked up as two men entered the house carrying a stretcher. I thought their feet were coming closer to me, but it seemed to take a long time for them to cross the living room. I decided to rest my eyes while they made the trip.

The phone rang ten times, eleven, twelve; I listened to it through the fuzz in my brain. *Someone should answer the phone,* I thought. *Why isn't someone answering?* I lifted my arm to seek the phone but, drained of energy, my arm fell, clobbering me in the face. Then I realized it was a pager hanging from one of the paramedic's belts. I was lying on a stretcher with two hefty straps clamping my chest down. Two brawny young men were lifting the stretcher into the back of an ambulance.

"You fainted," one of them said when he noticed I was awake. I felt like I'd slept for hours but the sun was still high in the sky.

"I fainted," I repeated, feeling stupid.

A third paramedic—a girl who looked younger than I was—said, "On the phone you wondered if you overdosed on something."

Suddenly unwilling to appear foolish in front of the girl, I defiantly said, "Yeah, I thought I'd taken more pills than I should have." I knew that story wouldn't hold water but I was determined not to be labeled as suicidal.

The Emergency Room doctor continued the same line of questioning while a nurse busied herself taking blood samples and shining a light into my eyes. "What were the pills?" the doctor asked.

"Wellbutrin. I have a prescription."

"How many did you swallow?"

I'd thrown up at least five, but I had no idea how many that left. The nurse was looking at me like I was some kind of circus freak, so I decided to lie. "I forgot if I took my prescription this morning, so I took it again and then I started to feel funny."

"You don't seem to be having bad side effects," the doctor said. "The fainting probably was due to stress or hyperventilating. Do you have a lot of stress in your life?"

"I'm a reporter," I said with a stupid grin, trying to be funny.

He grimaced. "Maybe you should look for a new job."

He scribbled something on a medical chart then turned to the nurse. "Put her in the psych hold," he murmured. I sneered. I could hear every word he said. "Watch her for a couple of hours to make sure she's not going to try to hurt herself."

The nurse led me to a small room with a tiny window that looked out onto the nurses' desk. More accurately, it was a small room with a tiny window for staff to look in at frightened figures banished to the psych hold.

"Sit down," the nurse said, motioning toward a cot with paper stretched from a bolt at the foot to protect the mattress. She rolled up my sleeve and wrapped the black blood pressure cuff around my arm. "One-twenty over ninety," she slurred, making notes on my chart. "Give me your wrist."

"I can't," I said, sliding my arms behind my back.

"Give me your wrist," the nurse repeated firmly. "I have to take your pulse."

I was stuck. I was found out. There was no way around it. I held out my wrist with the faded crisscrosses and newer scabs glaring up from a silent battleground. The nurse looked at me and then left the room quickly, shutting the door and locking it behind her.

I imagined the conversation on the other side, the doctor telling the nurse I was pathetic, stupid to want to die, that I needed to be under surveillance. At first I wanted to cry, but then I was angry. The doctor didn't care if I lived or died. I was just a number to him, maybe $250 extra on his paycheck. He didn't care that my insides hurt so badly they were going to burst, that remembering to breathe was so difficult some days that I wanted to die just to end the pain.

I'll show him, I thought. *I'll teach them who's in charge. If they want me to be crazy, I'll show them crazy.* I pulled all the Kleenexes out of the box on the desk. When the floor was littered with tissues, I picked them up two at a time and crafted them into tiny ghosts. Then I threw the ghosts all over the room.

The nurse had left my medical chart on the desk. I scanned the messy handwriting. "Patient is twenty-four-year-old female, claims she accidentally overdosed on Wellbutrin. No signs of overdose, but patient did lose consciousness. Denies she is suicidal. Recommendation is in-patient therapy in a psychiatric hospital." Sitting cross-legged on the floor and using the hard floor tiles for a folding surface, I tore my medical chart pages into smaller squares and turned them into origami animals.

When the nurse returned twenty minutes later, she stepped into a snowfield of Kleenex ghosts and paper cranes, attainments from my church craft classes. She stepped gingerly into the confetti, nervously trying not to show her surprise. I giggled gleefully at my private joke: I was crazy.

The nurse obviously hadn't dealt with crazy people before. She sat silently on a stool, took a pen from her pocket and pulled out a virgin medical chart. The only sound was the spring inside the pen as the nurse punched the button on its tip, propelling the ink out, then contracting it back in. Click-click, click-click. I waited for her to speak. "So how are you feeling?" she finally asked.

"Fine. How are you?"

"I'm fine."

After another long pause, she started again. "As far as hurting yourself, how are you feeling?"

I raked my fingers through the ghosts on the floor and threw one across the room. "Do you like my ghosts?" I knew I was being a jerk but I didn't care. I also knew I'd pay for it later—in my room, alone with a blade. The punishment was coming anyway so I kept up the act. "Can I go now?"

"No," she said. "I need you to answer some questions. As far as the cuts on your wrist go . . . do you feel like doing that now?"

"As far as doing that now," I mocked her. "As far as . . . what? What does that mean, anyway? *As far as?*"

My punishment was getting more severe by the moment. I decided to be nicer.

"We can't keep you here unless you're actively trying to hurt yourself," the nurse said. "Are you feeling at all like you might do something?"

"No, I'm fine. All I did was take my prescription twice. I don't know what all the fuss is about."

"You have scars on your wrist. You obviously cut it recently."

I started to feel nasty again. "And?" I challenged.

"Nothing. You're free to go, but the doctor wants you to see a psychiatrist. He has some recommendations. There's actually a hospital in Phoenix he wants you to check into."

"Can I go home now?" I asked again.

The nurse sighed and left the room, locking the door behind her again. It was fifteen minutes before the door opened. This time it was the doctor.

"I really think you should check into a hospital," he said, but I knew what he was thinking. It would make him look bad if one of his patients killed herself. Besides, death is messy and someone would have to clean up after me. The doctor's lips were still moving but I didn't listen.

When he was done talking, I told him I wanted to go home. He sighed. People were doing that a lot around me. I signed myself out of the hospital four hours after I'd arrived.

I decided the next time I tried to kill myself, I would go somewhere else, somewhere no one could find me.

After the report from the ER made its way into my regular doctor's hands, his receptionist called to schedule a follow-up visit. I slumped into the office, knowing what awaited me. By that time, my doctor and I were on first-name terms, and conversations were preceded by five or ten minutes of off-the-wall joking before he got down to the meat.

"How's the cutting?" he asked suddenly. I appreciated the way he trumpeted into tough subjects like a herd of elephants into a nursery.

Wordlessly, I pulled the band of my watch away from my skin, exposing my rubber wounds to his scrutiny. He shook his head but his voice was more optimistic than his expression. "At least there's no blood," he chirped.

"Yep."

"Did you take the antidepressants?"

"I did." I hesitated. "For a couple of days."

"And then . . ."

"Well, I took the rest of them all together." He grimaced. "What?" I demanded. "Say something."

"I don't know what to say. What am I supposed to do with you?" I counted the tiles on the floor. "So you called 9-1-1?" he asked.

"Yes."

"And?"

"I threw up most of the pills before I called," I said. "They made me sit in a room for four hours."

The doctor sighed. "And then they sent you home." It was a statement, not a question, so I didn't answer it.

I often went to the tiny, ill-stocked local library and hid in the stacks of books, the thick smell of sweat and rotting paper caking the walls of my throat. It was a quiet place to hide during a hard afternoon, and no one questioned me for sitting among the unread books, leafing through obsolete art or autobiographies of presidents' wives.

One day, a book called *Ordinary People* jumped out at me from the shelves. I started at the beginning, hungry for the kinship that came from its pages. I read about a teenage boy who, after the death of his brother, tried to kill himself. Finally, I came to a line that stopped me. "Motion before motive," it said. When you can't remember the motive behind something, do it first, and the motion will remind you. The line seemed important, and I read it several more times before continuing.

Ordinary people. Who are these ordinary people? Ordinary people are those who live without questions, without pain, those who share Jell-O salads with relatives on holidays. Ordinary people are those who don't have to remind themselves to breathe in the morning or to comb their hair or to eat three times a day. Ordinary people simply live, unscathed in their perfect, predictable, ordinary lives. At that moment, sitting in the library, I would have given anything for such a life.

Later that evening, I perched in the rocking chair in the Sicoras' living room, finishing the final chapters. The front door burst open as Neil returned from his nightly visit next door. He demanded of me, "Are you happy?"

"No."

"You need to stop moping," he said, violently taking a seat on the piano bench and leaning toward me. "You're wasting your life and you're wasting mine. You sit here like a shadow, your face long and your eyes sad. Snap out of it! Most of the things you worry about aren't worth it anyway."

I crumpled under Neil's gaze, afraid my heart would seep through the soles of my feet and melt into the carpet. I stared at my bare feet and his work boots, unable to look up. My book slipped from my fingers and dove to the carpet. We sat in silence for a couple minutes before Neil tramped from the room. Moonlight drifted through the translucent curtains and the muted outdoor sounds filtered into the room as I sat, curled up on the rocking chair, too tired to move.

Later on, I wandered into the kitchen and found Neil and Halley sharing a plate of biscuits. Neil offered me one, oblivious of my still festering wound. I envied his ability to lash out and move on. As far as he was concerned, the friction that had raged between us only an hour before was forgotten.

When Neil handed me the biscuit, I set it on the checkered tablecloth in front of me. What was I supposed to do with a biscuit? I couldn't remember. I had the vague feeling I should eat it, but I couldn't remember why. I just stared at it, paralyzed with apathy.

But then I thought: *motion before motive.* I raised the biscuit to my lips and bit into it.

15

I decided to shoot for a geographic cure again. Alaska seemed like the biggest, craziest thing I could aim for, so rugged and far away that it was almost a foreign country. There was no way I could live in such a place and still be myself.

I began a search with two words: Alaska and jobs. When the printer regurgitated its list, it didn't take long for me to realize that the easiest way to get a job was through the government. Most positions offered reimbursement of $800 or so a month, just enough to survive. Within a week, I had three offers. A week later, I signed a contract to work for a non-profit alternative high school in Juneau.

On my last day of work in Grant, I woke early. Carrie was visiting and already arguing with her father in the kitchen. I was starving so I got dressed and headed into town. It had been a year since my arrival, and the Arizona heat was still unbearable, so I cranked up the air conditioning for the short drive. Two or three men in tight dirty T-shirts and greasy overalls whistled at me from a service station across the street. Ignoring them, I gathered my long red hair into a loose ponytail. The back of my neck was sweating.

The small diner had already been open for hours and it was easily ten degrees cooler than outside. I'd been there before, but this time I noticed a red dust coating everything. My feet even left prints as I shuffled toward a vacant booth. Avoiding the idle stares of diners, I made a point of examining my fingernails until a waitress appeared with a menu and water. Standing too close to my table, with one hip jutting out unnaturally, the waitress pulled a straw from her red apron pocket and jammed it unceremoniously into my glass.

"Hot enough for you?" she asked, talking around a wad of gum. Coffee stains made her name tag hard to read. Tam, I finally decided. She smelled like stale cigarette smoke and sweat, but the odor was familiar to me and I realized I'd miss the shaky sense of security I'd found in Grant.

"Do you know what you want?" Tam pressed. I shook my head in response.

The waitress turned on her heel and headed back to the counter, calling over her shoulder, "I'll be back." I watched her poor posture as she leaned against the counter and I could see the tops of her nylons cinching into the flesh on her thighs. The frailty of humanity depressed me and I looked away. Suddenly a man came teetering in through the front door and Tam yelled out, "Hey, Danny, you're late." Laughter erupted from several tables.

Danny eased himself onto a stool and slapped a dirty hand sharply on the counter. He was obviously suffering from a mean hangover. "Knock it off, Tammy," he said. "I'll have the regular."

The waitress curtsied flirtatiously, flashing a grin that was missing more than one tooth, and then shouted into the kitchen, "Danny's here!"

Tam pirouetted with a mug of coffee in her hand and delivered it to the countertop in front of Danny, asking him, "Did you quit your AA meetings again?" Danny was quiet.

I skimmed the menu absentmindedly, more interested in the diner. Strange hieroglyphs and Indian artifacts decorated the walls and shelves behind the counter. A huge cracked mirror stretched the length of the room, endlessly reflecting the ketchup and mustard settings at each table and making the diner seem twice as big. Behind the counter, waitresses in dirty white and red uniforms filled glasses from the soda fountain and called out orders to the cook in code, things like: "One number five rare with a side of fries to walk," or "Three jimmies, hold the sauce, extra cheese with the second." Through an open door a large man sweated over a smoking grill and shoved plates of food through a window for pick-up.

A row of blue stools lined the near side of the counter, occupied by elderly men sitting with their backs to me. They ignored each other and read papers, gulped down coffee, and shoveled runny eggs into their mouths. Danny sat among these men but his attention was focused on me. He had worn Levis and a T-shirt that was missing its top ribbing, revealing a portion of his chest. Self conscious, I ran my fingers through my hair and looked down.

When I looked up a second later, he was still staring at me, but now with a grin. Then he stood and shuffled toward me. "Mind if I join you?" Danny slurred. His teeth were covered with coffee and tobacco stains, and he hadn't shaved in several days.

"No," I mumbled and meant Yes. I'd been in the diner before, and a dozen others just like it. Next the man was going to ask if I wanted to go somewhere with him. I looked toward the exit. Just then the waitress returned with her pad and another glass of water. I hadn't touched the first. I ordered my breakfast to go.

"What's a nice girl like you doing here alone?" Danny asked after Tam left.

"Leaving," I said, appreciating the double meaning only I knew. I paid for my breakfast, picked up my Styrofoam-packaged scrambled eggs and toast and left without looking back.

But I might belong in Grant, I thought. *These people could be my friends; or if not friends, at least fixtures, as familiar to me as the furnishings of my bedroom. I could become a regular, eating breakfast every day with last night's drunks. I could belong.*

Of course, I was lying. I was glad I'd kept my expectations of Grant low so I wouldn't be disappointed when it was time to leave.

Unsurprisingly, moving to Juneau didn't cure anything either. My feet walked a different set of streets but my heart beat the same rhythm. Still, it was a difference.

I traveled with a group of eight other government volunteers from the lower forty-eight. As we dropped into the capital city, trees stretched up to meet the underside of the plane. Blue-green water surrounded the city on three sides, and a slope of green mountains punctuated with white fields shot up from the fourth. As I stared out at the wilderness of my new home, my year in Grant became distant and inconsequential.

A former volunteer met us at the airport. After we deposited our things at a faded blue house, she led us on a walking tour through downtown, from the steep metal steps that spanned four blocks of homes built on a hill, to the wooden docks floating on the surface of the ocean. At the bottom we ducked from the sprinkling rain into an ice cream shop. Windows on the far side of the room framed a dazzling view of the Gastineau Channel. My neck was too sore to look up at the gondola threading its way up to the tip of Mount Roberts. *The view from the top must be incredible,* I thought idly, but I had no desire to witness it. Instead, I wanted to go to bed for a week.

I looked over the flavors at the shop, but I hadn't eaten ice cream since I broke up with Joel. Sugar made me sick; I could taste every ounce of poison in it. My dad's parents had served us ice cream every Sunday evening when we visited their home a mile from my parents' house. "Ice cream and cake or your windows will break," Grandpa chanted as Grandma got the ice cream and a stack of bowls. My grandpa was a strong man, having spent most of his life farming sod. His hands were work-worn and chapped and he lived in grubby overalls, always ready to rush out to fix a sprinkler head or chase off a herd of cows. His silly rhymes contradicted his physical bearing and always made us laugh. From the first time Joel visited my grandparents' house with me, I'd been unable to eat any ice cream.

But Juneau seemed so far removed from my former lives in Arizona, Massachusetts, and Utah that I decided my aversion to sweets must be over. I had my first ice cream in six years my first day in Juneau. Then I started back up the enormous staircase I couldn't see the top of, and I felt suddenly claustrophobic. My stomach boiled and I threw up a puddle of bright pink ice cream on the side of the road.

Six days after arriving, reality threatened to shift and the risk was great because I was so isolated. Swallowing became difficult and I had to force myself to eat. The muscles in my neck tightened, threatening to cut off blood circulation to my brain. I walked around in a stupor, too involved in surviving each minute to notice my surroundings. I persevered partly because I was holding on to the image of being brave enough to survive alone in Alaska, but more because I feared the alternative. As the days grew shorter, my determination to be a survivor grew more intense.

I boarded with a recent college graduate named Jerome, who'd moved to Alaska for adventure. He worked at a health food market, played the banjo, and wrote poetry in the morning while sucking on marijuana and coffee. When I left for work at seven thirty a.m., he'd be sitting glassy-eyed, lost in thought over a verb or phrase, a cigarette burning toward his long white fingers.

Mornings were still painful, the cold fingers of panic grasping at my lungs during my first waking moments. But then Jerome would get out of bed and bustle around the kitchen and bathroom. Just the sound of a warm human being in the house broke the chain of panic, and I could climb out of bed.

I hated relying on someone else to keep me alive, hated my parasitic life.

I learned later that my brain was in survival mode. The traumas

I'd experienced years earlier had reduced me to little more than a machine. I ate. I slept. I breathed. My brain was only capable of dictating the basic functions to keep my body alive. When I researched Post-Traumatic Stress Disorder, I found that survivors of trauma can go long periods without symptoms, only to have them pounce on their victims years later. It helped me to understand the escalating panic attacks.

I envied the way my roommate lived without boundaries, trusting people at face value and shrugging off disappointment or pain like snow from his shoulders after an afternoon walk. Everything Jerome needed to live fit into his backpack and one other, smaller knapsack he carried during the day. He accepted me absolutely. I couldn't tell if he was naive or simply unscathed by the world, but I decided to trust him.

"What's this?" Jerome asked one evening, stepping toward me. Instinctively, I stepped back. An unspoken question on his face, Jerome again stepped forward. I cringed as he drew an imaginary line under my left eye with his forefinger. He repeated the motion under my right eye where the gray-black bags of weariness hung.

"What's wrong? Aren't you sleeping?" he asked.

"I'm OK," I answered quickly, turning my head away. "I'm just tired."

It seemed I'd been tired for a long, long time.

But after surviving for a year in Arizona, I thrilled at the chill in the Juneau air as autumn approached. I breathed long and deep outside, watching the steam rise from my lips to float into the air. Gradually, the pain lessened and I fell into a routine. As a reporter, I'd worked odd hours, juxtaposing school board meetings that dragged late into the evenings with early-morning field trips with the Bureau of Land Management.

Alaska was as far away from Joel as I could get—further than Arizona—and I clung to that idea. And if geography didn't provide

234

enough of a partition between my two lives, the climate clinched the deal. Joel hated cold weather. Ten minutes after he proposed to me six years earlier, he told me he'd purchased a cruise to Bermuda.

"I can't stand the snow," he said. "We're going to Bermuda for our honeymoon. You'll wear a red bikini. We'll swim in the ocean during the day, and during the night . . . Well, you know, we'll work on our honeymoon baby."

I grimaced every time I thought about that. If I were married to Joel, I'd be the mother of six by then. The cold Alaska air smelled even better, and I felt safer in the small wilderness town with my job as an art teacher assistant.

My corner desk at the school allowed a view of the channel on one side and swelling cliffs on the other. During rainy days, a heavy whipped-cream mist covered the tip of the mountain. As the day progressed, it trickled down into the streets ghostlike until the sun melted it away. The window also welcomed the sparse sunlight into the school. Aware of the shadow it cast across my face, I plastered a green sheet across the glass so no one could accidentally catch a glimpse of my profile or the bump in my forehead.

During the first week of class at the high school, the art teacher assigned her students to design a cover for their notebooks with words or pictures of the things that defined their lives. I decided to join in. I looked at the orange poster board sitting in front of me on the desk and swiveled the base of the glue stick, watching the glue emerge and retreat from its plastic container. I couldn't remember what I was passionate about. I couldn't remember where I came from or where I was going. I didn't feel anything. I knew my name and I knew I was in Alaska, but beyond that, a big blank canvas seemed to stretch out before me like the ice field I could see out the window. I panicked. My life consisted of keeping myself alive. And I'd been so busy not dying, I'd forgotten who I was. I was a stranger in my own skin.

Most of the students were absently leafing through magazines, but none had started on the assignment yet. One girl said, "I don't know what I like."

"Think abstractly," the teacher offered. "Think of the words or objects that can describe who you are inside. What do you dream about? What kind of sports or food or animals do you like? What are your fears?"

The girl continued to stare blankly at the teacher. Finally, she picked up a magazine and began to search, but she kept one eye warily on the teacher and the other students. I smiled in recognition.

"Alysa," the teacher said. "Will you help us with some ideas? You're a writer. How would you describe yourself?"

I swallowed. "I write. So I guess I'd start by cutting out different letters and words, just to show that I like words. . . . I also play the piano and like the Beatles," I continued. "Not that anything I do is unique, but that's what I'd put on my cover."

I suddenly remembered myself the summer I turned six. I was wearing a blue tank top and yellow shorts and dipping my bare feet into a vigorous stream of water shooting from a sprinkler head. My older brother and the boy next door were under the picnic table in the backyard, an old bedspread draped over the top. I crawled into the back of their fort and crouched uncomfortably, ducking to keep from hitting my head. A neighbor girl was also under the bedspread and the two boys were trying to persuade her to take off her clothes.

"Come on," the neighbor boy prodded. "You have another shirt underneath anyway."

The girl reluctantly stripped off one of her shirts. "I can't stay," she kept saying. "My mom wants me to go home."

I'd wanted to come to the girl's rescue, knowing somehow what the boys were asking was wrong, but I was the little sister. I felt privileged to be there at all, so I kept quiet. A shiver of excitement swept through the little make-shift hut as the girl stripped off another layer. I could see she was running out of layers but the boys urged her for more. She floundered, anxious to please the boys but not prepared to expose herself.

Just then a boy my age paraded past on the sidewalk, pulling a red wagon stocked with pitchers of lemonade. He walked by every afternoon, hollering "Lemonade! Fresh Lemonade!" Scrawled on a piece of posterboard and pinned to the side of the wagon were the words "Lemonade—7¢ a cup."

With the special intuition lent only to children, the boy discovered our hut and peeked his head under the bedspread. "Lemonade," he announced, and the awful expectant moment was over. The girl pulled her clothes back on and we scuttled out from under the table.

"Can I have some lemonade?" I asked.

"Do you have seven cents?" the boy shot back sneering, knowing I didn't have it.

"No, but I have two cents, I think."

"No lemonade then," the boy said before continuing on his trek.

I knew he'd end up at home with the pitchers still full. My mouth was as dry as cotton as I watched him pull his wagon along the sidewalk, the wheels making a tap-tap, tap-tap every time they went over a crack. Where the sidewalk ended, the boy eased his wagon down the incline and into the street. But the wagon tilted and I watched as the pitchers of lemonade sloshed violently, and then spilled in slow motion as the wagon careened onto its side.

Stripped of the pride he'd demonstrated just moments before, the boy scooped the pitchers and the scattered cups from the asphalt and dumped them back into his wagon. Then, as if the burden of loss was too great, he left the wagon in the street and ran home teary-eyed to his mother. I remembered the conflicting emotions of satisfaction and pity as I stared at the wrecked wagon. It was the first memory of my childhood I'd indulged in for several years.

237

The whish-snip of a pair of scissors forced me back to the present, and I found myself suddenly surrounded by a crowd of high school students in Alaska.

"The only thing I care about is my boyfriend," a pregnant girl named Ruby was saying. She snipped letters out of a magazine and spelled her boyfriend's name over and over on her cover. Then she cut out babies' faces and plastered them over the top.

"Who are you besides a girlfriend?" the art teacher asked. But it was useless. The rest of the class was already bent on creating glue-and-paper shrines to their lovers.

I returned to my corner desk to concentrate on my own project. Who was I besides a cutter? Who was I under all the pain?

In December my landlord shut off the heat and water, a passive-aggressive suggestion that Jerome and I might want to move out. The legislative session would begin in January, and she could hike up the rent and offer the apartment to a man in a suit and tie. We started a search. We also left the oven on and bundled up in as many layers as we could. The stairs to the apartment froze over, and Jerome and I were forced to rappel down the front of our house to reach the street. I continued to work, making my way carefully down the streets. To stop working would be a death sentence; interacting with other people kept me alive.

As winter settled on Juneau, the daylight waned to about four hours a day. I left for work in blackness and returned home under the same sky. If I was lucky, I caught a glimpse of sun once a week or so. The dampness was contagious and everyone in the school caught it. Teachers stopped smiling at each other and students were cross, often arguing or fighting over meaningless differences.

Then December was half gone and I still didn't have a place to live. Every day as I trudged home, I passed the homeless in gray rags who begged for nickels. Some paid bus fare in the morning and rode from downtown to the valley and back all day, hovering over the bus's tiny heaters. I'd be among them in two weeks if I didn't find a place. Finally, a woman whose path I'd crossed several times doing business downtown rescued me. She offered me half of her room at minimal rent and, in sheer desperation, I accepted.

A drunk driver had lost control of his vehicle and plowed into the front of Heather's apartment building more than a year before. The landlord's insurance company paid him for lost rent every month, and he found it hard to summon up the ambition to repair the building. The bedroom in the back, where Heather lived, was undamaged although a gaping hole covered with clear plastic tarps and duct tape defined the front room. The arctic wind found its way through, casting a permanent chill on the apartment. Even inside the bedroom with the door shut and blankets crammed into the cracks, the outside got in. But I had a roof over my head.

My days consisted of nine hours inside the school and fifteen hours a day in a box, wrapped in blankets to ward off the cold. Even inside the bedroom I could see my breath. Outside, I had to cover my face with scarves to keep the moisture in my mouth and nose from freezing. Fifteen hours a day is a lot of time to think. I needed a hobby. Running was out of the question on the icy streets, so I signed up for the women's hockey league.

I had no idea what I was getting into. The first night at practice, I pulled on all the protective clothing I thought I'd need. After half an hour, I had padding everywhere and looked eighty pounds heavier than I was. As I walked toward the rink, a dozen women dressed just like me in tow, I had time to rethink my decision. We were all going to die.

"You are invincible," the coach yelled at us as we felt our way carefully out onto the ice. "I want all of you to skate as fast as you can to this point." He motioned to a line under the ice. "Then skid and fall down."

When we hesitated, he added, "It won't hurt. Trust me. You have enough padding on to survive a train wreck." Sure enough, when I finally got the courage to thrust headfirst into the ice, I came up unscathed. I wished I could wear the protective gear every day.

Adrenaline pulsed through my veins every Sunday night as my team met another on the ice, and for my two minutes of ice time every quarter I thought about nothing but the tiny puck and the stick in my hand. Twice a week, I practiced with my team and once a week we beat our opposition until, at the end of March, my team was proclaimed unbeatable and awarded a trophy.

It wasn't until the season ended that I realized I'd stopped cutting.

The nature of my job was healing, too. Students at the alternative school were there because of problems in their lives. Most had been expelled from the regular high school and were on drugs. Half the girls were pregnant and the other half had eating disorders. Many of the students were homeless. I found kinship with the students and they began to seek me out to talk. I never shared my own pain, but I listened when they told me about their parents divorcing or kicking them out of the house. I listened when they talked about turning to drugs or alcohol to drown their pain. I listened as girls sobbed about being pregnant and their babies' fathers disappearing.

In the middle of listening, something changed. I felt an emotion other than pain. During the nine months I worked with alternative students, a piece of my heart awakened and I remembered how to love. I was able to erase the seven years between my own high school time and the adult I'd become.

I bought a leather band to wear on my wrist. That way, I couldn't see the cuts and I could pretend I was cured. The thick strip of leather covered years of scars, and with the band hiding my secret I masqueraded as a whole person.

16

I met Brent at a Laundromat called The Dungeon in downtown Juneau. The entrance was below street level, and the only windows were tiny squares near the ceiling. It was a rainy day in late spring, and I was watching my clothes tumble in the dryer. He came in with both arms full of dirty clothes, propping the steel door open with one foot as he maneuvered his body through the doorway. After setting down his piles, he grinned at me. "I'm down to the old holey underwear and mismatched socks," he said. I smiled back. I was there for the same reason.

He stuffed the washers and smiled again. "You look bored. I could lend you a book if you want."

I pointed at the digital clock on the dryer and said, "I'm almost done."

"I just live upstairs," he said. "Be right back." He ran up the stairs and returned out of breath to hand me a book. "By the way, I'm Brent," he panted. "I've seen you around and wanted to meet you, but my life has been a little complicated recently."

I took the book and offered him my hand. "I'm Alysa." The book was called *Under the Midnight Sun*, a murder mystery set near Fairbanks. It wasn't really my type but I figured I'd try it. "How am I going to get it back to you?"

Brent laughed. "You're going to have to call me." He wrote his number on a slip of paper and handed it to me.

The timer buzzed on my dryer and I pulled out my clothes,

stuffing them into my laundry bag. A pair of underwear fell to the floor and Brent pounced on them, held them out for me as he commented, "Nice panties." I blushed, grabbed them back, and promised to call as I let myself out the door.

Brent was twelve years older than I was. I found this out when I called him a week later. After telling him I hadn't liked the book, he demanded, "How could you not like it? It's one of the best books I've ever read. I even met the author. He signed inside the front cover."

I flipped the book open to find a black scribble spanning the first page: To Brent, one who knows the truth. At a loss for something useful to say, I managed, "Cool. So do you want the book back?"

He said, "Meet me at the Fifth Street Bridge. How's ten fifteen?"

It was nine thirty. "Fine," I said.

Time dragged for half an hour. I paced the floor, getting increasingly nervous, but instead of analyzing why, I used the time to put my hair into French braids. Brent was at the bridge when I got there, looking at the moon. But he turned toward me as I approached, the slap, slap of my flip-flops echoing in the still night. He asked in a hushed voice, "Can you see the North Star? I love the night sky."

I looked up at his face, half a foot higher than mine, and saw a kind of reverence. I followed his finger to the North Star, the big dipper, and several other constellations. The bridge spanned the road going past the governor's house, and the white-pillared mansion was illuminated by the same streetlights that dimmed the constellations. The night was beautiful and silent, and Brent asked quietly, "Do you want to go for a walk?"

"Sure," I said, following as he headed for the steep hill that was Main Street.

Suddenly, with a playful grin on his face, Brent asked, "Ever played stealth?" Before I could answer, he pressed his index fingers together into a pistol and stalked off into the darkness. "Watch out," he called. "The KGB is after us."

I slunk after Brent, staying close to the fence and bushes of the houses we passed as we made our way up the hill. From the top, a steep metal staircase led down to Cope Park. Brent stopped, waiting for me to catch up before starting down. I took the stairs every day when I walked to work, so I was comfortable on the familiar path. But at the bottom, he took a sharp right and made his way through dense underbrush, ducking to keep from hitting his head on low-hanging branches. When he emerged in a semi-clearing, he waited for me again and we exploded into giggles. We were like children on a playground, except that it was dark and I was alone with a man who was very much a stranger. Despite the whispered warnings in my head, I followed Brent because he expected me to and, despite being a twenty-five-year-old woman, all my years of deferring to men still made it hard for me to say no. I also craved human companionship, simply wanted to have some fun.

When the path ended, we found ourselves behind the dugout of a baseball diamond. Brent took me by the hand to lead me toward a bench by the back wall, the deepest part of the shadows. "Look at the sky," he breathed, resting an arm around my shoulder.

The night had blackened and the stars shimmered like diamonds in silk. Brent moved his hand from my shoulder to my back and started to rub gently up and down. *This is OK*, I thought. *He's not too close.* I was nervous anyway. I shifted my position slightly but he moved closer. The rubbing became vigorous and he moved his hands up and over my shoulders to begin massaging my chest. I tried to figure out the exact moment he should have stopped. I couldn't remember. And I couldn't feel. I knew his hands were on me, rubbing my breasts through my shirt with both hands, but I couldn't feel it at all. I wondered about that and then I decided I should ask him to stop. But it was too late. I should have stopped him before he got that far. But when had that been? I was frozen in my black and white childhood, where there was one right and many wrongs for everything, and I couldn't find the one

243

right thing to do in the situation. I couldn't unravel the problem. So I emotionally froze, mentally disappeared.

In frustration, I just sat there watching him grow more aggressive. Then he pulled my chin toward him and forced his lips over mine, plunging his tongue deeply into my mouth, demanding a response. I lacked the energy to turn my head away, so I kissed him back. Then I felt his hands on me again, pulling my bra down so he could massage my nipple. He grabbed my inner thigh and pulled me toward him, forcing my body to recline.

With a huge effort, I finally took hold of Brent's hand and lifted it from my chest. I pulled away from him and stood up, feeling wobbly. He followed me and asked if I wanted to continue our game of stealth. I went along listlessly, in a daze.

"Wanna rent a movie?" he asked.

What I really wanted was to go home, curl up in the corner of my room and cry. Instead, I said, "OK." Afterward, I wondered why I'd agreed, why I'd so completely submitted to Brent. The awful truth is that I never realized I had a choice. All those years of conditioned compliance were rote grooves in my brain, so deeply entrenched that I still yielded to any man's desires with a sort of passive and—to my mind—philanthropic obedience.

He took my hand and led me down the street to a video store. "Let's get a horror movie," he suggested, pulling me toward the back section.

We were almost there when I caught a glance of myself in one of the mirrors on the ceiling and cringed. I wasn't worth taking out on a date. I wasn't worth the money Brent was spending to rent the movie. It was obvious what he wanted. Why didn't I just let him take it? I joined him in the corner of the room, sick to my stomach and trying to hide my face from him as he scanned the videos. He finally settled on *Halloween.*

"This OK?" he asked.

"Sure." I wished he wouldn't look at me. Maybe if he didn't notice I was ugly, I could go home.

Brent paid for the movie, took my hand again and started to walk briskly up the street, bragging about his enormous entertainment center and the quality of sound we'd have. "Remember, if you get too scared, you can grab onto me," he said. Hadn't I heard that from boys in high school? I couldn't remember, but I thought about that as I followed Brent to his apartment.

I thought I could see myself from far above—a little girl trailing behind a large man. The girl looked sad and was dragging her feet. I wondered why the girl was following the man if he was making her sad. I wanted to warn her, to tell her to run the other way, but I didn't have a voice. I wondered who the little girl was.

Brent and the little girl got to his apartment before I had a chance to say anything. He lived in a big apartment complex with glass doors in the front. He unlocked the door and led the girl through a lobby and into the elevator. He pushed the eight button and the doors closed. Brent's apartment door was next to the elevator. He unlocked the door and led the girl inside. He didn't turn on the light. She sat down on a chair by the window as he turned on the TV and busied himself with the video.

Maybe they're just watching a movie, I thought. But something about the little girl's face made me nervous. She was scared, so I was scared.

I felt nothing beyond my immediate terror of the situation. My readings about PTSD and dissociation were lost in the back of my mind, buried behind the adrenaline pumping near the front. What I didn't understand was that being with Brent was triggering past feelings, feelings that had nothing to do with the present situation. I didn't realize that I could speak, that I could tell Brent to stop, or that I could leave. Instead, I was frozen into emotions that had never been resolved, frozen into uprooted times I'd lost, times that refused to stay put in the past.

Brent went into a room for a minute and came out dressed only in shorts. He sat on the couch and picked up the remote, then waved the girl over to sit next to him. She went, like a child obeys her father. He pulled her close and tried to kiss her. She turned away.

"Come on, just one kiss," he coaxed.

Suddenly he was kissing her hard. He pulled her to the couch and positioned himself on top of her. His hand went under her shirt, and he kneaded her abdomen. Then both his hands went to her chest and he rubbed it. He put his mouth to it and began to suck. Then he pulled her legs down and lay spread eagle over the top. He started to hump. I could see him pushing himself into the girl, harder and harder as he grew more breathless and aggressive in his kissing. His hands and face were all over her, kissing, sucking, twisting skin. I watched from what felt like a great distance, feeling completely separated from the scene.

He pulled the girl's arms up to embrace him, trying to force her to participate. Finally, looking confused, he sat up and asked, "How do you feel?"

The sudden silence demanding a response broke my trance, and I fully grasped that I was the girl. Numbly, I looked around. What had happened? I mumbled in an unfamiliar voice, "I think I should go."

Brent stood up and went to the corner, standing in the shadow of a tall bookshelf. He watched me search for my shoes and smooth my hair. "Why are you going?" he asked.

I could barely hear him over the growing noise in my head. I realized it was my turn to speak. "I'm, um, just a little bit confused."

With a hint of anger in his voice, he said, "*You* are?"

I opened the door and turned to the elevator. I pushed the down button and willed the doors to open.

"You don't have to go," Brent said. He'd followed me to the hall.

"I'm sorry." I couldn't bear to look at him. "I'm just going to walk around and think."

The elevator door opened and I stepped in, but Brent put a hand on the door and watched me for half a minute. "You'll be back," he promised.

He moved his hand and let the door slide shut. Trembling, I reached out to press the button but hesitated, thinking of Brent's promise. What had he seen in me? Pain throbbed against the inside of my skull. I knew it would be worse if I faced it alone, but I finally pushed the button and slumped against the wall. Mentally, I knew that I was in no danger but it didn't *feel* that way. The fear and pain rose up again from somewhere deep inside of me, and wouldn't be denied. When the doors opened on the main floor, I knew what I had to do. I was going to walk to the edge of the ocean and slit my wrists. Then I'd jump from the dock. If the bleeding didn't kill me, hypothermia would quickly claim me.

As I walked through town though, I got distracted. Smudged people-shaped objects moved up and down the streets. Laughter spilled out from bars and two natives argued at the bus stop. Something in my head started screaming but I cut myself off from that part, separate from it, numbed. Then I actually began to laugh because I couldn't feel anything. I laughed harder. I laughed until tears starting falling and the late-night crowds blurred like oil in the street when it rains, merging in bright patterns. Finally, I found my way back to my apartment. It was 12:58 a.m.

I sat outside in the dark hours of the early morning and rocked. Arms wrapped around my knees, I let my body tilt gently back and forth. I tried to cry silently, breathing through my nose in a controlled way so I wouldn't wake my roommate. As morning sunlight crept inch by inch along the cold cement, the night grew more distant. But my pain didn't lessen; the sunlight was too cheerful and I knew the day would stretch on. I panicked thinking about going to work and acting normal.

I went into the bathroom to splash cold water on my face and I didn't like the person who looked back at me in the mirror. A pair of toenail clippers sat on the bathroom counter and I tested the tension by pushing up and down a couple of times. I'd just cut until I bled. I'd just cut as long as I could stand the pain.

I used the clippers to grasp a fold of skin on the inside of my wrist and pulled on it gently. The skin around the area stretched and wrinkled. I pressed the small slabs of the clippers together. Pain shot up my arm but I pressed harder and then let go. A wedge of skin stood out from my wrist. It was pinched at the bottom and I could see a thin line of blood at the base. I put the clippers over the wedge and pressed as hard as I could, traveling back in time to the day I'd clipped off the mole on my face for Joel. The wedge came off and a tiny gaping hole appeared beneath. Blood oozed from it, forming a bubble.

I wondered if I'd ever possessed anything but the enormous pain in my heart and the lesser corresponding pain on my wrist. Even before Joel. Had I felt anything else before Joel? Then I positioned the clippers next to the red bubble and pinched another wedge of flesh, this time a little bit thicker, thinking about Joel as the current of pain surged up my arm. The pain was greater when I pressed the clippers together slowly, and less intense if I cut circulation off quickly. I moved faster, grabbing chunks of skin at random. One after another, wedges of skin died between the jaws of the clippers and, with an extra cinch, the wedges came off. Deep pools of blood attached themselves at the edges, spanning my wrist, but I couldn't stop. I ripped out bigger and bigger chunks.

The further I dug, the more blood I wanted to see. I wanted to get to the vein and determine if I was still alive. Finally, the blueness of the vein gaped at me from under surging red blood. It was raw, simple, mocking. I nudged it with a bloody blade, watching it pucker under the pressure. I recognized my heart beating in the exposed vein and in several places in my hand. Again, I dug the blades of the clippers into the wound, poking at the vein, craving the comfort of death. Pain soared up my arm.

In the end I couldn't cut it. That way, I would lose.

I washed the clippers with a thoroughness that surprised me. I washed and dried it as the red bubbles on my wrist burst and slid in plasma-like plates to my hand, and in rivulets up my arm. They dropped in tiny explosions on the floor and my clothes. Even as I watched the blood and puss and pieces of skin slide from the wound, I wanted to cut again. Instead, I gingerly washed the stinging wound in warm water. It continued to bleed. I dabbed at it with a washcloth, glimpsing the raw meat-loaf look of the inside of my arm in the brief instant before blood swelled in, filled the holes and overflowed again.

I grabbed a wad of toilet paper, pressed it to my wrist and then staggered to my room, where I bandaged it with gauze and athletic tape. Around and around my wrist I wrapped the tape; blood soaked through every layer. Finally the stain was only a dull pink, so I stopped wrapping and curled into a ball on the floor. My face was hot and the coolness of the linoleum floor calmed me. The last thing I heard before I fell asleep exhausted was my roommate's alarm clock.

I woke once during the mid-morning to pull a dirty sweatshirt off the floor and put it under my head. Several hours later I woke again, my wrist throbbing. Blood had seeped through to the top layer of bandage and left an ink blot that only began a story. Memories of the cutting came back all at once, and I felt like I'd been punched in the stomach.

The ache in my wrist was so intense it choked me. I raised my hand above my heart and ran to the bathroom. Each layer of gauze I removed stung as I eased it from the cut. The closer to my skin I got, the more painful it was to remove the bandage. Tears of agony washed my face as I peeled off the last layers. The bottom strip of gauze was embedded into my flesh. As I coaxed it away, the bleeding started all over again. For a second, I saw the white cauliflower rawness of torn skin before it flooded again with rich gooey blood.

I threw up.

I washed the wound again and rewrapped the dressing. Exhaustion overcame me and I lay on my bed, its softness enveloping me in a way I didn't deserve, but I was too tired to argue. I rested my injured wrist on a pillow to keep it above my heart, and escaped into a deep and dreamless sleep.

For days, I didn't let the wound heal. Every time a new layer of onion skin began to form over the war zone, I picked at it until it bled.

I decided to stay in bed. If I fell asleep again, when I eventually woke up things might be better. Each morning, I hid my head under the covers and listened from another dimension as Heather showered, dressed, and left the house for work. A bitter cold breeze percolated through the blanket during the interval when the front door was open. I'd punch the numbers of the school into the phone, wait for the secretary to answer, and listen to a voice that was not mine tell her that I was sick. Then I'd go back to sleep, dreading the hour I'd wake and find the fog unlifted.

A week later I woke to the familiar sense of being a stranger in my own life. Colors and sounds were muted. My roommate's lips moved out of synch with her speech, like a character in a low-budget film. At noon I'd stumble around the tiny apartment, foraging for food and ignoring my hands. If I looked directly at them, I wouldn't recognize them. I already knew the rules; I just needed to stay calm and follow them. I'd curl up on my bed again to sleep the afternoon away. I was not going to survive the shadow world again. The last time had almost killed me.

Two weeks later, I broke down and went to the doctor. "Can I have a prescription for Paxil?" I blurted out.

A physician's assistant asked, "Have you taken it before?"

"Yes. I felt like this last time and Paxil helped."

Without further questioning, the man wrote me a prescription. An hour later, I had a small orange bottle of salvation. Along with the bottle came the familiar temptation to swallow all the pills at once. Once a person has done that, bottles and pills communicate a different story.

⌁⌁

In March, Jason fell into my life like a bomb. He moved to Juneau from San Francisco, where he spent six months in jail for blowing up a car. His explosive temper preceded him, and people instinctively shied away. He was sentenced by the California courts to three years probation near his mother in Juneau, and he wasn't happy about it.

The first thing I noticed about Jason was the leather band he wore around his left wrist, a near replica of the one on my own. I'd never before met a cutter. Until Jason found me, I thought I'd invented it. After introducing himself, Jason said, pointing to the leather on my damaged wrist, "You play the game, too." I nodded, fingering the stiff band. Jason's looked softer, more broken-in. I wondered how long he'd been wearing it.

"Why do you call it the game?" I asked.

"Easy. You feel the pain, you cut. But if you cut, you keep cutting. If you don't cut, you know you're going to cut and it will be worse for waiting. You play the game. You strategize. You negotiate what hurts more—pain inside or pain outside. Then you play. Will you win or will the pain win?"

I envied how Jason put it into words. I'd searched for a description for a decade and he'd just spit them out without effort. Then I realized the words worked only because our identical scars had already made us blood brothers. For the first time in my life, I felt completely understood and I hadn't even said anything.

Jason dressed in black and had greasy hair hanging in his eyes and over his ears. Black combat boots boxed his feet and he stomped everywhere he went. He carried a dirty backpack stocked with notebooks of various sizes and colors. From the first time we met, Jason was at my side, offering dark and cynical remarks about the world around us.

A week after we met, we were walking along the wooden dock in downtown Juneau. He hunched forward from the weight of his backpack. He hadn't put it down since I'd met him. The sky was clear and the air was the warmest of the year. Jason was explaining his jail time. "This guy tried to rape this girl I knew, so I blew up his car. I put a rag into the gas tank and lit it."

I didn't know that actually worked. I played with images from movies where the car goes up in a ball of orange flames, usually flipping over onto its hood from the blast. "It works that way?" I asked.

He nodded. "The sad thing is, I'd do it all over again. In fact, if castrating myself would keep men from treating women like that, I'd get it done in a second."

Based on that statement alone, I decided Jason was my soul mate. In the following weeks I spent more and more time with him. He walked through downtown Juneau like he owned it, glaring at tourists and residents until they shied away. His very presence commanded a general fear and vigilance. I stayed by his side, holding his hand and feeling completely safe. I was attracted to Jason's outlook on life, his overuse of the f-word, his dark gothic appearance, the black eyeliner that made people uneasy. And I felt honored that he chose to spend most of his time with me.

"Outward appearance has to echo what you feel inside," Jason explained. "Otherwise you're lying. You're nothing but a poser in your own life." I had enough darkness inside to justify an equally dim outward appearance. Jason gave me a stick of black lipstick and eyeliner and helped me choose clothes from thrift stores. A week after I met him, I'd mastered the look he shot at every living being, warning them before they approached that they'd better not. Being with Jason was a lot like having a force field around my body. Nobody dared even knock on it.

I decided to invert night and day. By night Jason and I tramped the streets, smoking marijuana and throwing rocks at the sides of buildings and through windows of broken-down shacks. We scaled fire escape staircases onto mold-covered rooftops to watch the flashing lights as cops rounded up early-morning drunks and carted them off to jail. From the rooftops, we watched the enormous cruise ships glide silently into the channel and dock, wisps of smoke curling up from their smokestacks like cotton spires.

Jason and I were the first to see the sun creep over the horizon and shoot its white rays across the water. We toasted the morning with clove cigarettes and shots of whiskey. We listened to the daily serenade of cars starting, front doors slamming, and church bells chiming the hour. The aroma of fresh bagels and coffee permeated the air, and it was time to go home.

Because day was night in our world, Jason and I went to bed at dawn. I arose again at seven thirty and tramped the mile to work. Bags formed beneath my eyes and sentences swam in the air before I said them, but the lack of sleep forced my body into a state of hyper reality, and I preferred it to the alternative.

I attained the same level of euphoria by starving myself. I went three or four days without eating and then binged, feeling my body inflate with carbohydrates and sugars. Then I'd go another week without food. Jason and I existed on caffeine, nicotine, alcohol and lack of sleep, and I had the time of my life.

Out of the blue one day in early July, Reggie called from the *Gazette*. "I have an opening right now. If you want it, I'll hold it for a month."

I hadn't given Grant much more than an occasional passing thought in Juneau. It was in the past and it hadn't been pleasant.

I didn't take the prospect of returning seriously at first, but as I weighed my job options, or the lack of them, I began to think about giving the small desert town a second chance. The only thing keeping me in Juneau was Jason, but he didn't need me. Or maybe he did, but the need to move forward with my life was suddenly more urgent. So soul mate or not, I left Jason behind with the promise that we'd stay in touch by mail.

I had a long conversation with Neil on the phone. "I'm sorry about the way things ended before," he said. "I still want my house to be a haven for you. I want you to find safety here. You're welcome to stay as long as you want." I decided to take Neil up on his offer.

Once I decided to say good-bye to Juneau, I couldn't leave quickly enough.

17

When I walked off the plane in Phoenix, I was no longer the girl people remembered. I found Halley waiting for me near baggage claim and, when she finally recognized me, her expression read disappointment and something else. She even took a step backward as I approached, though I pretended not to notice.

My hair was ratty and tangled and a silver stud punctured my nose. A thick chain hung from my belt loop and brushed the bare knee that protruded from a ragged hole in my jeans. I wore a tarnished metal skull on a silver cable around my neck. I watched through heavily made-up eyes the bustle of people disentangling themselves and groping for their luggage. My lips, colored black, stayed pressed together as I made my way expertly through the crowd without so much as brushing an elbow or meeting an eye.

I walked with a practiced sullenness, my feet clomping deliberately on the floor. The world was my enemy and I scrutinized humanity's every movement for signs of betrayal, like an antlered deer during hunting season. The three-hour drive back to Grant was familiar and foreign at the same time because I looked out from different eyes. Halley attempted small talk but I resisted, choosing instead to gaze morosely out the window.

My first day, I dressed in bondage pants and a baggy black gothic tee, my neck covered in silver chains. Then I stomped through a grocery store seeming pissed off, enjoying the harmony of looking exactly how I felt. The second day I went to the doctor for a tetanus shot. I sat on the floor and stared at his loafers, their tassels dangling and taunting as he berated me. I'd unwound the gauze and infection bubbled from the straight-edged holes on my wrist.

Swiveling slightly on his short stool, he asked himself, as usual, "What am I going to do with you?"

"Can you please wrap it?" I asked, jabbing my wrist at him. "I can't bear to look at it."

"You should have thought of that before you did it," he said. "You have to stop this. I'm going to give you a referral to a treatment program."

I avoided his eyes and my wounds. "I can't go," I said to the floor, my face burning with shame. "I have to work."

The doctor sighed, pulled on rubber gloves, dabbed ointment on the wounds and wrapped them with gauze and blue tape. "I can force you to go," he said. "All I have to do is sign a form that says I believe you're in danger of hurting yourself."

He wasn't a gentle man by nature, but my doctor set aside his usual sarcasm and spoke to me softly, the way a father would to his small daughter. He rolled his stool to the middle of the room— strategically between me and the door. "You need to get better," he urged. "Let me send you somewhere."

"If I don't work," I thrust back, "I'll end up back at my parents'. Besides, I don't have any insurance to pay for it." A tear inadvertently slid down my face, which angered me. I wiped it quickly with the back of my hand and stood up. "I have to go."

The doctor hesitated, but then stood and moved aside so I could stomp out the door. I could feel his eyes on my back as I slammed my way down the hall. My job was waiting for me, though I felt more like swallowing a wire clothes hanger than going back to the office.

Even with the ointment slathered on my wrist, my arm ached with every beat of my heart. The surge of blood through my veins twice every second screamed when it reached my wrist, causing the entire left side of my body to throb. I needed help with it, so every night for two weeks, I even let Neil wrap my wrist and give me an ice pack to elevate it before I went to bed. When I held my hand above my heart, the pulsing pain was less intense and it was the only way I could sleep.

"Oh, Alysa," Neil sighed as he dressed my wound. "I can understand the physical pain, but I can't even imagine what the inside looks like."

"You can see the inside," I pointed out. "You can see the vein."

"I meant your heart."

I tried to imagine what my heart looked like. I knew what it felt like—a bludgeoned piñata. How was it still working?

Panic ensued every morning I woke up, but I didn't dare make it public. I'd talked too much before. This time, I'd be quiet about my personal life. That resolution lasted about four days, until I thought I was going to burst. I decided to find a therapist. The yellow pages listed three local ones. I started at the top of the alphabet. An answering machine asked me to leave my name, a message and what sort of medical insurance I had. "None," I said at the end of my message. "I don't have insurance." The therapist never returned my call.

A week later, I tried the second one. Before even giving her my name, I told the receptionist, "I don't have any insurance."

"No one has insurance," she said. "What can I do for you?"

"I just need to talk to someone."

"He could see you this Thursday." She paused. "At ten. Will that work for you?"

Thursday was two days away, so I decided to pace myself. Two days meant 2,880 minutes. My frantic heart was still pounding away at 120 beats per minute. After I'd counted 345,600 pulses, I could talk to someone.

Derek Saunders was a huge man towering half a foot over me, and he was easily double my weight. His office was inside a partially renovated home. The waiting area consisted of a long velvet couch and a couple of stiff chairs. When he came out of his office, I shook Derek's hand and followed him into a small room furnished with two plush chairs. I shut the door behind me and sat down.

He asked, "What can I do for you?" How do you put your life into a sentence? How do you explain to a stranger that you're about to fall? After several moments of awkward silence, Derek tried again. "Tell me a little bit about yourself. How old are you? Where do you work?"

Those were easy questions and the answers fell out of my mouth.

"You're twenty-six and you're living in Grant?" Derek repeated. "Why?"

I didn't have an answer for that. I wanted to live among my peers and experience life, culture and happiness, not rent a bedroom in a house in Grant. I wanted to tell Derek about how I was slipping from reality, about how it hurt to wake up, and that I couldn't move or recognize my own face in the mirror. Derek had a different agenda. We could talk about more personal things in the visits to come. We wouldn't even try to open the can of worms I was carrying around until we were ready for it.

I left the office in a daze, more hopeless than when I'd arrived an hour before with $55 more in my bank account.

Demons followed me around that day, threatening to choke me if I thought too much. I functioned on the surface of my workday, waiting to talk to Neil. As I drove into the carport that evening though, I saw an unfamiliar BMW that I guessed was Carrie's, so I entered the house with caution. Neil, Halley, Carrie and Jane sat around the table. From the entrance, they looked a mile away. I skirted the table and went to my room.

Before I could close the door though, Neil called after me, "Are you hungry? We can get you a plate."

"Dad . . ." Carrie started reprimanding.

A sense of urgent stubbornness turned me around and forced

me back into the kitchen. I hadn't eaten all day and I was, after all, paying for room and board. It wasn't a matter of me invading Carrie's personal space; eating dinner was a privilege I paid for. Recalling Jason's lessons, I pulled a chair up to the table. Solid food in my stomach would have helped me, but I just couldn't eat while Carrie was murdering me with her eyes, so with the faint impression that I was giving myself whiplash, I again pushed away from the table and started for my room.

I fell asleep fully dressed and woke around ten with the ceiling light burning down on me. I could hear voices in the kitchen and I unashamedly pressed my ear to the door. Carrie was saying, "No, I don't understand why you have her here again. I thought we were done with that when she moved to Alaska."

"Alysa has certain needs . . ." Neil started, and I suddenly felt like a cripple or an infant.

Carrie then threw out, "Jane said she and Alysa had a sleepover. In Jane's *room*. How do you know she's not a . . . *lesbian?*"

Jane and I had shared her queen-sized bed a couple weeks before when she was having a hard time; we'd stayed up late talking. But I heard Neil suddenly ask his youngest daughter harshly, "Jane, did you and Alysa sleep in the same room? In the same bed? That's entirely inappropriate!" Neil's voice grew louder with each successive word and my heart sunk inside of me. "I don't want you spending too much time with Alysa. And I don't want you to ever share a bed or a room again. *Ever!*"

Neil's shoes came clomping toward my room. I shrunk away from the door as he approached. He didn't knock; he *banged* on the door, paused for a second and then banged again.

"Coming," I said, making a point of taking my time. I opened the door hesitantly to Neil's angrily contorted face.

He spat, "You are living in my house, under my roof. And under my roof, there are certain rules that will not be disobeyed. I don't want you in Jane's room. From now on. Period!" He turned and stormed away with no opening for me to speak.

My eyes stung and my heart ached, and in the small crack before the door shut completely, I caught Carrie smirking at me.

The world was different the next day. My co-workers were the same, the community was the same, the same blistering hot sun beat down on sweaty residents, but the eye holes I looked through were different. I breathed shallowly because filling my lungs with oxygen made them ache. I stared bleary-eyed at the monitor in front of me as minutes and then hours ticked by. My head had no room for intruding thoughts, so I stared contentedly at nothing.

Then a call came through from a new counseling clinic hoping to open its doors soon. I drove out to interview the owners. Bells jingled as I pushed the front door open, and the company's director approached me. A second man was lying on the floor under a desk rewiring a computer, and the director had to step over his legs to get to me.

I started to explain my mission and the older, well-dressed man underneath the desk stood up to listen. "This is Viktor," the director said, motioning to him. As Viktor began introducing himself, the director faded from the room.

Shortly, he said in his unrecognizable accent, "You have a sadness about you. Let me guess; you've been sexually assaulted." The way he said it made me feel like he was seeing right through me. I nodded and slipped my watch band down so he could see the series of bulging scars. They glowed one shade whiter than the rest of my skin. A shadow crossed Viktor's face as he stared at my wounds and scars.

Then his eyes met mine, some communication passed between us, and I knew he could help me. "I'm not officially certified yet," he told me, "so I'll have to see you as a friend rather than as a therapist."

I nodded again. Viktor gave me his business card, on which he also wrote his home and cell phone numbers. "Call me," he said. "I will help you." Something lifted from my shoulders at that moment.

By the next morning, however, the pain was back, so I picked up the phone in the back room of the *Gazette* office and dialed Viktor's home number. "Allo?" The accent was unmistakable.

"Hi," I said quietly. "It's Alysa."

"Hello, dear," the man said. The familiarity with which he addressed me already made me feel protected.

"I'm sorry for being so eager," I started to say, but Viktor cut me off.

"It's OK, it's OK. When can you meet me? Today? Later this afternoon?"

"Yes, yes," I said, wiping at my face, embarrassed at the sudden escape of emotion.

"Meet me at the office at, say, four then?" Viktor asked.

After hanging up, I sunk to my knees on the concrete floor and cried for a minute before I could stand and make my way back to the desk. At a quarter to four, I grabbed my car keys and a stack of paper to look busy and left through the back door. I had to ease up on my right foot to keep from speeding. My heart and head were racing by the time I reached the office, but the door was locked.

An eternity passed before I saw Viktor pull up in his silver truck and get out. He glanced at his watch as he approached me. "Sorry, I'm running a little late," he said as he unlocked the door and held it open for me.

The gap between us was suddenly huge and I doubted I could span it. I thought about all the normal everyday things Viktor probably did between my phone call and our scheduled appointment. Most likely he'd eaten lunch, run a few errands, maybe phoned a friend. All I'd done was watch the clock.

I followed him down the dark hallway into a room decorated with colorful clowns—clowns on the wallpaper, clown faces framed on the walls, and tiny porcelain-faced clowns with their feet dangling over the edges of shelves and desks. "I hate this room," Viktor said. "Bloody clowns all over the place." I surprised myself by laughing at his expression. "Makes you think the whole world is a circus." I giggled again.

"You, sit here," Viktor instructed me, pulling a chair away from the wall and sitting in another one with a comfortable space separating us. He leaned forward and took both of my hands in his. "You're going to be OK," he said. "I am going to help you."

Tears threatened but I laughed nervously instead. "How do you know you can help?" I asked.

"I look at you and feel I know you already. You're a good kid and you've been hurt. We're going to get into everything. There will be a lot of tears, a lot of yelling and swearing, a lot of pain, but when I'm through with you, you'll be OK." His brown eyes, unblinking and full of empathy, reflected sincerity as he sat back in his chair and said, "Let's begin."

I told my story in a way I'd never told it before. I told Viktor about Joel and Russ. I told him about hating myself, about pounding my head with a hammer, cutting and banging to make the pain go away. I showed him my scars and identified each with a man or an incident. Viktor sat quietly, occasionally murmuring a "Damn" or "Shit" after I admitted a certain detail. I stared at my lap as I talked but every time I looked up, Viktor's kind eyes met mine to reassure me that he was still listening.

When I got to explaining my move back to Grant, Viktor interrupted with a simple, "Walk with me."

The sun was going down and I felt like I'd been in the building for years. Viktor lit a cigarette and paced the sidewalk in silence for several minutes. Finally, he spoke. "You're lucky to be alive. I've never met someone like you. Usually, with that kind of abuse, women don't function without a lot of medication and therapy."

262

As I prepared to leave, Viktor told me, "I'm not working yet. I don't have any clients except you, so I can talk whenever you want."

After the first session, we didn't meet at the office anymore. "Too sterile," he said. "Too official. And too many clowns." So we met at parks and all-night diners for a couple weeks. I trusted him more than I'd ever trusted anyone.

Finally, Viktor asked me to meet him at his house. He gave me a tour of his simple place scattered with European tapestries, wooden statues, and ashtrays overflowing in every room. The smell of tobacco radiated from the walls and furniture. Then he informed me, "I want to do more aggressive therapy tonight."

He circled me slowly. I turned with him, always facing him, trying to trust him, but simultaneously listening to the warnings in my head. Although I'd ignored those inner voices for most of my life, they persisted, and I heard them as I faced Viktor in his living room. He continued, "I didn't want to try this until I got to know you better, but I think you're ready for it now. When a person has been touched sexually in a negative way, the only thing that can repair the damage is to be touched in the same way positively."

My brain raced to keep up with Viktor's logic, and when it finally caught up, his words actually made sense to me. At that point, I was willing to try anything. My anguish was so intense by the time I went to Viktor that I might have chopped off my own fingers if he'd prescribed it. By comparison, what he suggested seemed harmless. So as absurd as Viktor's method sounded, I held on to it; at least I was doing something constructive by trying to stop the inner torment, trying to live. I hesitated anyway. I'd never freely given of myself sexually, and I was scared.

Motion before motive, I reminded myself. Then I told Viktor, "OK."

He added with reassurance, "I've studied with the Native Americans, and I've been recognized as a spiritual healer by them. Your problem is that you've been brought up in a man-made religion that teaches sex is bad. That's why rape has damaged you so much. Other victims don't take as long to heal."

"Don't you believe in God?" It seemed an important question to ask.

"God is everywhere," Viktor said. "You believe in God as an individual being, a creator. But God is in me, and I can heal you." He breathed in deeply several times and stretched his muscles. Then he pounced on me, pulling me down to the Persian rug in his living room. A ceiling fan whirled above us.

I protested stupidly, blurting out things like "Clothes are good" as he skillfully undressed me. Then I lay under him too tired to move, letting my mind drift away. A thought began and vanished—something about not fighting back and it would be over sooner. Half an inch from my physical self, my brain told me to move but I pretended not to hear. Instead, I tried to remember a song lyric and the name of the boy who sat next to me in kindergarten. In a jovial sing-song voice, I said, "This is a bad idea." But by then it was too late. I felt my shirt sliding over my head and fingers unzipping my jeans.

I don't know how long I stared at the ceiling fan, seeing it and not seeing it at the same time. Finally, bathed in saliva, I sat up and stared at Viktor, feeling both safe and violated. His eyes had the same sincerity and caring in them as before, but my skin still stung with a sense of betrayal. Then Viktor handed me my clothes and, whistling a song, went into the kitchen. "I'm going to make you dinner before you go," he said. "And you have to eat it. I'm not having an anorexic patient on my hands."

I had to do what he said; he was my therapist.

Our "hands-on sessions" continued, and so did my ambivalence about them. "How does it feel?" he'd ask me after our daily appointments. "To finally be able to trust someone and to lie naked with a man?"

I didn't have answers, but I didn't tell him to stop either. It was nice to be wanted. It was nice to trust a man enough to let him touch me without dissociating. Unlike the men in my past, Viktor made me happy. But I also thought of him as my therapist when I allowed him to caress my skin. The goose bumps of pleasure I felt weren't anything I could have control over, but I'd still feel a sense of guilt, of something not quite right.

Carrie visited her parents often that fall. She had a one-year-old son and was filing for a divorce. She'd sleep on a made-up bed in the living room. Whenever I got a drink of water from the kitchen or took a shower in her bathroom, I felt like an intruder. I spent all my time trying to disappear.

I walked in one night when she was having an argument with her dad. "I don't know why you have her here, but I can guess. Why the hell would you have a younger woman in your house if you weren't having an affair? Or at least *wanting* to have an affair?"

I was apparently both a lesbian and a marriage-wrecker. I held my breath on the other side of the wall, wanting Neil to defend me, but he said nothing. "Just get in her face," Carrie steamed. "Tell her to get over whatever she's dealing with and get out. If you don't tell her, I'll do it for you."

"It's really none of your business who I have living under . . ." Neil began, but Carrie interrupted.

"It's inappropriate for her to be here, and I want her out!"

I slammed the door shut and walked noisily into the room, feigning surprise. Then I darted through the living room and dressed for bed silently, too scared to sneak into the hall and use the bathroom. I got into bed dirty and put the pillow over my head, but I could still hear the murmuring voices.

I started spending more time at Viktor's house. It got to be a habit—whenever Carrie visited, I moved in with Viktor. He was accommodating when my home turned into a prison. After a few weeks of therapy, however, he fired me as a client.

"I want you to be my friend," he explained. "I can't legally or ethically be your therapist if I want to see you socially." Viktor laughed. "The look on your face," he said. "You'd think I just slaughtered your pet cat. Nothing's going to change. I'll still help you. I'll still be here for you. You just won't have to pay me."

As Christmas approached, Neil's married children began coming home for the holidays. I had to work the day before and the day after Christmas, so I couldn't leave the area. Besides, I didn't have anywhere to go. For what seemed like hours on Christmas Eve, people piled into the house. I spent most of the time staring at the walls in my room, wishing I'd had the foresight to find a place to go.

As night approached and Neil's family got busy spreading blankets on all the available floor space, I sat awkwardly on a kitchen chair and made friends with the children. Curious about the new addition to their family, they surrounded me and begged me to play. So for half an hour, I led them in a riotous game of hide-and-go-seek. Then Carrie's older son asked, "Mom, can I sleep with her?"

Carrie answered stiffly, "No, you cannot. She's the reason we're all sleeping on the floor."

One of her cousins jumped in. "Who do you think you are, anyway? You can't just join someone's family."

Carrie's son continued to pester, "Mom, why can't I sleep with her?"

Suddenly the room snarled into chaos and all fingers pointed at me. I retreated to my room, intending to spend the rest of the evening in solitude. But it was Christmas, so I decided to go to the spare bedroom at Viktor's house, the only safe place I knew. I didn't end up in the spare bed, though. Viktor answered my knock dressed only in a robe, sleep clouding his eyes. When I explained, he picked me up and carried me, kicking and beating him, into his room, and threw me on his bed. "I don't know why people treat you the way they do," he said as he stripped and climbed in next to me.

He held both my wrists in one of his hands and began to undo my jeans. "You are beautiful, and I'm going to make you believe it." I began to protest as he undressed me, but then I decided to give up. What hadn't he seen already anyway? When I lay there naked, he stood above, surveying me and gesturing at my exposed body. "You call this ugly? You have long beautiful legs and perfectly curved hips. I want you to stand in front of the mirror until you see what I see."

I didn't move. I couldn't. I lay there under Viktor's gaze like a display in a museum. His voice came through a dense fog and filtered through my ears like they were full of cotton. "Oh, you poor thing," I heard him say from a distance. "This really is difficult for you, isn't it?"

He covered my body and slipped under the blanket with me. I allowed him to wrap his arms around me and pull me close. My skin, betrayed and clammy, clung to his warm sweaty body as he persuaded mine to respond. It went further than touching that time.

When it was over, I asked, "Do you love me?" The question immediately felt stupid and I wanted to retract it, but it was too late. It was the result of my parents not having even kissed when they married; it was my sister Sarah singing, "If you kiss me, you have to marry me," right before Joel put his tongue in her mouth; it was all the Sunday sermons and my ward's Wednesday evening classes for girls.

I'd already moved far beyond that world. I'd trampled all my former boundaries and beliefs in the name of therapy, though they still cried out. But Viktor's love would be justification. Viktor's love would not be betrayal.

"I don't make half commitments," he answered.

267

In the gathering silence, I suddenly felt mean. "What if I tell? What if I tell your boss?"

"You're not my client," Viktor said. "You've never paid me. We never filled out the paper work. There's no record. As far as I'm concerned, this was all consensual."

Driving back from Viktor's that final time, my foot hard on the accelerator, I played the scenario through my head over and over. "I don't make half commitments," I whispered out loud. Then why did I hurt so much?

I slowed down as I approached the house and its driveway crowded with cars. Carrie, no doubt, was waiting to accuse me of sleeping with her dad again. I wished I had a blanket and a change of clothes; I'd just spend the night in my car. But the only way to get to my things was to walk past Carrie. "Not worth it," I said out loud, turning the car around.

I hadn't gone far when vomit curled up in my throat. I stopped at a gas station and stumbled into the unisex bathroom. The floor was grimy, the air rank with urine, and blemishes covered the walls. I didn't care. I put my face over the toilet and gagged so violently that cold sweat spilled from every pore.

My teeth chattered and I wrapped my arms around my knees to stop the shivering. I was crying by then, and tears mixed with mucous from my nose trailed down my chin, but I didn't move to wipe it off. Cowering in the crevice between the toilet and the sink, I fished the toenail clippers from my purse and dug them immorally into my skin. I hacked at the crude uncovered flesh again and again, willing the pain to seep through the growing hole. And it did, until I could stand to live.

When I was finished, I stood to wash the wound in the sink. A flesh-colored blob appeared in the mirror, a spongy hideousness I didn't want to recognize as my face. Looking closer, I saw the bulbous shape of my nose, my forehead protrusion, red-rimmed eyes that cried over a lost cause. A selfish screwed-up monster glared pitifully back at me. My heart did its familiar dive as a wave of vomit forced its way up.

I screamed and hurled the bloody clippers as hard as I could into the mirror.

18

Shortly after the incident with Viktor, falling apart and unable to function, I called him for help. In a cold and distant tone, he refused to see me as either a therapist or a friend. "I don't know you," he said to me. Apparently the possibility of legal repercussions had come to him at that late date. In turn, I felt all stability yanked out from under my feet. During the following weeks, my entire life disintegrated. I dreamed I was screaming but no sound came out. I dreamed it so often I forgot it was a dream.

A month later, Neil asked me to move out to relieve the turmoil among his children. He gave me three days to find a place and rentals were hard to come by, so I jumped on the first one I found. I transported two carloads of my things into a dilapidated brick building crouched at the edge of a trailer park, and dumped all my belongings just inside the front door. I always planned to organize, but I never did get around to it. A neighbor brought over a mattress she'd salvaged from the dump and helped me wedge it through the front door. A week after I met her, her husband tried to kill her and ended up in prison for assault.

Alone in my house, my emotions were amplified. A broken record of guilt played constantly in my head. Had it not been tragic, I might have laughed at my predicament. I'd aged six years since my relationship with Joel ended, but my stress reactions were the same, only deeper. Life seemed bent on teaching me a lesson, but I never learned.

In June, after months of not sleeping, I tried therapy again. This time I chose a woman nearby. In response to her question of why I sought therapy, I giggled. My reason suddenly seemed hilarious. "To recover from going to therapy," I said. But then I was crying.

The therapist's stiff silver hair glistened in the light of an overhead lamp. She leaned back in a soft armchair with her yellow notepad to consider me. "I don't understand."

I began to tell her about Viktor. Then I realized I had to back up and tell her why I saw Viktor in the first place. It felt futile. She wouldn't be able to help me, either. There was no magic bag of cures.

But then I decided to try a different approach and held out my bared arm, pointing to a red and pink scar. "I named this scar Viktor." Then I pointed to a white bulge on the inside of my wrist. "And this one is for Joel." I rattled off names as I moved across the collection of tally marks carved into my skin. "And this one," I said, fingering the thickest scar, a swollen mass of discolored skin, "this one is for me."

The therapist closed her legal pad. "I don't do outpatient therapy with clients who are actively injuring. I can't see you until you get more intense help."

She recommended I check myself into a rehabilitation center where specialists would be on hand twenty-four hours a day to help me address my issues. As I left her office, she slipped several brochures into my hands—embossed covers with smiling adolescent girls staring out of a background of flourishing foliage. She walked me to the door and patted me on the shoulder. "Do something good for yourself for once."

I scoffed. Reggie would never let me take time off. And if I did take a break for a month or two months or six months, where would I be when I got out? Homeless. Jobless. Friendless. Back in Utah.

That was a Friday afternoon. By early Sunday afternoon,

while lying on my bare mattress in a room saturated with heat, I reconsidered. The brochures were strewn across the dirty carpet among piles of discarded clothing. I was having trouble breathing and my heart raced. I longed to drag the cool metal of a blade across my wrist, but I resisted. As I stared at the sagging, water-stained ceiling, hundreds of arms seemed to be holding me down, pressing me into the decaying mattress. My heart thudded against my chest as my breathing grew shallow. Suddenly my muscles seized together, making my arms and legs convulse. For hours I skimmed consciousness like a pebble skipping across the placidity of a pond. Asleep for several moments at a time, I dreamed I was screaming, but the sound got stuck in my throat. While awake, I panicked and stopping breathing, sending my body into shock.

Finally, feeling that I might die, I rolled onto the floor, crawled toward the phone, and dialed the emergency number to the therapist's office. When the on-call therapist answered, I sobbed, "I can't do this by myself. I need help."

Admitting my weakness brought relief, which was swiftly followed by shame, and I stammered when she asked where I was. After she said she was sending an ambulance, I hung up and immediately left the house. I spent the rest of the day driving and berating myself for giving in.

I walked into Reggie's office the next day, tears hovering on my lashes. I closed his door after me and sat on the same hard yellow chair I'd taken almost three years before, when I first met Reggie. After I explained my condition, he said, "Legally, I can't penalize you for taking medical leave. But if you have to go to the hospital, I'd ask as a personal favor that you forfeit your position. I need an editor I can rely on, not someone who's going to succumb to mental illness."

I felt slapped across the face, and quickly backtracked. "I'm actually feeling a lot better than I was. Maybe it was just stress. I think I'll be OK." I hung my head and returned to my desk.

I was emotionally and physically spent. Each day I endured took me closer to an end I both dreaded and longed for. I'd survive until I had nothing left and the choice would no longer be mine. I'd never even have to sign myself into the hospital. One day, I'd just run out of strength and someone else would have to step in. To speed the inevitable process, I took to wandering the streets and broken sidewalks of Grant in the middle of the night. An assault or rape would certainly send me to the hospital, and it wouldn't be my fault.

It was after midnight sometime in the middle of July when Ryu found me. Our paths had crossed more than once, and I'd interviewed him several times for the newspaper. A police officer with more than a decade of experience, Ryu refused to leave me standing on the sidewalk. "Get into the car," he told me, and I obeyed. "Now, tell me what you think you're doing on the street at this time of night."

"I'm just wandering."

"In the middle of the night? By yourself?"

"I don't really care anymore." I looked out the corner of my eye to gauge his response, but it was too dark to see his face.

Ryu said, "There was a welfare alert for you going out over the scanner a week ago."

My face burned. "What did the dispatcher say?"

"Nothing really. I mean, no specific details, just that someone was concerned about you."

"Well, no one found me," I said.

"I was worried."

I turned in surprise. "Were you really?"

"I tried to find you," he said. "I drove around looking for you."

"Oh." I couldn't think of anything else to say. After a couple minutes of silence, though, I added, "Well, I'm OK."

"I see that." Ryu was driving again, up and down the silent streets. "Fasten your seat belt, please."

Several more minutes passed. I gazed out the window until I couldn't stand the silence anymore. "I was just having a bad day," I explained, then paused. "Or days. . . . Or maybe life."

Ryu listened quietly, and then finally said, "I know what you mean. I'm having a rough time, too. I'm getting a divorce." It was my turn to listen. "I mean, the divorce isn't the bad part. It was the marriage, really. It hasn't been a real marriage for a couple of years now."

"How long were you married?"

"Five years, but she kicked me out of the bedroom after about three, and she hasn't spoken directly to me for the last year. I was living in the guest bedroom, and she'd have her boyfriends stay over. She even took the sheets and towels from my end of the house and replaced them with the old linens, the ones with holes in them."

I chuckled. "Really? That's stupid."

"We didn't talk," Ryu continued, and I sensed that he needed to hear his words out loud. "Sometimes we bumped into each other in the kitchen, like in the morning when we were both getting coffee, and she just looked right through me. Finally, she said she wanted a divorce, so I'm giving it to her."

"Why did you stay with her for so long?"

Ryu shrugged. "I made a commitment."

That I understood. I hated going back on my word. Even worse, I hated feeling that I'd hurt or even inconvenienced someone. Ryu and I talked and patrolled for another hour before he asked if he could take me home. "I want to make sure you're safe," he said, "and I don't want you out walking the streets alone like this anymore."

His voice carried genuine concern and my heart fluttered with hope that I had a friend, one who needed me as much as I needed him. That night, I slept.

Although a substantial age difference separated us, we understood each other, and I began to look forward to my time with Ryu. We continued to talk, often driving around in his patrol truck long after the town went to sleep. He began showing up at my doorstep every night he was on duty to ask if I wanted to keep him company.

On the day his divorce was finalized, Ryu asked, "Can I take you out sometime?"

I'd known the question would come, but I was caught off guard anyway, and hesitated. I decided to avoid his question by asking him one. "How old are you?"

"Fifty-two."

"Oh," I said. "One year younger than my dad."

That didn't faze him. "So, can I take you out?"

"OK." I instantly regretted my answer, certain I was about to ruin our good friendship.

"I'd like to take you to dinner tomorrow," he said. Then he hugged me before saying goodnight.

I could hear Ryu turning his patrol truck around in the gravel parking lot as I entered my dark house. I began repeating to myself, "What am I doing? What am I doing?" I decided to dedicate the next day to finding a reason I couldn't go out with Ryu. I'd check his references.

"What do you think of Ryu?" I asked the town clerk, the mayor and the police chief. Their answers were resoundingly positive. "He is a police officer," the chief pointed out. "Did you expect me to hire someone I didn't think was up to par?"

As the hour of the date loomed closer, I decided not to call it off. Ryu picked me up at six, looking surprisingly safe in his civilian clothes. He led me to his shiny black Monte Carlo and opened the door for me. It was so clean that I hesitated, afraid I'd soil it. I asked, "Are you sure you want me in there?"

Ryu gave me a confused look. "How else are we going to get dinner?"

After I got in, he closed the door. Only two minutes into the date and already Ryu was treating me better than anyone ever had.

I decided not to push my luck. I kept my feet firmly planted on the mat inside the car, making sure I didn't get dust anywhere else. I vowed not to talk too loudly, laugh too long, or eat too much.

Ten minutes later, we pulled up in front of an American diner. "I hope you like spaghetti," he said, shifting the car into park and reaching for the door handle.

"Wait." I grabbed his arm and he eased back into his seat. "I have to tell you something first. I've been sexually assaulted. I have to tell you now because I like you, and I don't want you to find out later and decide you don't want to be with me. It's messy, and my life is all screwed up, and I just need you to know that now before anything happens between us."

Ryu was quiet.

"Say something," I urged. "Just say anything."

"Thank you for telling me."

"That's it?"

"Thank you for trusting me enough to tell me that."

I thought I was going to cry. "I understand if you don't want to hang out with me."

"Look," Ryu said. "None of that matters. The only thing that matters is the future. I've liked you from the first time I saw you. I may not be your knight in shining armor, but I want to try."

"Well, the thing is," I said, "I'm not really looking for a knight in shining armor. If I'm looking at all, it's for a knight in busted armor. I want someone who's been through a fight and has the battle wounds to prove it. I don't want someone who sits at home buffing his armor. I want someone who understands that life hurts."

Ryu said, "Let's go get something to eat."

"Wait," I urged. "There's more. Do you remember that day when the welfare alert went out for me, that day when someone called the police? I was a danger to myself that day. I was going to cut my wrists." When Ryu didn't respond, I slid the watch from my wrist and shoved the exposed scars under his eyes. "I was going to do more of this."

Ryu gazed at my arm for a long moment and then put his hand over my scars. "I thought it was something like that."

"And you're not scared?"

"I've got my own busted armor."

"The last person to assault me was a therapist," I blurted out. I'd opened the floodgate, and there was a lot that needed to be said.

Ryu let me talk until I was done, and then he took my hand. "I don't care what you've been through," he said. "I told you before, I'm only interested in the future."

During the following week, I told Ryu everything, and he urged me to file a complaint against Viktor at the sheriff's office. So for two hours, I let the details of my relationship with Viktor pour from my mouth while a special investigator took notes. When I finished, she put her notes into a folder, wrote "Under Investigation" on it with a black marker and stashed it in a file drawer. Two months later, when she was promoted, the investigator threw all her files away.

For our second official date, Ryu took me to the Tasty Freeze on the highway. He bought me ice cream and I didn't throw up.

<hr />

I was terrified of marriage, so when Ryu proposed three months after we started dating, I put my fingers in my ears and sang, "I can't hear you. I can't hear you." Later, I added, "I don't want you to marry me just because I'm crazy and you feel sorry for me."

Ryu stared at me for a long time, and then cupped my chin in his hands. "Look at me. I want to marry you because I love you, and because you make me happy."

"How can I make you happy?" I argued. "I'm miserable, and I still want to die half the time."

"You can't die," Ryu insisted. "You're my life."

He asked again two months later. That time, he used the air horn on his patrol truck and I said yes. Despite the age difference, Ryu and I found common ground. He held me during my panic attacks, and I held him when the traumas of his failed marriage trickled in. For the first time in my life, I felt needy and needed in the same proportions.

Because of my repulsion to marriage, a regular wedding would never work. At first, we planned it for a year in the future, but even that upset me enough to confine me to bed for a day or two. I thought about all the traditional duties of a bride—the cake tasting, dress shopping, flower picking—and I wanted nothing to do with it. The thought of being bound to a man until death did us part was causing a perpetual migraine headache. But at the same time, I craved the security and companionship marriage offered. I knew it wouldn't be the cure to my ills, but it could be the beginning of a gradual healing. Eventually, I decided the only way to combat my anxiety was to sneak up on the marriage. It'd have to be on the spur of the moment.

So that's what we did. Five months after Ryu and I started dating, there was a quiet afternoon at the newspaper office when I decided I was ready. I gave Ryu twenty minutes warning, and twisted my hair into a bun on my way home to change into a dress. We met at the half-trailer that passed for a courthouse, and the judge pronounced us man and wife as the clock struck five. Ryu caught my hand and pulled me close, and we toasted each other with paper cups full of sparkling apple cider.

AFTERWORD

When I was four years old, my preschool class took a field trip to the zoo. I wore yellow straight-leg pants with embroidered flowers on them and a yellow T-shirt. Grasping a paper sack full of popcorn, I eagerly fed handfuls to some baby deer. My fisted hand was small enough to fit through the holes in the chain-link fence, and the deer nuzzled my skin tenderly. Lost in the moment, I suddenly saw myself from above and wasn't sure on which side of the fence I belonged.

Similarly, I have two lives—one on each side of the fence. My interior life will be foreign to most readers, who only look in and move on, though I cannot. I have cut, burned, gouged or otherwise mutilated myself more than two hundred times. Most of the scars will fade with time. Some will not. Those I will wear as a badge for the rest of my life; they reflect my inner pain. I have seen therapists and psychiatrists in four different states over the years. So far I have only narrowly avoided going to the hospital. Psychiatrists have variously diagnosed me as bipolar, borderline, schizophrenic, obsessive-compulsive, and a victim of post-traumatic stress disorder (PTSD). The only one I'm sure about is the last.

People who haven't experienced the cycles of abuse, or who don't understand environmental conditioning, ask me why I didn't just leave the cult, and why I kept getting involved with abusive, power-hungry men. The water wasn't boiling when I stepped in. Or maybe the water was boiling but I just didn't notice because that was all I knew. Either way, by the time the hot water began to endanger my life, I was too weak to climb back out. Abuse is a circle with no corners in which to hide and no obvious way out. There was no break in the circle; nothing in my experience suggested a healthier way of being. I existed in perpetual fear for most of my life; I sought abuse because it was familiar, and because pain masked itself as the equivalent of love.

Trauma changes people. The world moves on around us, but for a trauma victim, time creeps by or stops altogether. Trust and security are stolen, and it hurts to smile. The desire to continue is drained. I completely lost six years of my life—six years of darkness so thick that it smothered my dreams and choked every emerging blossom of hope. I became a cut-out paper doll of the person I once was.

I've learned to function better in the world because I've nearly mastered the art of hiding my emotions. While turmoil rages inside, I can appear perfectly calm on the exterior. It's strange how inconsequential and invisible something can be one day, then how fear of it absolutely governs my life on other days. I spend some days checking my appearance in every store mirror, car window, and even shadows, hoping something will change and I won't be ugly anymore. To some extent, the level of recurrent trauma I experience depends on how much I indulge in it. The world is full of reflective objects and I still slip into it, but I can't indulge. I have to tell myself to stop.

I can pick out a sexual perpetrator from a mile away. His posture, the way he walks, the proximity between him and another person on a public bus, or something as little as a look in his eyes or a particular smell can identify him as an offender. Whatever it is, I'm aware now that I can sense it on a subconscious level, just as he senses that I'm a victim, like a bleeding, wounded animal that is easier prey. When I pass these people on the street, work next to them in an office, or view them from afar, a piece of communication passes between us as perpetrator and victim. We recognize each other, but I stay away.

Any cycle of abuse is difficult to stop, and it is further complicated when it involves self-abuse. This is the unkindest abuse, because a self-injurer becomes both the abuser and the victim. Self-abuse leaves scars that other kinds of abuse do not, and it can continue long after the immediate danger of being victimized by another person has passed. My life circled eternally between psychological abuse, sexual abuse and self abuse. Every time I was victimized, my life tilted, and every time I victimized myself, my life tilted the same way, until it lay permanently on its side.

In high school I listened to a motivational speaker who sat in a wheelchair, a microphone propped next to his mouth so he could speak without moving. The legs of his jeans were wound into thick knots to cover the stumps where his legs should have been. As a teenager himself, he'd climbed a power pole during a game of hide-and-seek in a cornfield. He grabbed the top line to steady himself, and the electricity blew off both of his legs at the hips. "It really, really hurt," he told us. Then he paused and backtracked. "That is, I remember that it hurt, but I don't actually remember how it felt to hurt."

The human mind has the inability to remember pain, whether that pain is physical or mental and emotional. I remember that my pain was excruciating, sometimes intense enough that I lost consciousness. But I don't remember exactly how it felt.

Like that rotting apple at the end of Elysium Drive, the pain with which I defined my life festers, succumbs to time and elements, and will gradually disappear into the earth. Though I don't have a happy fairytale ending to write, I did eventually learn to smile again. I can't say I'm cured. I can't say things are all better and I've moved on. I still have days I can't get out of bed. Sometimes I still hold a blade against my skin and wait for the courage to press in. Then I look at my hundreds of scars and decide against it. I don't have to act on that impulse anymore. Deeper than that, though, is the absence of the black-hole pain, that urgent craving to find someone or something to heal me. For years I wandered around zombie-like, searching for that person or thing that would make me whole. I never found it because it was in myself.

One key to healing, though, is to find a person to trust. Ideally, this person has scars of his or her own, or at least is able to suspend judgment long enough to listen and experience the pain secondhand. A roomful of rowdy teenagers with healthy imaginations will agree that having their legs blown off by a surge of electricity would probably hurt, but they're unlikely to have a frame of reference to truly empathize.

I can't say I'm grateful for the raw hand life dealt me. I don't know if I'm a better or a wiser person because of it. Sometimes I watch children or teenagers or young adults with their families or in groups at the park, throwing a Frisbee or barbequing or just eating Jell-O salad, and I think, *Why isn't that me?* I may always have a hard time trusting people, and view the world through a veil of suspicion. I refuse to be fooled by humanity's sugar coatings or pretty appearances anymore, and I realize I may never be among the lighthearted people sharing a joke on a hot summer day.

One of the few things in my life that makes sense is my need to write this book. Since I was very young, I've remembered everything and guarded my memories with a kind of hyper-vigilance. Some of the things I experienced were horrible enough that I had to remember every detail to convince myself of their reality. Perhaps with this book I can finally put some of my experiences away. Since they're written down, I no longer have to hold on to them so tightly.

I also wrote this book with the hope that it would find those who need a friend. In my life, certain lyrics of a song or the particular words of an author, spelled out with the right rhythm, have calmed my heart and given me courage to go on for another day. I can already pick out offenders; maybe with this book I can begin to find other survivors.

Self-harm often stems from intense or long-term sexual abuse. It can also stem from more temporary problems, such as loneliness or stress. But it is always a symptom of deep inner pain. There are people among us whose voices ache as they describe their experiences with self-injury and the incidents that led up to it. It's an epidemic so brutal that it seems impossible to ignore. Yet mainstream society continues to do so, as if pretending it doesn't exist will make it go away. It's time for us to rise up and stop *all* of the abuse.

Unfortunately, it's a reality that some of our health professionals harm more than heal. I've been shocked to hear some educators and doctors refer to self-mutilation as an attention-getting ploy or as "pretend suicide." Even more alarming, I've heard some of them mocking victims and calling them weak for not completing the task. If you're looking for professional help for self-injury, please don't stop until you find someone you feel good about, someone worthy of trust. They are out there.

What about the cult of "lymphnogenesis"? The cult is real, but that is not its true name. The names of all places and people have been changed in the book, except for David and Elidah, whose names are a matter of public record. Members of the cult still exist around the world. Though some left after Elizabeth Smart returned home, those closest to the center of power still honor their vows of poverty and wander the streets dressed in robes, begging for coins.

I learned that "Joel" took away the medication that regulated his wife's schizophrenia and she attempted suicide. When she got out of the hospital, he forced her to get pregnant, which resulted in three miscarriages and then twins that died days after they were born. She then had a healthy pregnancy and gave "Joel" a daughter, whose name he cannot spell. When he received revelation that the world would be destroyed, "Joel" built an underground shelter. As the world continued to remain intact, he joined the Army and his wife moved in with his parents.

I don't know whether "May" is still alive, but "Dr. Adams" died in 2004 following complications from a fall. He was in court defending the tax-exempt status of the "International Academy of Lymphnogenesis." Moments after a ruling not in his favor, "Dr. Adams" lost his balance and hit his head on a low bench. After waking up at the hospital, he suffered a stroke, and he died a few weeks later.

Elidah, or Wanda Barzee, as the world knows her, was found mentally incapable of standing trial. She divorced David and resides in a mental hospital.

David, a.k.a. Immanuel David Isaiah, or Brian David Mitchell as his birth certificate states, was also found mentally incompetent. He faces charges of aggravated kidnapping and sexual assault, but the judge consistently dismisses him from the courtroom when David begins chanting and singing.

The faithful followers of "lymphnogenesis" still insist their religious science will heal the world, and they dedicate their lives to saturating it with this good news. The last I heard, cans of government food still lined the shelves in the storage room of the "Adams" sub-basement. As far as I know, however, no one has yet eaten the whole chicken in a can.

Alysa Writing

Resources

National Suicide Hotlines U.S.A.
Toll-Free / 24 hours a day / 7 days a week

1-800-SUICIDE (784-2433)

1-800-273-TALK (273-8255)

1-800-789-4TTY (4889—deaf hotline)

For local centers: suicidehotlines.com

National Domestic Violence Hotline
1-800-799-SAFE (799-7233)
www.ndvh.org

Rape, Abuse & Incest National Network
1-800-656-HOPE
www.rainn.org

Teen Online Support
www.teenadviceonline.com

In Canada—Counseling Hotline
for youth to 19 & referrals for adults
1-800-668-6868, 24 hours

In U.K.—A Key Information Resource
for those who self-harm, their friends and families,
and professionals working with them:

http://www.selfharm.org.uk

Upcoming: Book of Essays by Slug, MC of *Atmosphere*

Coming from a family with black jazz trumpeters and an ancestral line of Irish hereditary bards and minstrels, Sean Daley, a.k.a. "Slug," emcee of Atmosphere, accidentally meets his destiny in the essential world of hip-hop. One of the sublime results is a series of passionate, sure-to-be-controversial essays. In the tradition of street zines, this book comes complete with artistic Slug-projects, including cut-and-paste. While it's true that Sean is not an "unheard voice," which is what we mainly aim to publish, he's kin to the spirit of Word Warriors and has been kind enough to lend support to a great new press that can't afford to advertise.

Yesterday's Warrior

Hey, this is Heather Harrison and *Yesterday's Warrior* is my book. If you're looking to read a story with lots of fluff, then my book is definitely not for you. You will find no mercy in my words, only gut-wrenching honesty about my experiences. I'm told that my story is unique, but I'm sure there are millions out there who've suffered similar heartbreak. Among the tales of pain, you will also find my spirit that refuses to die. I hope this book offers a source of hope to all who have been dealt a raw hand in life and think there is nothing they can do about it. —Author, Heather Harrison

In *Yesterday's Warrior*, a memoir both heartbreaking and disturbing, Heather Harrison gives us the account of her teenage years with grit and unflinching honesty. A gifted girl expelled from school at fourteen, Harrison is alienated from her family and friends, struggling with addiction, street living, the dispassionate reality of government institutions, and puzzling psychological events. On her own, the world becomes her battlefield and this memoir is her brutally candid account of how she came to survive.

"Emotionally intense!" — Slug, MC of *Atmosphere*

"Heather Harrison's spellbinding tale of personal transformation is an essential read, not only for those of the 'lost generation' but for anyone who has ever risked a journey to the raw mirror of self and the world. The power, nuance and clarity of Harrison's voice reveal a wisdom far beyond her years."

— Leif Utne, *Utne Magazine*

Excerpt from *Yesterday's Warrior*

Memories from my childhood flashed through my mind in group each time one of the other kids talked about theirs. The fragmented images bothered me. I willed them to stop but they were stronger than I was. I hated the way Hank attacked the kids and crumbled their insides.

In one of my daily private sessions with Hank, I challenged him, "Why do you always have to make everyone feel like shit?"

"Because kids like you guys have a lot of pain."

"But what's the point in talking about it and feeling like shit? I don't see how it does anything."

"I think you're just scared." He moved his chair closer to mine.

I shrieked, "Don't come near me!" Pushing my chair back against the wall, I continued, "Seriously, stay away."

"Whoa, whoa." He moved his chair back, further than it had been. "What are you so afraid of?"

I snapped, "I just don't like people in my space."

"Okay." He leaned back. "Kids don't run away if there's nothing to run from. Drugs help you run away. If you deal with what you're running from, then maybe you won't have to run anymore."

I do drugs because I like them. But why does it scare you to live without them? I just like my life better that way. Really? Do you really like puking, getting into trouble, losing time, and being up for days? It's not that bad. Oh yeah, do you really like the guys who put their dicks in your mouth when you're passed out in the back of a trailer someplace you don't even know? Shut up!

At that moment, I split into two completely distinct voices in my mind. The voices argued back and forth with each other. I don't know whose voice was the real me or if they both belonged to a part of me. I just know that two voices were born. They began a dialogue that would torment and haunt me until I sat with the barrel of a gun in my mouth, contemplating pulling the trigger to shut them up.

Outlet or a Heaven Full of Televisions

"A memoir with elaborations." Are you being cheated? Conned? As you read, will this categorization force you to stop and ask, time and time again, *Did this really happen?* It did. It's true. Have certain things been enlarged or reduced, colored according to my desires, painted over or made transparent, wrapped up in blue bows and sent out for Christmas? Yeah. How is it possible not to do this? We remember people and events the way we want to remember them, not the way they really are or the way they really happened. Memoir is always a creative art. —Author, Scott Sundvall

As a lowly shoe pimp in an outlet mall, Scott Sundvall casts a lyrical and interrogative eye on American culture. With both searing drama and comedic irony, the author: takes a road trip to Mexico, where the meaning of life can be had for one dollar; meets Newt Gingrich in a divinely metaphorical D.C. bathroom; indulges in vodka and psychedelics to within three yards of death; faces one friend's suicide attempt and another's disappearance into rehab; and finally undergoes observation at a psych ward in the midst of an emotional epiphany. Full of yearning and anger in an existentially indifferent world, the 20-year-old author of this "memoir with elaborations" ultimately finds some clarity and purpose amid dead pigeons and clearance leather shoes.

"Sometimes it takes a work of fiction to provide insight into the real world. *Outlet or a Heaven Full of Televisions* by Scott Sundvall is just such a minor masterpiece of literate fiction."

— Midwest Book Review

Excerpt from *Outlet or a Heaven Full of Televisions*

At the height of all this, the police stormed into Matthew Felts' house to make the arrest. What they found was Matthew Felts hanging by a rope from the chandelier, shirt removed and his pants soaked in piss and shit. Something was written on his chest. In red. Below Matthew and over to the right—by the television—a cat was sprawled out on the floor. A cat obviously dead, with blood slowly trickling out from what looked to be its anus. The police all grabbed their mouths, though mutters of *Oh God* and *My God* and *Oh Jesus* and *Mary Mother of God*—whatever God phrase they fancied—came out anyway. A couple turned away, walked away, not believing. One, feeling truly sorry, vomited. One of the muttering cops walked over to the cat to examine it. By the time he realized what had happened to it, another cop had read the message scrawled on the chest and belly of Matthew Felts.

On the top of the message a line was drawn, pointing to his right, all of it crafted in lipstick:

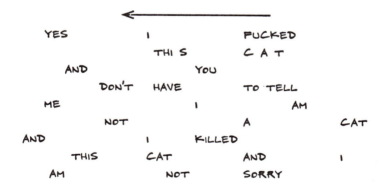

And that was that. Matthew Felts fucked the cat, killed the cat, and killed himself. He was not sorry for it and nobody could hold him accountable for it. Nobody could keep him from anything forever because he took it away first. The debates hushed as the funeral procession began, as the organ began to beckon and the dirge began to carry, and the eulogies were short and simple. Silence grew large in a small time; a full, voluptuous silence where opinions were rendered obsolete and morality grew mortal, where sinners and saints alike pondered Matthew Felts, never knowing exactly how to ponder.

WORD WARRIORS PRESS

Welcome to the world of Curb Lit. Word Warriors books are literature of the street—of the people—out of the garden, not quite in the gutter. Think of our literature as where the sidewalk ends, on the edge of the main flow, at the threshold of something new.

Word Warriors Press publishes edgy trade paperbacks of creative nonfiction by authors primarily in their twenties and late teens. We especially want to hear new and emerging voices from people whose stories aren't often told in the mainstream, the stories that are all too common but that rarely get talked about or reported on the news. By publishing unheard voices, Word Warriors Press seeks to empower, educate and entertain those whom society ignores. We believe in the power of this generation's truth-telling words to change the world, one page at a time.

Social and political change begins with psychological change: a sense of individual and group power and the realization that change is possible. Through its books and interactive website, this press hopes to help engender such changes. We invite you to visit our website for more information, for discussion in its forums, and to become a part of this process.

www.wordwarriorspress.com